Tania Pattison

# Critical reading

English for
Academic Purposes

PEARSON

Montréal Toronto Boston Columbus Indianapolis New York San Francisco Upper Saddle River
Amsterdam Le Cap Dubaï Londres Madrid Milan Munich Paris
Delhi México São Paulo Sydney Hong-Kong Séoul Singapour Taipei Tōkyō

Managing Editor
Sharnee Chait

Project Editor
Tessa Hearn

Proofreader
Brian Parsons

Coordinator, Rights and Permissions
Pierre Richard Bernier

Text Rights and Permissions
Rachel Irwin

Art Director
Hélène Cousineau

Graphic Design Coordinator
Lyse LeBlanc

Cover Design
cyclonedesign.ca

Book Design and Layout
4B Communication

The publisher thanks the following people
for their helpful comments and suggestions:

Cecilia Aponte-de-Hanna, Seneca College

Joanna Daley, Kwantlen Polytechnic University

Roisin Dewart, Université de Québec à Montréal

Michelle Duhaney, Seneca College

Pamela Gifford, Brock University

Brianna Hilman, University of Calgary

Marcia Kim, University of Calgary

Izabella Kojic-Sabo, University of Windsor

Cyndy Reimer, Douglas College

Mary Tang, Centennial College

Text Credits

Chapter 1, pp. 9–11 "Igopogo: The Monster of Lake Simcoe" by Rob Morphy © Rob Morphy. pp. 14–16 "The call of the weird: In praise of cryptobiologists" by William Laurance, © William Laurance.

Chapter 2, p. 24 Excerpt from "Pressor responsiveness to angiotensin in soy-fed spontaneously hypertensive rats" by Douglas S. Martin, J.L. Williams, Nikolai P. Breitkopf and Kathleen M. Eyster. Reprinted by permission. p. 24 Excerpt from "The Tofu Trap" by Erin Barnes © Featurewell.com. p. 24 Excerpt from "Decoupling of deforestation and soy production in the southern Amazon during the late 2000s" by Marcia N. Macedo, Ruth S. DeFries, Douglas C. Morton, Claudia M. Stickler, Gillian L. Galford and Yosio E. Shimabukuro reprinted with permission of *PNAS*. p. 25 Excerpt from "A Guide to Growing and Harvesting Edamame: The joys of edamame" by John Navazio reprinted with permission of *Mother Earth News*. pp. 27–30 "The Caveman Diet: Meat-eaters love it, critics call it 'a craze'" by R. Shore © *Vancouver Sun*. pp. 34–35 "There's No Reason to Eat Animals" by Lindsay Rajt © *Earth Island Journal*. pp. 38–42 "Obesity: A public health failure?" by T. Glassman, J. Glassman and A. J. Diehr. Reprinted with permission of Torstar Syndication Services.

Chapter 3, pp. 54–57 "MMA for Kids: Teaching violence, or values?" by Paul Hunter. Reprinted with permission of Torstar Syndication Services. pp. 61–63 "Sports Doping Should Be Legal and Controlled" by J. Savulescu. Reprinted with permission. pp. 66–69 "Why the Olympics Are a Lot Like 'The Hunger Games'" by Samantha Retrosi. Reprinted with permission from the January 22, 2014 issue of *The Nation*.

Chapter 4, p. 77 "How Safe Is Nuclear Power?" by Dietrich Fischer© Dietrich Fischer. pp. 80–81 "Panda Poop Power Promising for Biofuel Production" by James A. Foley © *Nature World News*. pp. 84–85 "Living off-grid" by Deborah Carr reprinted by permission. pp. 88–93 "Adverse health effects of industrial wind turbines" by Roy D. Jeffery reprinted by permission.

Chapter 5, pp. 104–107 "Top 10 Qualities That Make a Great Leader" by Tanya Prive reprinted by permission. pp. 110–112 "Why we need quiet, introverted leaders" by Ray Williams © Raymond B. Williams. pp. 114–117 "MIA: Women in the Executive Suite by "P. Galagan. Republished by permission of T + D.

Chapter 6, pp. 129–131 "Swimming against the tide of PowerPoint" by Clifford Orwin © Clifford Orwin. pp. 134–135 "Students Want More Mobile Devices in Classroom" by Ellis Booker. Copyright © 2014 UBM Electronics, A UBM company, All rights reserved. pp. 138–141 "Facebook as a formal instructional environment" by Bahar Baran. Reprinted with permission of *British Journal of Educational Technology*.

Chapter 7, pp. 153–156 "Ancient Chinese Wisdom for the Modern Workplace" by Kirsten Lagatree republished with permission of *Training & Development*. pp. 159–161 "Sitting Too Long Is Bad for You, but a Treadmill Desk Left Me Cold" by Christie Aschwanden © Christie Aschwanden. pp. 163–167 "Workstation design for organizational productivity" reproduced with the permission of National Research Council of Canada and Public Works & Government Services.

Chapter 8, pp. 178–181 "Can Money Buy Happiness? An examination of happiness economics," by Tim Mak. Reprinted with permission. pp. 185–187 "Denmark Is Considered the Happiest Country. You'll Never Guess Why." © AOL Inc. All rights reserved. Used by permission. pp. 190–193 "Is Bhutan the happiest place in the world?" by Andrew Buncombe © *The Independent*, Used by permission.

Chapter 9, p. 202 "Social networking leads to isolation, not more connections, say academics" by Ethan A. Huff / *Natural News*. Reprinted with permission. pp. 205–208 "The Magic Number" by Professor Robin Dunbar, University of Oxford—*RSA Journal* 2010. Reprinted by permission. pp. 212–214 "Is Dunbar's Friend-Limiting Number Still Relevant in the Facebook Era?" by Rik Lax / Wired.com © Condé Nast. pp. 216–218 "Social networks: a learning tool for teams?" by Patrick Tissington and Carl Senior © 2010 The Authors *British Journal of Educational Technology* © 2010 Becta.

Chapter 10, pp. 226–227 "NASA's SpaceX, Boeing deal a giant leap for space flight" by Bob McDonald, © Canadian Broadcasting Corporation. pp. 232–235 "Why It's Important to Look at the Stars—Literally" by Conor Farrell. Reprinted by permission of the author. pp. 237–240 "Does Mars Have Rights?" by Ronald Bailey reprinted by permission.

Introduction

Critical Reading presents a systematic approach to the reading and analysis of written text.

Intended for higher intermediate to advanced students in EAP studies, the book takes the learner through the skills fundamental to developing critical awareness: considering place and date of publication; identifying author bias and purpose; evaluating scope of research; distinguishing fact from opinion; comparing the author's argument to other points of view and to the reader's own experiences; and ultimately, evaluating the strength of argument and validity of the text with the goal of writing a critical review of an article.

This is achieved through the reading of authentic texts on a variety of subject areas, including nutritional science, environmental science, business, anthropology and more. Addressed here are topics as diverse as the caveman diet, new forms of energy, cheating in sports, computers in education and the effect of social media on human relationships. Texts are taken from academic journals, professional and general-interest magazines, opinion columns, websites and other sources. Materials from Canadian, American, British, Australian and Irish sources are used.

Throughout, the book aims for a balance between "standard" reading skills (pre-reading, comprehension and vocabulary development) and the development of higher-order critical thinking skills. Each chapter follows a similar pattern: pre-reading discussion questions to stimulate interest; comprehension and analysis of the text; and a follow-up section that provides opportunities for synthesis and further research. This final section allows learners to work with the themes and skills of the chapter through oral presentations and/or written tasks.

Critical reading skills are recognized as a crucial component of postsecondary learning skills. *Critical Reading* aims to set university- and college-bound students on the path to developing the skills they will need for academic success in a variety of disciplines.

Acknowledgments

Many people have provided support and encouragement at various stages of writing this book. These include former teaching colleagues at Sir Sandford Fleming College and Trent University, fellow ELT materials writers, and EAP teachers who responded enthusiastically to my various conference presentations on teaching critical reading. I am grateful for all the words of encouragement I received. I would also like to thank the Pearson team for their enthusiasm for this project, most notably my editor Tessa Hearn for her guidance. Last but not least, I would like to express my gratitude to my husband Tom Milburn and my children Adam and Sophie for bearing with me during the writing of this book; I could not have done this without you.

Tania Pattison, Peterborough, Canada

Highlights

Warn-up provides general discussion questions to stimulate students' interest in the topic(s) to come.

In this chapter introduces the critical reading skills taught in each chapter of the book.

The **Introductory pages** of each chapter provide clear instruction in the focus points of each chapter. Focus points cover stance, bias, fact versus opinion, types of evidence and more.

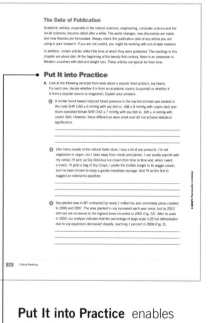

Put It into Practice enables learners to consolidate the knowledge they have acquired through guided practice activities and independent research.

Each chapter contains two or three **reading texts from authentic sources** (magazines, newspapers, websites and academic journals). These are thematically related and allow students to develop their understanding of the skills taught in the introductory pages.

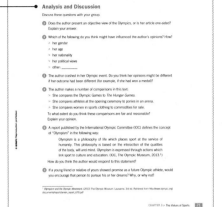

Questions on comprehension and vocabulary are followed by **Analysis and Discussion** in which students must use higher-order thinking skills to address the issues raised in the reading.

Focus on Language enables students to explore word families as a means of developing their vocabulary. Each chapter also features a quick look at another aspect of language use.

Independent Research provides an opportunity to expand on the topic of the chapter. Students have the chance to develop their research skills and to pursue an independent investigation of a topic that catches their attention.

In **Synthesis and Written Response**, students consolidate their understanding of the theme and skills presented in the chapter with the production of a short written assignment.

Every chapter ends with **Review** questions that allow users of the book to check their comprehension of key points.

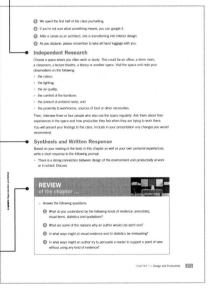

Scope and Sequence

CHAPTER AND SUBJECT AREA	FOCUS	CRITICAL READING SKILLS
CHAPTER 1 **MYTH OR REALITY** Subject Area: Life Sciences	Introduction to Critical Reading	• how different reading strategies can be used for different tasks • what critical reading is (and what it is not) • why critical reading is an important skill to have • the key questions you will answer as you read critically • how critical reading goes beyond reading strategies you already know
CHAPTER 2 **WHAT IS THE BEST WAY TO EAT?** Subject Area: Nutritional Science	Academic or Not?	• how to tell whether or not a text is academic • how the peer-review process works • why peer-reviewed texts are preferable for academic study • why the publication date of a text is important
CHAPTER 3 **THE VALUES OF SPORTS** Subject Area: Sports Studies	Author Credentials and Bias	• why it is important to know something about the author of a text and the people quoted by the author • what bias is and how to recognize it • why an author may be biased
CHAPTER 4 **APPROACHES TO THE GLOBAL ENERGY CRISIS** Subject Area: Environmental Science	Stance, Audience and Purpose	• how to identify the author's stance • how the author's intended audience influences the text • why the author's purpose is important
CHAPTER 5 **LEADERS AND LEADERSHIP** Subject Areas: Business Studies, Leadership and Management	Fact or Opinion?	• how to distinguish facts from opinions
CHAPTER 6 **TECHNOLOGY IN EDUCATION** Subject Areas: Education, Computer Studies	Interpreting Evidence 1: Casual Observation and Empirical Research	• how to evaluate conclusions drawn from author experience • how to recognize the steps of the scientific method • what to consider when reading reports of empirical research
CHAPTER 7 **DESIGN AND PRODUCTIVITY** Subject Area: Interior Design	Evidence 2: Other Forms of Support	• how to identify and evaluate evidence not based on author experience: anecdotes, visual items, statistics and quotations from others • how authors try to persuade readers using no evidence at all • how to evaluate these kinds of evidence
CHAPTER 8 **INEQUALITY, WEALTH AND HAPPINESS** Subject Areas: Economics, Psychology	The Text in Context 1	• why it is important to consider the text in its broader context • what a school of thought is and why it is important to know the schools of thought in your area of study • how to approach a text that presents an opinion or theory very different from anything else you have read
CHAPTER 9 **SOCIAL NETWORKS: A MAGIC NUMBER?** Subject Areas: Social Anthropology, Computer Studies	The Text in Context 2	• why it is important to ask yourself whether the text supports your own experiences • why it can be difficult to do this
CHAPTER 10 **LOOKING AT THE STARS** Subject Area: Astronomy	Bringing It All Together: Writing a Critical Review	• the key components of a critical review • how a critical review is different from a research essay • how to structure a critical review

READINGS	INDEPENDENT RESEARCH	SYNTHESIS AND WRITTEN RESPONSE
1 Igopogo: The Monster of Lake Simcoe 2 The Call of the Weird: In Praise of Cryptobiologists	Mythical creatures	The search for mythical creatures is a waste of time and money. Discuss.
1 The Caveman Diet 2 There's No Reason to Eat Animals 3 Obesity: A Public Health Failure	Popular diets	Meat is an essential part of a healthy diet. Do you agree or disagree?
1 MMA for Kids: Teaching Violence, or Values? 2 Sports Doping Should Be Legal and Controlled 3 Why the Olympics Are a Lot Like *The Hunger Games*	Sports	Sports are about more than just winning and losing; issues related to values and ethics also need consideration. Discuss with reference to one sport or sporting event.
1 Panda Poop Power Promising for Biofuel Production 2 Living Off-Grid 3 Adverse Health Effects of Industrial Wind Turbines	Alternative sources of energy	How can we solve the energy crisis? Compare and evaluate two or more possible solutions.
1 Top Ten Qualities that Make a Great Leader 2 Why We Need Quiet, Introverted Leaders 3 MIA: Women in the Executive Suite	Influential thinkers in business	What qualities, skills and personal characteristics should successful leaders have?
1 Swimming against the Tide of PowerPoint 2 Students Want More Mobile Devices in Classroom 3 Facebook as a Formal Instructional Environment	Applications of technology in education	Technology is a key component of education in the twenty-first century. Discuss.
1 Ancient Chinese Wisdom for the Modern Workplace 2 Sitting Too Long Is Bad for You, but a Treadmill Desk Left Me Cold 3 Workstation Design for Organizational Productivity	Work and study spaces	There is a strong connection between design of the environment and productivity at work or in school. Discuss.
1 Can Money Buy Happiness? An Examination of Happiness Economics 2 Denmark Is Considered the Happiest Country. You'll Never Guess Why. 3 Is Bhutan the Happiest Place in the World?	Wealth and happiness	What is the relationship between the wealth of a country, its economic policies and the happiness of its citizens?
1 The Magic Number 2 Is Dunbar's Friend-Limiting Number Still Relevant in the Facebook Era? 3 Social Networks: A Learning Tool for Teams?	Social networks	What is the value of social networks?
1 Why It's Important to Look at the Stars—Literally 2 Does Mars Have Rights?		Critical review

Contents

Myth or Reality?

FOCUS ## INTRODUCTION TO CRITICAL READING

What is critical reading? How is it different from the kind of reading you might have done until now? What kinds of questions do critical readers ask?

In this chapter

YOU WILL LEARN ...

> how you can use different reading strategies for different tasks;

> what critical reading is (and what it is not);

> why critical reading is an important skill to have;

> the key questions you will answer as you read critically; and

> how critical reading goes beyond reading strategies you already know.

Warm-up

Discuss the following questions with your group.

> What do you understand by the word *myth*? Can you think of any well-known myths from around the world? Share your ideas.

> Now, take one of the myths you have identified. Imagine you are reading an article that tells you that the myth is actually true. How would you know whether or not to believe it? What questions might you ask about the article?

Critical Reading: an Overview
Review of Reading Strategies

> The search for mythical animals is a waste of time and money. Discuss.

Imagine you have been given this essay topic in a course entitled *Introduction to Biology*. Your first task is to do some reading on the topic.

When you first studied academic reading in English, you probably learned some different reading strategies. You almost certainly learned that different strategies work best in different situations. Complete the chart with the correct information. The first example has been done for you.

STRATEGY	WHAT IT MEANS	WHEN I WOULD USE IT
Predicting	Looking at the title, subtitles, pictures, maps and other visual clues to guess what might be in the article.	When I have a long article and I need an idea of what will be in the article. Predicting gives me some clues about what I can expect to learn.
Skimming		
Scanning		
Careful reading for total comprehension		

These strategies will have served you well, but as you approach university or college study, you will find that they are not enough. To succeed in academic studies, you need to read *critically*.

What Is Critical Reading?

Everyone knows what reading is, but what is *critical* reading? What does *critical* really mean? It can mean several things; take a few minutes and brainstorm how many uses of the word *critical* you can think of. You might come up with examples similar to these:

> You may know that to *be critical of* someone or something is to "disapprove of" or to "have a negative response to" that person or thing. Example:
> *Some people are critical of the government's economic policies.*

> You may also know that *critical* can mean "very important," rather like *crucial* or *vital*. Example:
> *Today's meeting is critical to the future of the project.*

> You may refer to a situation as *critical*, meaning that the situation is very serious. Example:
> *The situation in the Middle East has reached a critical point.*

> If a patient in a hospital is in *critical* condition, you can guess that things are not looking good for him or her. Example:
> *The survivors of the plane crash are in critical condition in the hospital.*

These are all useful meanings of the word critical, but none of these explains what we mean by *critical reading*. There is another meaning of the word *critical*.

Think about the word *critic*. What does a movie critic do? He or she watches a movie—often a newly released movie—and writes a review of the movie. This review might include comments about the acting, the plot, the directing, the soundtrack, the special effects and more. This report might be negative, or it could just as easily be positive; no matter what, it expresses a **judgment** about the quality of the movie.

> **Be careful!**
>
> You probably know the verb *to criticize* (= say something negative about a person or situation). Don't let this confuse you; critical reading does not have to be negative. Your critical analysis of a text might actually be quite positive!

The key word here is **judgment**. When you read critically, you do similar things to those a movie critic does. In your case, you do not notice or comment on actors or special effects; you notice and comment on the text you are reading. Specifically,

> you **analyze** the circumstances of the publication of a piece of writing: *who* wrote it, *when* and *where* it was published and *why* it was written;

> you **question** how the author reaches his or her conclusions and on what evidence these are based; you **evaluate** any original research the author might have done, as well as any other sources the author uses to support his or her points;

> you **compare** and **contrast** this piece of writing with what you already know about the topic; you **consider** whether it supports what others have written or whether it presents a new opinion;

> you **assess** the strengths, weaknesses and general validity of a piece of writing, based on your careful reading of it. Your response may be positive, or it may be negative; your evaluation of a text is your own, and it may not be the same as that of your friend, your classmate or even your teacher.

Be careful!

A critical response is not an emotional response. There are some topics that people will always have very strong feelings about; these feelings are sometimes based on religious or political beliefs. You may read an article in which the author presents an opinion very different from your own. It is easy to become angry with the writer and to dismiss the text as nonsense. Instead, you need to look objectively at the author's argument. Come to a reasoned analysis, not an emotional reaction.

An example of critical reading

Look at the following text.

The First Moon Landing

On July 20, 1969, two Americans named Neil Armstrong and Edwin "Buzz" Aldrin did what no other humans had ever done: they walked on the moon. They had travelled to the moon in the Apollo 11 spacecraft; attached to Apollo 11 was a smaller Lunar Module, which made the landing. A third team member, Michael Collins, piloted the main spacecraft and did not walk on the moon.

Armstrong stepped onto the surface of the moon and made his famous statement that the moon landing was "one small step for man, one giant leap for mankind."

The 1969 moon landing was a key event in twentieth-century history. This was the era of the Cold War, and the USA and USSR were engaged in a "space race" to achieve supremacy in space exploration. In 1957, the Russian satellite Sputnik 1 had orbited the earth; however, by landing on the moon on that July evening, the Americans claimed victory in the intense competition.

If you are asked to write a paper *describing* the moon landing, you will find some useful information here. You will be able to answer the following questions:

> Who first walked on the moon?

> What were the first words spoken on the moon?

> When was the first moon landing?

> Where did the astronauts come from?

> How did they get to the moon?

> Why was this event important?

You read this information, and if you trust the author, you accept it. Your goal is to learn the facts, not to question them.

However, as you read more, you might learn that not everyone accepts the moon landing as the truth. Some people believe it never happened and that it was filmed on a movie set or in the desert of the western USA.

What evidence do they put forward to support their claim? Here are some points:

> First, the astronauts who landed on the moon took a photograph. The flag in this photograph appears to be waving in the wind; there is no wind on the moon.

> Second, no stars are visible in any of the pictures taken on the moon, even though the pictures were taken in space.

> Third, close examination of the pictures and footage from the moon landing appears to show everyday items. There is a rock with the letter *C* on it (which suggests it may be a film prop). A woman in Australia claimed to see a Coca-Cola bottle roll across the ground as she was watching the footage on television.

These are only a few of the points made by those who do not believe the 1969 moon landing happened. Other events in recent history have attracted similar controversy. Here are some examples:

> Some people think the assassination of President John F. Kennedy in November 1963 was not the work of a single gunman but was part of a larger plot.

> Some people think the death of Diana, Princess of Wales, in 1997 was not an accident and that she was murdered by representatives of the British government or royal family.

> Some people think the American government knew in advance about the terrorist attacks in New York and Washington on September 11, 2001.

As you read about these events, you discover that different writers have different opinions on all this. You find yourself wondering who is right. You ask yourself, does this author have a good point, or does that one? Is this argument stronger than that one?

Do those who deny the moon landings have a point? You must decide, and your decision must be based on your *critical* reading of the writing in question.

The Importance of Critical Reading

In your courses at college or university, you might be asked to respond critically to a written article, a video, a website or a piece of art. Your instructor will want to see that you have not only *understood* the work but that you can *respond* to it, discuss its strengths and weaknesses and make your own decision about the merit of the work.

However, you need to apply critical reading skills to *any* research you are doing. As you research and write papers, you are not just collecting facts; you are dealing with opinions, theories and your own analysis of what you have read.

You might be reading critically for the first time when you take courses in university or college. You might feel that critical reading is a "Western" skill, or something that is not expected in higher education in your own country. You might even feel that critical reading is disrespectful; you might wonder what gives you the right to make judgments about something that a respected academic has written, or to disagree with the opinions of someone much more knowledgeable than yourself.

You need to keep in mind that in Western countries, critical reading is encouraged and expected within higher education. Your university or college professors will be looking for evidence of critical analysis when they evaluate your work, so don't be afraid to show your own thoughts on a topic or a reading.

Questions to Consider

When you read, you should think about the following questions. Keep in mind that you do not need to answer these questions in order.

Before you read the text, you can think about these questions.

> Where was this text published? Was it published in a **peer-reviewed** academic journal, or somewhere else? How can you tell? Why does it matter?

> When was this text published? Is the publication date important? Is the material still relevant, or is it dated?

> Who wrote the text? What do we know about this person? What **credentials** might this author have? What **biases** might he or she have?

> What is the author's opinion of the topic being discussed? Why did the author write this text? Who is the text intended for? What does the author want the reader to do as a result of reading this text?

As you read the text, you can think about these questions.

> Is this a purely factual piece, or does the author present a personal opinion here? How can you tell what is a fact and what is an opinion?

> Does the text present a convincing argument about the topic in question? Has the author done **empirical research**, and if so, what conclusions are reached? Does the research methodology justify the conclusions presented? Are charts and graphs used? What information do they give?

> If the author is not presenting the results of his or her own empirical research, how are the author's points supported? Are there **statistics**? If so, where from? How about **quotations** from others? If so, who is being quoted? Does the author rely on **anecdotes**? If so, are these convincing? How effective is the author's use of supporting detail?

> How do you respond to a text that has no supporting evidence at all, but is simply a well-written presentation of the author's own opinion?

After you read the text, you can think about these questions.

> What is the larger **context** of this work? How does the text support or contradict other opinions on this topic? Who might agree with the text? Who might disagree? What should you do if a text presents an opinion that is very different from those presented

in other articles you have read on the same topic? Should you ignore it, or should you consider it?

> How does the text compare with your own experiences and opinions? Does it support your own experiences, or does it contradict them? Does the text contain information (for example, about your home country) that you know to be incorrect?

Put It into Practice

Discuss the following questions with your group.

1. A website from the United Nations Educational, Scientific and Cultural Organization (UNESCO) gives some statistics about the level of education reached by young women in Indonesia. Is this a reliable source?

2. You find an interesting article about addiction to online gambling. The article has some interesting statistics, but it was published ten years ago. Is it worth using?

3. You find a book about World War II that presents a different opinion from your other sources. What would you like to know about the author before you decide whether or not to take him seriously?

4. You are writing an essay on the importance of sports in elementary school. You have found a newspaper column that presents a convincing argument about this issue; however, the author has not given any evidence. Are you going to use this column as support in your essay?

5. An article tells you that research into space exploration is a waste of money. Do you think this article is presenting facts or opinions? How can you tell? What might you look for in the article?

6. You find some research that states that people who own dogs generally live longer lives than those who do not. The author has some convincing arguments, but you are not sure whether or not she has enough evidence. How much is enough?

7. A newspaper article tells you about human rights abuses in a certain country. The writer of this article has never visited the country in question; his claims are based on interviews with other people. How would you evaluate his information?

8. You find two websites about the use of seaweed as a source of energy. One is full of long words and complicated sentences; the other uses simple, clear language. Is the first one a more reliable source?

9. You have read nine different articles that tell you that there is no connection between wealth and happiness. The tenth article gives the opposite opinion: rich people are happier than those who are poor. What questions would you ask yourself about this article before you decide whether or not to consider it?

10. You come from a country in sub-Saharan Africa. A magazine story about communication technology in this part of the world has information that you know to be out of date. What does this tell you about the article and/or the publication?

Igopogo: The Monster of Lake Simcoe

The following text describes a mythical creature in Ontario, Canada.

FOCUS **As you read the text, think about the "Questions to Consider" on pages 6–7.**

Before You Read

Work in groups of three or four. Discuss the following questions.

1. Do you know what the following creatures are? What do you know about them? What do they have in common?

   a) Loch Ness monster

   b) Chupacabra

   c) yeti

2. Can you think of any other creatures whose existence is uncertain? Are there any mythical creatures in your own country or culture that may—or may not—really exist?

3. This reading is about a strange creature that is said to live in the waters of a lake north of Toronto, Ontario. What would you like to find out in this reading? In pairs, write six questions.

   We would like to find out …

   a) _____.

   b) _____.

   c) _____.

   d) _____.

   e) _____.

   f) _____.

Key Vocabulary

The words below are all in the reading. Fill in the space in each sentence with the correct word.

NOUNS	rivalry	skeptic	spectator	
VERBS	settle	speculate		
ADJECTIVES	aboriginal	canine	controversial	notorious
ADVERB	allegedly			

1. If something is _____, it is famous in a negative way.

2. A person who watches a sports event, such as a soccer or a tennis match,
   is a _____ .

3. If something _____ happened, people *say* that it happened,
   but there is no real proof of this.

4. If you doubt claims and statements, especially those that are generally thought to be true,
   you may be called a _____.

5. A _____ is a situation in which two or more people
   or organizations compete with each other, usually over a long period of time.

6. To _____ about something means to make guesses about
   something without knowing all the facts and details.

7. A _____ topic is one that causes a lot of disagreement
   because people have different opinions about it.

8. While *feline* is related to cats and *equine* is related to horses, _____
   is used to describe features that are typical of dogs.

9. The _____ people of Canada are those people whose
   ancestors lived in Canada before explorers arrived from Europe.

10. People who _____ in a particular region are people who
    move there from somewhere else.

Igopogo: The Monster of Lake Simcoe

By Rob Morphy

This long-necked, dorsal-finned, **canine**-featured critter[1] is one of the most unusual lake beasts reputed to dwell in North America.

Located in Southern Ontario—just 40 miles north of Toronto—Lake Simcoe is the fourth-largest lake in the province and a remnant of the colossal, prehistoric freshwater
5 sea known as Lake Algonquin. Algonquin's basin also included Lake Huron, Lake Michigan, Lake Superior, Lake Nipigon and Lake Nipissing.

⟶

---
[1] *Critter* is an informal word for an unspecified animal or other creature. The word is a variation on *creature*.

When the ice dam melted at the end of the last ice age, it dramatically reduced water levels in the region, leaving behind the lakes we see today.

This relatively small, island-riddled, oval-shaped body of water, which is approximately twenty miles long and sixteen miles wide, is known for its clean water, fantastic fishing and, most notably, the bizarre beast that's said to lurk within its gloomy, freshwater depths.

This unusual animal was dubbed Igopogo by the local fishermen—no doubt, in honour of her famous cousins Ogopogo of Lake Okanagan and Manipogo of Lake Manitoba. That having been stated, there seems to be a bit of a **rivalry** over the beast's appellation as, depending on whether or not you hail from Kempenfelt Bay or Beaverton, the monster has a few alternate *noms de plume*, including "Kempenfelt Kelly," "Beaverton Bessie"—which is, in and of itself, an homage to Lake Erie's more **notorious** Bessie—and even "Simcoe Kelly."

Considered by many cryptozoologists[2] to be unique, even amongst her amazing peers, Igopogo is a rarely seen beast, which has been described as having a neck resembles a "stovepipe," crowned by an unusual canine-like head. This ostensibly mammalian description—which, it must be admitted, has in no way remained consistent throughout the many years of Igopogo sightings—has led some to **speculate** that this creature may be biologically akin to aquatic enigmas such as the notorious "Irish crocodile" the dobhar-chu or even the Australian bunyip.

While tales of this cryptid go as far back as **aboriginal** legends and accounts from the earliest Europeans to **settle** the area, the first modern report hails from July 22, 1963.

The eyewitnesses involved with this sighting, including one Reverend L. B. Williams, claimed that they saw not a typically mammalian, but a serpentine creature with multiple dorsal fins, that was anywhere from thirty to seventy feet in length, undulating in the water. It was also described as having a "charcoal covered" epidermis.

This creature was **allegedly** captured on film while two, uncharacteristically calm children watch from the shore. While there is no written account of when or by whom the obviously aged, black and white image was snapped, it remains an intriguing—if somewhat **controversial**—piece of potential photographic evidence of Igopogo's existence.

---

[2] *Cryptozoology* is the study of animals whose existence is not certain, known as *cryptids*. The word comes from *crypto* = "secret" and *zoology* = "the study of animals." Someone engaged in cryptozoology is called a *cryptozoologist*. Another word with the same meaning as cryptozoology is *cryptobiology*.

Two decades later, on June 13, 1983, William Skrypetz, a sonar[3] operator with Lefroy's Government Dock and Marina, took a sonar reading which revealed a creature with a massive body and long tapering neck that seemed to look very much like the archetypal
50 lake monsters such as Champ or the Loch Ness monster.

During the 1980s, author, cryptozoologist and president of the BCSCC (British Columbia Scientific Cryptozoology Club) John Kirk III investigated this phenomenon and came to the conclusion that whatever might have lived in the lake had either migrated or had become deceased.

55 Kirk's assessment of the situation was not without merit, as the sightings of this animal—with the notable exception of Skrypetz's sonar hit—had dwindled to virtually nothing since the 1970s. Kirk's opinion of this creature's status changed in 1991, however, when he was given a copy of a videotape by former British army officer and fellow cryptozoologist Don Hepworth. The video—which was purportedly shot from the shores
60 of Lake Simcoe during that same year—apparently shows a terrifying lake demon rearing its head during a hydroplane race.

According to the unnamed videographer's account, one of the racers suffered a mechanical breakdown while on the south end of the lake and was forced to halt and make repairs. Just as the racer lifted the engine hatch in order to assess the damage, a
65 large animal suddenly surfaced directly in front of him, stunning the racer as well as the **spectators** on the shoreline.

The landlocked crowd began to panic, fearing the worst for the downed competitor. The racer himself would later claim that this possibly prehistoric apparition would continue to stare at him as it slowly lowered its head, finally submerging completely
70 beneath the water.

Apparently, Kirk, upon repeated viewing of the controversial footage, confirmed that this creature was between nine and twelve feet long and had what he believed to be pinniped (seal- or sea lion–like) features. Unfortunately the quality of the video and proximity of the creature to the camera did not allow for a more thorough
75 investigation of its species.

This video evidence—which is infamously difficult to find—has raised the profile of this creature considerably, yet **skeptics** continue to insist that what people are seeing is nothing more than normal seals who have slipped into the lake via the rivers that connect it to Lake Huron. Still others think it may be related to the now famous Pacific
80 Ocean-dwelling sea monsters known as cadborosaurus.

While the "seal" theory may debunk some of the unusual sightings, it in no way explains away the strange sonar hit reported in 1983. Even now, a decade into the twenty-first century, Lake Simcoe remains one of the most underexplored cryptid habitats in North America.

(957 words)

Morphy, R. (2010, Nov. 13). Igopogo: Canada. *American Monsters*. Retrieved from http://www.americanmonsters.com/site/2010/11/igopogo-canada/

---

[3] *Sonar* is an acronym of the term *Sound Navigation and Ranging*; it is a technique whereby sound is used to detect underwater objects.

Check Your Understanding

A. How many of your questions from "Before You Read" were answered in the article? Go back to your questions and fill in the answers where you can.

B. Answer the following questions in your own words using information from the reading.

1 What does Igopogo look like?

_____

_____

2 Where does it live? What do you learn about this place?

_____

_____

3 The first sighting of Igopogo occurred in 1963: true or false? Explain your answer.

_____

_____

4 In all eyewitness accounts, the description of Igopogo has been the same: true or false? Explain your answer.

_____

_____

5 Describe briefly what happened on

a) July 22, 1963: _____

_____

b) June 13, 1983: _____

_____

6 Why did cryptozoologist John Kirk change his mind about the existence of Igopogo?

_____

_____

7 What do skeptics think Igopogo really is? _____

Analysis and Discussion

Discuss the following questions with your group.

1 Where do you think this text was published?

> In an academic journal for animal experts

> In a daily newspaper in the Lake Simcoe area

> In a magazine for tourists visiting Lake Simcoe

> On a website for people interested in cryptozoology

Explain your answer.

2 How might the text be different if it had been published in one of the other sources listed on the previous page?

3 Do you think the author, Rob Morphy, personally believes in the existence of Igopogo? Explain your answer.

4 Why do you think Rob Morphy chose to write this article? What did he hope to achieve by doing so?

5 Based on what you have read, do you think there is sufficient evidence that Igopogo exists?

6 Which of the following pieces of evidence would convince you *with 100 percent certainty* that Igopogo exists?

	Yes	No
> A live Igopogo pulled from the waters of Lake Simcoe	○	○
> Igopogo footprints in the sand around Lake Simcoe	○	○
> A colour photograph taken by a tourist	○	○
> An eyewitness account from a local person	○	○
> An eyewitness account from a police officer	○	○

> Other: _____

7 What question(s) would you like to ask the author of this article?

8 Does Igopogo remind you of any other mythical creature you may have heard of? Tell us about it.

READING 2

The Call of the Weird: In Praise of Cryptobiologists

Now read another text on the same topic.

FOCUS **As you read, consider how this article compares to the previous article.**

Before You Read

Work in groups of three or four. Discuss the following questions.

1 Why do you think scientists might be attracted to the study of mysterious animals like Igopogo, the Loch Ness monster and others?

2 What could be gained from attempting to find one of these creatures?

3 The subtitle of this reading is *In Praise of Cryptobiologists*. Why do you think the author might want to write an article with this title? What might he say?

Key Vocabulary

The words below are all in the reading. Match each word with the correct definition.

1. conventional (adj. line 16) _____   a) a substance that carries genetic information within the body

2. credible (adj. line 8) _____   b) an animal that kills and eats another animal

3. DNA (n. line 12) _____   c) considered to be normal or usual

4. eccentric (n. line 16) _____   d) without any written record of existence

5. intrepid (adj. line 76) _____   e) an animal that carries its young in a pouch or pocket on its body

6. isolation (n. line 41) _____   f) able to be believed or trusted

7. mammal (n. line 2) _____   g) someone who acts in a way that is different from most people, or whose behaviour is considered strange

8. marsupial (n. line 5) _____   h) exclusion or separation from other members of the group

9. predator (n. line 5) _____   i) a member of a group of animals that give birth to live young and whose young are nourished by their mother's milk

10. undocumented (adj. line 50) _____   j) daring; willing to take risks or put oneself in danger for the purpose of adventure

The Call of the Weird: In Praise of Cryptobiologists

By William Laurance

Last December an 8-second amateur video went viral. Shot in remote northern Tasmania,[1] the blurry footage featured a long-tailed mammal trotting across a meadow with an oddly stilted gait. According to the filmmaker, Murray McAllister, the animal was a Tasmanian tiger.

5   The Tasmanian tiger, or thylacine, is a wolf-sized marsupial predator that has been presumed extinct since the last known specimen died in Hobart zoo in 1936. Yet despite its apparent demise, reports of Tassie tigers refuse to die. Hundreds of sightings, many from seemingly credible observers, have been recorded, both in Tasmania and on the mainland.

  When I saw the video there was something vaguely familiar about it. Then it hit me:
10 the animal moved like a red fox. I'd raised a fox as a boy in the western US, and they have a peculiar way of trotting. Soon, others were saying the same thing. Then a fecal sample McAllister collected was analyzed for its DNA: it was a red fox.

---

[1] Tasmania is a state of Australia; its capital city is Hobart. Tasmania is an island, lying to the south of the mainland. The island is mountainous and is known for its unusual wildlife.

McAllister has been searching for the Tasmanian tiger since 1998. Though he might not describe himself as such, he is a cryptobiologist, a chaser of mythical, mysterious or supposedly extinct species. Cryptobiologists are a diverse lot, ranging from conventional scientists to eccentrics far from the mainstream. All share a dream of discovering elusive or unknown creatures unrecognized by conventional science—and with it their share of instant fame.

Everyone knows about fabled creatures like Nessie and Bigfoot, but cryptobiologists actually chase a far larger menagerie of exotic beasts, which they collectively term "cryptids." Some, like the Tasmanian tiger, clearly once existed. Others, such as giant vampire bats, conceivably might exist, having somehow escaped the attentions of conventional scientists. The third category, oddities such as the Jersey Devil and the Mothman, are strictly on the fringes.

The more credible side of the cryptobiology crowd can be a pretty serious lot. Some, such as tropical ecologist David Bickford of the National University of Singapore and Aaron Bauer, an evolutionary biologist and herpetologist[2] at Villanova University in Pennsylvania, are respected mainstream scientists. Bickford has discovered a number of previously unknown species, including a bizarre lungless frog that lives only beneath waterfalls in Borneo.

The most committed cryptobiologists spend big sums of their own money to finance their quests. Being outside the realm of traditional science, they don't usually have a choice. For example, the late Grover Krantz, a physical anthropologist at Washington State University, invested around $50,000 for a light aircraft, infrared heat detector and other expensive gear in a decades-long search for Bigfoot in the Pacific Northwest.

But for mainstream scientists, being a cryptobiologist isn't easy. Some have paid for their efforts in more than money. Roy Mackal, a dedicated chaser of Nessie and Mokelem-bembe, an aquatic dinosaur that supposedly lives in the Congo basin, was booted out of the biology department at the University of Chicago; few if any dispute that his cryptid-seeking was the chief cause. Others endure sneers from their colleagues, a loss of credibility and even academic isolation.

Why tolerate such treatment? "The search for the fringe and fanciful captivates many people," says Mike Trenerry, a biologist with the Queensland Department of Environment and Resource Management who uses automatic cameras to search for rare beasts. "We want to believe there is more out there than what we already know about."

And the truth, of course, is that even in the twenty-first century, the natural world is still brimming with mystery. Tropical biologists commonly find that half or more of the insect species they capture in the rainforest canopy are new to science. Undiscovered fish and other species are frequently found in the deep sea. Up to half of all the plant species in the Amazon are still scientifically undocumented.

Not all of the new discoveries are small or obscure. The Mindoro fruit bat, discovered in the Philippines in 2007, has a 1-metre wingspan. The same year saw the discovery of a venomous snake in Australia and a large electric ray in South Africa.

---

[2] A herpetologist is a scientist who studies reptiles and amphibians such as snakes, lizards, frogs, turtles and crocodiles.

And despite the misfire of the recent Tasmanian tiger video, there are many Lazarus[3]
55 species that have been rediscovered after having been presumed extinct. Until 1951,
the Bermuda petrel had not been seen by scientists for 330 years. The Javan elephant,

Coelacanth.

okapi, coelacanth, mountain pygmy possum, venomous Cuban solenodon and giant terror skink
60 were also erroneously consigned to oblivion. The Laotian rock rat, discovered in 1996, is now the sole known representative of a rodent family that was thought to have
65 vanished eleven million years ago. The Wollemi pine—the only known survivor of a 200-million-year-old plant family—was discovered in 1994 just a stone's
70 throw from Sydney, Australia.

It is the Lazarus species, perhaps more than any other cryptid group, that most inspire cryptobiologists. They give them hope by revealing that nature is still very much shrouded in uncertainty. From the coelacanth to the mountain pygmy possum, Cuban solenodon and giant terror skink, even dramatic species are sometimes wrongly
75 presumed to have vanished.

So we should celebrate the intrepid efforts of cryptobiologists. Yes, they chase bizarre creatures and flit around the fringes of conventional science, but we ought to appreciate their adventurous spirit rather than be disdainful.

(893 words)

Laurance, W. (2011, June 22). The call of the weird: In praise of cryptobiologists. *New Scientist, 210*(2817), 30–31.

---

[3] Lazarus species are species that were thought to be extinct, but which have been discovered to still exist.

Check Your Understanding

A. Are the following statements true (T) or false (F)?

	T	F
1 Murray McAllister made a video of a Tasmanian tiger.	○	○
2 All people who search for mysterious animals are eccentric.	○	○
3 Cryptobiologists often search for creatures that definitely existed at one time.	○	○
4 Cryptobiologists are highly respected by their academic colleagues.	○	○
5 There is much that scientists don't know about the world's animals.	○	○
6 Cryptobiologists have found creatures previously thought to have disappeared.	○	○

B. Complete each of the following sentences in your own words.

1. The author knew that the creature in the video was not a Tasmanian tiger because

   _____.

2. David Bickford has made a significant contribution to science because _____

   _____

   _____.

3. A lot of research into mysterious animals is funded by the researchers themselves

   because _____

   _____.

4. Roy Mackal lost his job because _____

   _____.

5. Even though cryptobiologists are not always treated well, they continue with their work

   because _____

   _____.

6. Cryptobiologists should be celebrated because _____

   _____.

Analysis and Discussion

Discuss the following questions with your group.

1. Which statement best summarizes the author's opinion about cryptobiologists?

   a) Most of them are not serious scientists. They are eccentrics who want instant fame by finding well-known mysterious animals like the Loch Ness monster. We should be disdainful of them.

   b) Some of them are on the fringes of science, but others are well-respected researchers. The discoveries made by these researchers can be valuable. We should encourage them.

2. In what kind of publication do you think this text was first published? Why?

3. Why do you think the video described in lines 1–4 went viral? Why did so many people around the world want to believe the animal was a Tasmanian tiger?

4. Do you think the author makes a strong case for supporting people who search for mysterious creatures? Why, or why not? Has the author convinced you of the value of this kind of research?

5. Imagine that someone who does not approve of cryptobiology reads this article. What do you think that person might say to the author? How might he or she argue against this kind of research?

6. Scientists who search for mysterious species often pay for their own research. What is your opinion about this? Do you think supporting this kind of research is a good use of a university's research budget? Why, or why not?

Going Further

Focus on Language

A. The following chart contains ten words from the readings. Complete the chart with related words in the other categories, and, where possible, in the same category. (There may not be a word for each category.)

	NOUN	VERB	ADJECTIVE	ADVERB
1				completely
2	conclusion			
3		describe		
4	discovery			
5			familiar	
6		inspire		
7		migrate		
8			modern	
9	science			
10	survivor			

B. The two readings in this chapter are about *cryptozoology*, or *cryptobiology*. If we look at these words, we can see that they can be broken down into three parts:

crypto   This is a prefix. Prefixes come at the beginning of words. The prefix *crypto* has the meaning "strange, unusual."

zoo/bio   Each of these is a stem (the main part of the word). *Zoo* means "related to animals"; (a zoo—or *zoological garden*—is a place where animals are kept.) *Bio* has the meaning "life"; *biology* is the "study of living things."

ology   This is a suffix. Suffixes come at the end of words. The suffix *ology* means "study of"; it is common in areas of education such as biology, psychology and geology.

The following chart shows some other prefixes, stems and suffixes, together with their meanings.

PREFIXES		STEMS		SUFFIXES	
Prefix	Meaning	Stem	Meaning	Suffix	Meaning
anti-	against	anthro	human	-able[1]	able to be
auto-	self	capit	head	-ate[2]	makes a word a verb
contra-	opposite	dict	say, word	-er/-or[3]	someone who
de-	opposite, less, removed	geo	earth	-ful[1]	full of
inter-	between	graph	writing	-ic /-ical[1]	of, relating to
mal-	bad	ling	language	-ify[2]	make, become
micro-	small	man(u)	hand	-ism[3]	belief or quality
multi-	many	path	disease	-ize[2]	cause, become
post-	after	ped/pod	feet	-less[1]	without
sub-	under	port	carry	-ness[3]	state, quality
tele-	far	psych	mind	-ology[3]	study of
trans-	across	terr	land	-tion[3]	state, quality

[1] Words ending in these suffixes are usually adjectives.
[2] Words ending in these suffixes are usually verbs.
[3] Words ending in these suffixes are usually nouns.

Use the chart to figure out the meaning of the words in **bold** in these sentences.

1. **Anthropology** is a popular subject among students.

2. There are rumours that the novel is actually **autobiographical**.

3. The argument expressed in this article **contradicts** the textbook.

4. He died poor and **friendless**.

5. A **portable** stove is useful on a camping trip.

6 Some notorious world leaders might have been **psychopaths**.

7 The designer's work was **substandard**, so his contract was not renewed.

8 Many people living in Switzerland are **multilingual**.

9 Do you think human **teleportation** will be possible in the future?

10 The **postwar** period was a time of great economic growth.

11 Lions, elephants and giraffes are **terrestrial** animals.

12 The police have hired a **graphologist** to look at the handwritten letter they received.

Independent Research

Choose one of the following creatures and carry out some online research about your creature. You will present your findings to the class.

> Chupacabra

> Loch Ness monster

> Mongolian death worm

> Bigfoot

> Sewer alligator

Synthesis and Written Response

Based on your reading of the texts in this chapter as well as your own research into cryptozoology, write a short response to the following prompt.

> The search for mythical creatures is a waste of time and money. Discuss.

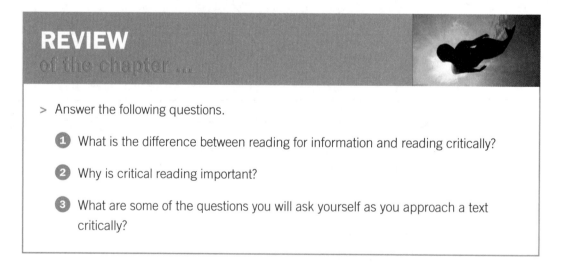

REVIEW of the chapter ...

> Answer the following questions.

1 What is the difference between reading for information and reading critically?

2 Why is critical reading important?

3 What are some of the questions you will ask yourself as you approach a text critically?

What Is the Best Way to Eat?

FOCUS ## ACADEMIC OR NOT?

When you read a text, you may ask yourself the following questions: Where was this text published? Was it published in a peer-reviewed academic journal, or somewhere else? How can you tell? Why does it matter? When was this text published? Is the publication date important? You will learn how to answer these questions, and you will apply what you learn within the context of three readings on food and diet and your own independent research.

In this chapter
YOU WILL LEARN ...

> how to tell whether or not a text is academic;

> how the peer-review process works;

> why peer-reviewed texts are preferable for academic study; and

> why the publication date of a text is important.

Warm-up

Discuss the following questions with your group.

1 What kinds of foods would you find in these categories: proteins, carbohydrates, fats?

2 Which way of eating do you think is healthiest—a diet based on meat or one based on vegetables? Why?

3 Where do you get information about food and nutrition? If you need dietary advice, what kinds of publications do you prefer to look at? Why?

Where and When Was the Text Published?

The Peer-review Process

> Is meat an essential part of a healthy diet?

Imagine you have been given this essay topic in a course entitled *Introduction to Nutrition*. As you search for information on this topic, you find many articles on the subject of meat and its health benefits or risks. Which ones are academic and reliable? Which ones can you trust?

Usually, an "academic" article is one that has been **peer-reviewed**. What does this mean?

> A person's *peers* are those people who are in the same area of study and who have a similar level of expertise.

> To *review* something means to examine something carefully and give an opinion on its strengths and weaknesses.

Here's how the peer-review process works.

1 An author—usually a professor or researcher—writes a paper showing the results of his or her research. The paper may have sections on how the research was carried out, the results obtained and the conclusions that can be drawn. It may contain statistics and specialized vocabulary. There will probably be an abstract (i.e., a short summary at the beginning of the article) and a long list of references. The article may be long, often up to thirty pages or more.

2 The author chooses a journal that is well-suited to the topic of the article. This is a specialized publication and will have a name like *Journal of ...*, or *... Quarterly*. The author sends the paper to the editor of the journal.

3 The editor receives the article and sends it to several reviewers who are experts in the same field as the author. They are usually university faculty, and they may be in different parts of the world.

4 These reviewers read the article. Often the editor has removed the name of the author, so they don't know who wrote the article. They examine the content and conclusions reached by the author. If there are any errors in the argument presented, the reviewers will find them. The reviewers send their comments back to the editor.

5 The editor decides whether the article should be a) published with no changes, b) published with some changes or c) rejected. The editor tells the author the decision.

6. The author makes any changes or corrections that have been requested and returns the paper to the editor.

7. The article is edited for style, grammar, spelling, punctuation, referencing, and so on. For example, references must be presented in the style (APA, MLA, etc.) preferred by the journal.

8. The paper is published.

By the time the article is published, it has been read and evaluated by other people who know a lot about the same topic. If the article was considered to have no academic value, or to contain inaccurate information, it would not have been published. A paper that is not peer reviewed does not go through steps 3 and 4. This paper is not sent to expert reviewers, and no academic feedback is received.

Academic or Not—How Can You Tell? A Checklist

Look at the following chart comparing academic journals with non-academic sources. You can use this comparison chart as a checklist for deciding whether an article is academic.

	ACADEMIC (peer-reviewed journals)	NON-ACADEMIC (magazines, newspapers)
Cover	simple	large, colourful, often photos and an attention-grabbing headline
Pictures	no pictures or very few, usually black and white	many pictures, often taking up a whole page or half a page
Advertising	very little, related to the subject of the journal	a lot, much of which has nothing to do with the topic of the magazine
Authors	often more than one author; sometimes ten or more authors in sciences	one or two
Length	long (thirty to forty pages is not unusual)	shorter (sometimes just one page of a magazine or a few columns of a newspaper)
Paragraphs, sentences	may have long paragraphs and can have complex sentences	shorter paragraphs and shorter, less complex sentences
Abstract	abstract which summarizes the methodology and findings of the paper	none
References	long list of references	maybe a few references, but no long list
Statistical analysis	complex statistical analysis; complex charts and graphs	some numbers, no complex statistical analysis
Vocabulary	specialized and technical; little or no use of the first person	more general; fewer technical words; idioms and other informal language; more use of the first person
Quotations	quotations from other published sources; the authors show how their own paper fits into a broader body of writing on the topic	quotations often from ordinary people talking about their own experiences (see **Anecdotes** on page 147)

The Date of Publication

Academic articles, especially in the natural sciences, engineering, computer science and the social sciences, become dated after a while. The world changes, new discoveries are made and new theories are formulated. Always check the publication date of any article you are using in your research. If you are not careful, you might be working with out-of-date material.

In addition, certain articles reflect the time at which they were published. The readings in this chapter are about diet. At the beginning of the twenty-first century, there is an obsession in Western countries with diet and weight loss. These articles are typical for their time.

Put It into Practice

A. Look at the following excerpts from texts about a popular food product, soy beans. For each one, decide whether it is from an academic source (a journal) or whether it is from a popular source (a magazine). Explain your answers.

1. A similar trend toward reduced blood pressure in the soy-fed animals was evident in the male SHR (160 ± 6 mmHg with soy diet vs. 168 ± 8 mmHg with casein diet) and sham-operated female SHR (162 ± 7 mmHg with soy diet vs. 169 ± 4 mmHg with casein diet). However, these differences were small and did not achieve statistical significance.

_____

_____

_____

2. Like many people at the natural foods store, I buy a lot of soy products. I'm not vegetarian or vegan, but I steer away from meats and dairies. I use vanilla soymilk with my cereal, I'll pick up Soy Delicious ice cream from time to time and, when I want a snack, I'll grab a bag of Soy Crisps. I prefer the buffalo burger to its veggie cousin, but I've been known to enjoy a garden breakfast sausage. And I'll be the first to suggest an edamame appetizer.

_____

_____

_____

3. Soy-planted area in MT contracted by nearly 1 million ha, and commodity prices crashed in 2006 and 2007. The area planted in soy increased each year since, but by 2010 still had not recovered to the highest levels recorded in 2005 (Fig. S2). After its peak in 2003, our analysis indicates that the percentage of large-scale (>25 ha) deforestation due to soy expansion decreased steadily, reaching 1 percent in 2009 (Fig. 3).

_____

_____

_____

4 There's another excellent reason to give edamame a try this summer. Many of us are eating more soy foods than ever before as we learn about the health benefits of this nutritious food. Aside from being a great source of quality protein and vitamin E, soy foods contain isoflavones, which seem to play a role in reducing the risk of heart attack, osteoporosis, breast cancer and prostate cancer.

_____

_____

_____

B. Imagine you are researching the following topics. Think about how old an article can be and still be useful. At what point does an article become outdated and no longer of any use to you?

MY ESSAY TOPIC IS ...	I WOULD NOT USE AN ARTICLE PUBLISHED EARLIER THAN ...
The health benefits of red wine	
Recommendations on salt consumption: an analysis	
The typical pioneer diet	
The use of arable land for raising beef cattle in Argentina	
Treatment for alcohol addiction: the best options	
The history of the fishing industry in Northern Europe	

Discuss your answers with your class. There is no "correct" answer here; you may have different opinions.

C. Consider again the question presented at the beginning of this chapter:

> Is meat an essential part of a healthy diet?

Find a published article on the topic of the nutritional value of meat. Answer the following questions.

1 Where was your article published? Do you think the article you have chosen is from an academic, peer-reviewed source? Why, or why not?

2 How recent is your article? Do you think it is still relevant and useful today?

3 You are writing an essay for your *Introduction to Nutrition* course, in which you argue for or against the health benefits of eating meat. Would you use the article you have chosen as support for your essay? If so, how would you use it? If not, why not?

The Caveman Diet

 FOCUS As you read this article, consider where it might have been published and whether or not this is a peer-reviewed source.

Before You Read

Work in groups of three or four. Discuss the following questions.

1 How much do you know about prehistoric people? Share your ideas about the way they lived.

2 This reading is about a diet that is based on the way prehistoric people ate. What do think this diet includes? What might be excluded? Write your thoughts below.

> We think this diet might include …

> We think it might exclude …

3 What do you think might be some health benefits of following a prehistoric diet?

Key Vocabulary

The words below are all in the reading. Fill in each space with the correct word.

NOUNS	addiction	ancestor	calorie	deficiency
	digestion	proponent		
VERBS	transition			
ADJECTIVES	abundant	lethargic	optimal	

1 If you have a/an _____ supply of something, you have plenty of it.

2 A/An _____ is a unit for measuring the amount of energy a food item produces.

3 A person who was a member of your family in previous generations is known as a/an _____. The opposite (i.e. someone of a more recent generation) is a *descendant*.

4 The _____ way to do something is the best or most suitable way to do it.

5 The process whereby food is changed to energy inside the body is called

_____ .

6 A/An _____ of something is a person who supports it or is in favour of it. The opposite is *opponent*.

7 People who _____ into a different lifestyle or career usually make a gradual but permanent change.

8 If you have a/an _____ to something, such as coffee or alcohol, you have a strong and often physical need for it.

9 A/An _____ is a lack or shortage of something that is necessary.

10 If you feel _____, you have no energy; you might want to sit on your sofa all day and watch television.

The Caveman Diet

By Randy Shore

Fruits, nuts, grass and whatever grubs, insects or game you can kill with your hands or a rock.

Our hunter-gatherer **ancestors** thrived on a daily menu of whatever was at hand until the development of agriculture about 10,000 years ago, and a surprising number
5 of dieters and fitness buffs are turning back their dietary clocks.

In a nutshell, the paleodiet[1] is an attempt to approximate the caloric and nutritional intake that human beings evolved to eat, before we started to plant grain and legumes for their easy, **abundant**, but largely empty, calories. Or so the theory goes.

The modern menu includes grass-fed meats, fruits, cooked and raw vegetables, wild
10 fish and unprocessed oils such as olive or avocado. Wheat, dairy and legumes, such as beans and peanuts, are not allowed because they are relatively recent additions to the human menu. Some versions forbid added salt. Most people limit or eliminate alcohol.

"It's really popular, at least half the people at my gym are eating something like the caveman diet," said Cassandra Kruger, a trainer at Momentum Fitness in Vancouver.
15 "It's in the same vein as the South Beach and Atkins diet in that they don't include any refined carbohydrates, so no grains, no sugar, no flour and no processed foods."

Some nutritionists warn that low-carb diets carry potential health hazards from kidney stones and low blood pressure to calcium **deficiency** and osteoporosis.[2]

Ultralow carb diets induce ketosis, a state in which the body burns fat for energy. You
20 will lose weight, but it is not without risk.

Warehouse manager Rahim Khan of Langley started on the paleodiet just before his twenty-seventh birthday. He weighed 250 pounds, heavy for his 5-foot-11 frame. →

---

[1] The prefix *paleo-* is used to refer to the time before agriculture, when stone tools and weapons were used.
[2] *Osteoporosis* is a medical condition, most often seen in elderly people, where the bones become weak and break easily.

"Less than a year later I hit my **optimal** weight of 173 pounds," said Khan, who lost weight even as he cut back on his workouts. "I used to be in the gym three or four days
25 a week and sometimes for two hours, now it's thirty minutes and I'm out."

Khan, his wife Liz and their three children all follow the paleodiet at home. Exceptions have to be made when the kids visit their grandparents, Khan laughed.

"I was skeptical at first," said Liz, who admits feeling sick and **lethargic** for the first two weeks after the change. "But I feel so much better now, I didn't even know how
30 lousy I felt before."

The Khans eat grass-fed beef, pork and chicken, usually the fattiest cuts they can find. Wheat in all its forms has disappeared, along with soy and corn. Dairy is confined to butter and small amounts of aged cheese.

Fruits and vegetables make up the balance of the plate, which Rahim says he usually
35 fills twice at supper time. When their personal workload gets heavy, the Khans will add a sweet potato with butter for extra energy.

"I like to just call it my lifestyle, it's the most logical way to eat," Rahim said. "What I do is based on the feedback my body gives. When I feel good I know I'm doing the right things."

40 The cavemen diet is an attractive weight-management program, because it is naturally low in **calories** and you are generally encouraged to eat whenever you are hungry. But the paleolithic menu probably has the most traction with people who have gluten sensitivity or celiac disease.[3]

"Just look at how many people are eliminating gluten from their diet," Kruger said.

45 Indeed, gluten-free foods are among the fastest growing product classes at the grocery store. And theceliacscene.com lists dozens of restaurants across Metro Vancouver that offer gluten-free meals.

Chilliwack mom Lori Wedel made some paleolithic adjustments to her entire family's diet to address her and her daughter Eva's gluten sensitivity.

50 "When Eva was three or four we started noticing that she was having trouble with her **digestion**," said Wedel, a community support worker.

Gluten sensitivity can cause symptoms including constipation, diarrhea and abdominal pain.

"We decided we needed to investigate what might be the problem, and we started to do an elimination diet," she recalled.

55 Eva showed no change when dairy was removed from the menu. "But when we got to gluten it was completely different and rapidly different," she said. "Within a week we noticed big changes, some we didn't expect."

"We thought she was a typical four-year-old until we started changing her diet," Wedel said. "She was a terror with concentration problems and aggression, but once we started
60 removing gluten it changed altogether."

---

[3] People who have gluten sensitivity (celiac disease) are unable to digest foods made from wheat and other grains.
  They typically experience stomach pains or diarrhea when they eat foods containing gluten.

Wedel's own allergies to nuts and to seafood meant there were few processed foods in the house anyway, but even fewer when the family began to eliminate sugar, artificial colourings and gluten.

"The difference in Eva made it impossible to go
65 back," Wedel said. "We can't eat another way."

Rather than keeping abundant carbohydrates in their diet with gluten-free breads and pasta, the Wedels just eliminated bread and grain-based foods such as pasta. At $7 a loaf for gluten-free
70 bread, it just didn't make sense.

"We eat meat every day and a whack of vegetables, usually in a stir-fry," she said. "We don't follow the strict paleodiet, if we have sushi we eat the rice and sometimes we have quinoa."[4]

75 Even though the Wedels don't consider themselves paleodieters, Eva likes to joke that she is a caveman child. Lori's husband Will, an engineer with the City of Chilliwack, is a big fan of the hefty portions of meat, usually chicken, pork and grass-fed beef.

"For me the biggest change was just deciding that not every meal had to be like my
80 mom taught me, meat, potatoes, grain, you don't need those to live," she said.

Wedel's sister Brittany Eidsness, a registered holistic nutritionist, helped tweak the family's menus.

When calories from wheat, rice, potatoes and refined sugar are eliminated from the diet, the ratio of fibre, vitamins, minerals and important nutrients per calorie consumed
85 goes way up.

The exception is vitamin D, which hunter gatherers produced in great abundance because they lived outdoors and spent long hours walking and foraging.

"People have a hard time figuring out what to eat and this diet is healthy and very clear," she said. "It removes all of the foods that cause us problems."

90 **Proponents** of the caveman diet point out that so-called "diseases of civilization"—heart disease, cancer, obesity and diabetes—were not a problem to people who lived in the Paleolithic period, which ran from about 2.5 million years ago until farming took hold about 8,000 BCE.

"The paleodiet is naturally low-carb and focuses on clean protein sources like grass-
95 fed beef, wild fish, naturally raised chicken and eggs," said Eidsness. "Then you are going to have as many vegetables as you can possibly eat, with the possible exception of nightshade vegetables[5] for people who are sensitive to them."

→

---

4 *Quinoa* is a member of the grass family that originates in South America. It is high in protein and calcium, and is considered to be a very valuable food.
5 *Nightshade vegetables* include tomatoes, eggplant and peppers.

People **transitioning** to the caveman diet can expect a minor rebellion by their body. Many people experience lethargy, headaches and flu-like symptoms that 100 Eidsness attributes to a withdrawal from the body's **addiction** to sugar and carbohydrates.

Critics of the paleodiet trend point to a long list of incongruities, knowledge gaps about the true nature of man's diet during the Paleolithic period.

A true paleolithic diet would probably include some wild game, tart berries, insects, 105 roots and wild tubers, shellfish, rodents and the occasional cache of honey. But it would also vary enormously from north to south, coast to inland and continent to continent, ranging from a chimpanzee-like diet of fruits to a very fatty meat-based diet of seal and caribou consumed by Arctic peoples.

The truth is that defining a true paleolithic diet is next to impossible.

110 In addition to the potential for health impacts from eating an ultra low-carb diet, a leading Canadian nutritionist warns that paleodieters often eat more meat than is healthy for them and the planet.

The environmental cost of a largely meat-based diet is probably the strongest argument against eating like a modern caveman, said David Jenkins, a professor of nutritional 115 sciences at the University of Toronto and Canada Research Chair in Nutrition and Metabolism.

"We just can't produce enough calories in meat protein and fat to feed the world's human population, it's not sustainable," Jenkins said.

Widely accepted estimates suggest it takes 16 kilos of grain to produce one kilo of 120 beef and at least 441 gallons of water.

Caveman diet proponents claim that eating what they believe to be the human ancestral diet will reduce their risk of disease, pointing out that Paleolithic-era people were not afflicted with today's most common ailments, many of which are associated with obesity and old age.

125 That idea might just hold water.

Pre-agricultural humans did live long enough to suffer from diseases of age, and there is evidence arthritis was common, though obesity, heart disease and diabetes were rare or entirely absent.

Jenkins is skeptical that such dramatic alterations in our modern diet are key to better 130 health.

"The first step in adopting a paleolithic lifestyle would be to throw away your car keys and walk everywhere," he said. "The diet we have adopted over the past 10,000 years suits our physiology just fine if we are exercising. The problem is we put all these starchy calories in our body and then try to burn them driving everywhere in 135 our cars."

(1546 words)

Shore, R. (2012, July 19). The caveman diet. *The Vancouver Sun*. Retrieved from http://www.vancouversun.com/health/cav eman+diet+Meat+eaters+love+critics+call+craze/6959423/story.html

Check Your Understanding

A. Go back to the predictions you made in "Before You Read". How many of your predictions were accurate? Did you predict anything that was not addressed in the reading?

B. Choose the correct answer for the questions below.

① Which of the following combinations is permitted by the caveman diet?

a) steak and potatoes   c) fish and rice

b) pizza and salad   d) chicken and broccoli

② Which is the main food group eliminated from the caveman diet?

a) proteins   c) carbohydrates

b) fats   d) vegetables

③ Which condition may *not* be helped by following the caveman diet?

a) obesity   c) gluten sensitivity

b) osteoporosis   d) diabetes

④ Which of the following statements is probably *not* true?

a) It is easier to produce grains than to raise animals for food.

b) The caveman diet will save you a lot of money.

c) Today's caveman diet may be different from our ancestors' diet.

d) We could get the same benefits by exercising more.

C. Answer the following questions in your own words using information from the reading.

① Describe some of the key features of the paleodiet. Which food groups do people who follow this diet usually choose from? What do they avoid?

_____

_____

② Consider the two people mentioned in the article, Rahim Khan and Lori Wedel. Fill in the chart below with information about them.

	REASON FOR TRYING THIS DIET	TYPICAL DAILY DIET	HEALTH BENEFITS
Rahim Khan			
Lori Wedel			

3 The paleodiet is useful for people who want to lose weight: true or false? Why?

_____

_____

4 What is meant by the term "diseases of civilization"? Give three examples.

_____

_____

5 Why might some people feel unwell after they start to follow the paleodiet?

_____

_____

6 How does today's version of the paleodiet differ from the way our ancestors probably ate?

_____

_____

7 What does David Jenkins think we should do if we really want to adopt a paleolithic lifestyle?

_____

_____

Analysis and Discussion

Discuss the following questions with your group.

1 Look again at the chart on page 23. Do you think this article came from a peer-reviewed source or a non-academic source? Explain your answer.

2 This article was published in Vancouver, Canada, in 2012. To what extent are a) the city and b) the date significant? Could this article have appeared in another country? Could it have appeared twenty-five years ago?

3 Why do you think the paleodiet is so popular today?

4 Why do you think the author included quotations from David Jenkins?

5 Which readers do you think might be interested in this diet and might want to try it? Which readers do you think might be skeptical?

6 How do you personally feel about the paleodiet? Could you happily eat in this way? Are you interested in trying it? Why, or why not?

There's No Reason to Eat Animals

This article presents an opposing point of view to the previous reading.

 FOCUS **As you read this article, consider again what type of publication it comes from. Ask yourself to what extent the information provided is reliable and trustworthy.**

Before You Read

Work in groups of three or four. Discuss the following questions.

1. Are you a vegetarian? If so, why? If not, do you have vegetarian friends? What reasons do they give for following a vegetarian diet?

2. How common do you think vegetarianism is around the world? How popular is vegetarianism in countries you know well?

3. How do you think a vegetarian might respond to the previous reading about the paleodiet?

Key Vocabulary

The words below are all in the reading. Match each word with the correct definition.

1. abolish (v. line 28) _____   a) without cruelty or causing suffering

2. authority (n. line 48) _____   b) make (people) calm or stop (them) worrying

3. betray (v. line 10) _____   c) officially end something

4. euthanize (v. line 23) _____   d) feel sad because a loved one has died

5. feasibility (n. line 52) _____   e) basic or common

6. grieve (v. line 5) _____   f) be disloyal to someone who trusted you

7. humanely (adv. line 13) _____   g) expert; someone whose opinions are respected

8. pacify (v. line 35) _____   h) kill in a painless way

9. staple (adj. line 57) _____   i) equivalent to

10. tantamount to (adj. line 70) _____   j) likelihood of being effective or successful

There's No Reason to Eat Animals

By Lindsay Rajt

If we care about the environment and believe that kindness is a virtue—as we all say that we do—a vegan[1] diet is the only sensible option. The question becomes: Why eat animals at all?

Animals are made of flesh, bone and blood, just as you and I are. They form
5 friendships, feel pain and joy, grieve for lost loved ones and are afraid to die. One cannot profess to care about animals while tearing them away from their friends and families and cutting their throats—or paying someone else to do it—simply to satisfy a fleeting taste for flesh.

What does it say about us that we're willing to give animals
10 a safe pasture and freedom from suffering only to betray them by killing and eating them in the end? Nicolette Hahn Niman argues in her recent book that it's acceptable to raise animals for food as long as they are treated humanely and killed quickly. But we wouldn't extend that philosophy to
15 dogs, cats or children. The inconsistency means that eating animals simply cannot be justified.

Ms. Niman assures consumers that the animals at the ranch that she manages with her husband, Bill Niman, have a "good life and an easy death." This likely conjures up
20 images of pigs frolicking together, getting belly rubs and playing in mud puddles while turkeys strut about, gobbling along to music and eating fresh corncobs, melons and grapes until they're peacefully euthanized at a ripe old age. Think again. While the animals at BN Ranch may have a better life and may face an easier death than the animals killed for Smithfield or
25 Butterball, "good" is not an accurate description. What kind of good life ends at age twelve, which is the human equivalent of the oldest non-breeding animals on farms such as hers? Niman's arguments are similar to those of slaveholders who advocated treating slaves more kindly but did not actually want to abolish slavery.

Ultimately, it's not our farming practices that need to change—it's our diets. As Niman
30 knows, we cannot use only pastureland to produce the amount of meat that is currently consumed in this country. Approximately ten billion cows, pigs, chickens and turkeys are killed for food each year in the United States alone. The sheer number of animals killed to satisfy people's taste for flesh makes it impossible to raise and slaughter them all on small family farms.

35 Claiming that meat eating can be ethical or eco-friendly tends to pacify people who want to feel as if they are doing the right thing but don't want to stop eating meat. Yet raising and killing animals is neither moral nor green. As Niman knows, meat

---

[1] While vegetarians do not eat meat, vegans do not eat any form of animal product. This includes milk, cheese, eggs and honey.

production is resource-intensive and plays a role in nearly every major environmental problem, including climate change.

40 Animal agriculture is one of the world's largest sources of CO_2 and the largest source of methane, which is more than twenty-three times more powerful than CO_2 when it comes to trapping heat in the atmosphere. Research by Robert Goodland and Jeff Anhang, the authors of *Livestock and Climate Change*, indicates that raising animals for food produces 51 percent of global greenhouse gas emissions each year. Of course,

45 animals on feedlots produce more greenhouse gasses than pasture-raised animals, but all farmed animals produce methane while digesting food, and their feces also emit methane.

One of the world's leading authorities on climate change—Dr. Rajendra Pachauri, chair of the Intergovernmental Panel on Climate Change and himself a vegetarian—

50 believes that everyone in the developed world should consume a vegetarian diet for environmental reasons. According to Pachauri, "In terms of immediacy of action and the feasibility of bringing about reductions in a short period of time, it clearly is the most attractive opportunity." The Netherlands Environmental Assessment Agency has reported that climate change mitigation costs could be reduced by 80 percent if everyone

55 around the globe went vegan.

Meat consumption is also a major contributor to food shortages. There would be more food to go around if more people went vegan because many staple crops are fed to farmed animals instead of to hungry people. This is especially wasteful considering that animals can only turn a small fraction of that food into flesh. It takes

60 about 700 calories worth of feed to produce just one piece of 100-calorie beef.

More food can be grown on a given parcel of land when we aren't funneling crops through animals. Vegfam, which funds sustainable plant-food projects, estimates that a ten-acre farm can support sixty people by growing soy, twenty-four people by growing wheat or ten people by growing corn—but only two by raising cattle.

65 The United Nations' special envoy on food says that it's a "crime against humanity" to funnel 100 million tons of grain and corn into ethanol while nearly one billion people are starving. So how much more of a crime is it to divert 756 million tons of grain and corn per year—plus 98 percent of the 225-million-ton global soy crop—to farmed animals? With 1.4 billion people living in dire poverty, reserving these harvests for

70 animal forage is tantamount to stealing food out of people's mouths.

Meat production is inefficiency at its worst. When you factor in all the water squandered on animal agriculture and all the fossil fuels needed to operate slaughterhouses and processing plants and to transport meat from the plants to the stores—not to mention the air and water pollution that results from it all—you'll

75 understand why it just makes sense not to eat animals. As Ms. Niman—who herself has been a vegetarian for years—can tell you, one can live quite healthily and happily without eating animals. (994 words)

Rajt, L. (2010 Spring). There's no reason to eat animals. *Earth Island Journal, 25*(1), Retrieved from 47–48. http://www.earthisland.org/journal/index.php/eij/article/campaigner/

Check Your Understanding

A. Are the following statements true (T) or false (F)?

		T	F
1	Animals can experience emotions.	○	○
2	The animals at BN Ranch live a long, healthy and happy life.	○	○
3	The writer believes meat production is related to climate change.	○	○
4	The writer thinks eating meat can be both ethical and eco-friendly.	○	○
5	It is more efficient to raise animals than to produce crops.	○	○

B. When you come to write a critical review of a text, you will need to include a summary of the text's main ideas.

How to Write a Summary

1 Read the text more than once, making sure you understand everything. Look up new and important vocabulary (key ideas, definitions or repeated words).

2 Write down the key points of the text. You will often find the key points in the first and last paragraphs and in the first sentence of two of each paragraph.

3 Write the first draft of your summary. Make sure that you include all the main ideas, not just the first or most obvious ones. Do not include small details. Ensure that your summary is not repetitive.

4 Read through your summary and check to see if a) you have included the main ideas and b) your summary is clear on its own. In other words, can someone who has not read the original text get the main points from your summary alone?

5 Read your summary again, and check to see whether it reads as a cohesive paragraph. Does the language flow? If not, consider joining sentences with conjunctions such as "because" or "whereas" or using transitional devices such as "however" or "therefore."

6 Write the final version of your summary.

Write down the key points of the following argument: "... raising and killing animals is neither moral nor green" (line 37).

It is not moral.

_____

_____

_____

_____

It is not green.

_____

_____

_____

_____

Now, use your points and write a summary of each argument.

Analysis and Discussion

Discuss the following questions with your group.

1 Look again at the chart on page 23. Do you think this article came from a peer-reviewed source or a non-academic source? Explain your answer.

2 The author uses several techniques to convince the reader to accept her argument. Find an example in the reading of each of the following.

a) A use of "you …" to address the reader directly

b) A quotation from an expert on the topic

c) A direct question she asks the reader to consider

d) An appeal to the reader's emotions

e) A shocking statistic

3 Where does most of the supporting detail in the article come from? Has the author done her own research, or does she rely on the findings of others? If she uses information from others, who are these people? Are they reliable sources?

4 How might a paleodieter respond to Lindsay Rajt's statement that there is no reason to eat meat?

READING 3

Obesity: A Public Health Failure?

 As you read this article, consider how it differs from the previous two texts; refer to the chart on page 23.

Before You Read

Work in groups of three or four. Discuss the following questions.

1 Is obesity a problem in parts of the world you are familiar with? If so, why do you think this is?

2 Who should be responsible for solving the problem of obesity: individuals, schools, governments, doctors or someone else?

3 Look at the reading below. In what ways does it immediately seem different from the previous two readings in this chapter? Give three differences.

Obesity: A Public Health Failure?

Tavis Glassman PhD, MPH, MCHES, Jennifer Glassman M.A., CCC-SLP, and Aaron J. Diehr, MA

Abstract: Obesity rates continue to escalate, bringing into question the efficacy of prevention and treatment efforts. While intuitively appealing, the law of thermodynamics represents a gross oversimplification for weight gain, as calories represent only one variable of the multifaceted issue of weight management. From a historical perspective, the recommendation to eat a low fat, high carbohydrate diet may have been the wrong message to promote, thereby exacerbating the obesity epidemic. Suggestions to address the obesity epidemic include taxing, restricting advertising and reducing accessibility to sugar. Communities must employ these and other strategies to curtail sugar use and reduce obesity rates.

Obesity represents an immense public health threat to the welfare and prosperity of the nation.

With one-third of its population overweight and another one-third obese (Ogden, Carroll, Kit, & Flegal, 2012), America has the highest obesity rate among developed countries in the world (Popkin & Gordon-Larsen, 2004). These rates reflect a nation's inability to meet the *Healthy People 2010* National Health Objectives to reduce the prevalence of obesity among adults to less than 15 percent. As a response to this lack of progress, the revised goal for 2020 was a little more modest, calling for a 10 percent improvement (U.S. Department of Health and Human Services, 2010a). The list of ailments associated with obesity includes heart disease, diabetes, sleep apnea, hypertension, asthma, stroke, infertility and some cancers. In spite of vast prevention and treatment efforts, obesity rates have been increasing since the 1970s (U.S. Department of Health and Human Services, 2010b). The future does not look promising, with approximately 18 percent of the children in this country classified as obese (Centers for Disease Control and Prevention, 2012). This may be the first generation of children with a shorter life expectancy than its parents. What caused the spike in obesity rates, and why has such little progress been made? More importantly, what approaches can health educators and others take to remedy this public health dilemma?

Perhaps the shift in dietary focus began in the 1950s with Ancel Keys, when he theorized a diet low in animal fat would reduce cholesterol[1] and thereby reduce the risk for heart disease. In an attempt to prove his hypothesis, his research team collected data from twenty-two countries, but curiously only reported on the results from seven of them. He incorrectly concluded from the study, now called the *Seven Countries Study*, that a strong association existed between serum cholesterol and coronary heart disease and maintained a reduction in animal fat intake would reduce cholesterol levels (Werkö, 2008). Subsequently, the American Heart Association (AHA), World Health Organization (WHO)

---

[1] *Cholesterol* is a fat produced in the body. Too much cholesterol is related to heart disease and other illnesses.

and Centers for Disease Control and Prevention (CDC) cautioned the public to avoid or limit the consumption of butter, eggs, lard, whole milk and other high fat foods. These recommendations then spread to the general public, due in part to tenacious health education efforts.

In the 1980s and 1990s, low fat, high-carb diets became the prevailing trend. In response to these public recommendations, fat was removed from refined carbohydrates, which resulted in a less-than-desirable taste. To compensate for lost taste, food manufactures added sugar, and lots of it. Consider a present day example; a certain brand's Skinny Latte Fat-Free French Vanilla instant coffee mix has 0 grams of fat and 23 grams of carbohydrates. The regular French Vanilla has 4.5 grams of fat but only 19 grams of carbohydrates, meaning that the "skinny" version actually has four more grams of carbohydrates. Today, though sugar is ubiquitous, it is often disguised by various euphemisms on the food ingredients label— high fructose corn syrup, cane juice and sucrose, to name a few—potentially confusing well-intended laypersons. Americans dramatically changed their dietary habits during this time. The proportion of calories from carbohydrates increased significantly among males and females, from 42 percent to 49 percent and from 45 percent to 52 percent, respectively. Meanwhile, the percentage of calories from fat decreased approximately four percent for males and females, whereas protein intake remained stable (Centers for Disease Control and Prevention, 2004). This combined proportional shift in macronutrient consumption cannot be ignored when examining obesity rates over the last twenty-five years.

Further complicating matters was the introduction of high-fructose corn syrup (HFCS) to the market during the mid-1970s. Manufacturers produce HFCS by milling corn to produce corn starch and processing the starch into corn syrup, whereby enzymes then change the glucose into fructose (Marshall, Kooi, & Moffett, 1957). HFCS's development occurred, in part, due to the escalating costs associated with imported sugar. It is more economical to produce high-fructose corn syrup because of the government subsidies paid to farmers to grow corn (Tyner & Quear, 2006). Incidentally, in an effort to maximize bushels of corn per acre, chemical manufacturers created seeds with pesticides developed to work in conjunction with particular herbicides (Shelton, Zhao, & Roush, 2002). The consequences for these biological interactions are unknown, as is the impact to the environment. However, corn production has never been more efficient, and subsequently, the percentage of added sugars to the American diet increased 25 percent since the 1970s (Bray, 2007). In fact, people today consume an average of more than 500 calories per day from added sugar (USDA, 2002), due in part to HFCS.

As blood sugar levels rise, the brain sends a message to the pancreas to stimulate insulin;[2] high insulin levels cause a precipitous drop in blood sugar, resulting in hunger. Ironically, this drop can lead to hunger cravings that can surpass fasting levels. All things being equal, the more sugar a person eats, the hungrier he or she becomes, thus disrupting homeostasis.[3] Sugar consumption is critical because emerging research indicates that sugar interferes with the hormones *leptin* and *ghrelin*, which influence satiety (Ribeiro et al., 2011). In experimental animal and human case studies, reduced leptin has been linked to weight gain and distorted ⇥

---

[2] *Insulin* is a hormone produced in the body. When insulin levels are not controlled, the result may be diabetes.
[3] *Homeostasis* is the process by which the body keeps conditions within the body relatively stable and balanced.

regulation of food intake (Lustig, Schmidt, & Brindis, 2012). Additionally, some argue that sugar consumption elicits addictive responses by activating the brain's reward centre, causing the release of the neurotransmitter dopamine, among others (Davis et al., 2007). The user develops tolerance similar to addiction and requires more and more of the substance to obtain the same pleasurable feeling (Sartor et al., 2011). With homeostasis disrupted, the individual feels lethargic, decreasing the likelihood of engaging in physical exercise. Ironically, conventional wisdom puts the onus primarily on the individual, placing self-control ahead of biology. Indeed, Ebbeling et al. (2012) found that patients placed on a low fat diet, after achieving a 10 percent weight loss, produced changes in energy expenditure and serum leptin levels associated with weight gain. No wonder so many people regain weight after losing it.

Whereas scientists are making significant advances, sugar is so pervasive in the food supply that it adds another layer of complexity to the research not often addressed. Consider the following example. In what some refer to as "The Big Study," Sacks et al. (2009) sought to determine to what extent the proportion of fat, protein and carbohydrates affected weight loss. Participants were followed for two years, and the researchers concluded reduced-calorie diets resulted in weight loss regardless of which macronutrients are emphasized. However, in each of the four cohorts, at least 35 percent of the diet came from carbohydrates. More importantly, with the exception of fruits and vegetables, almost all other carbohydrates contained some form of sugar. Thus, it is not surprising that a significant weight loss did not occur among any of the cohorts. The average weight loss was only about 9 kg among participants who attended two-thirds of the sessions over the two-year period. The point is that each of the diets contained too much sugar to achieve meaningful weight loss, sabotaging dieters' efforts and confounding research results.

Critics of nutritional research believe the medical community and the federal government relied upon misinterpreted scientific data to define what constitutes healthy eating (Lustig, et al., 2012; Taubes, 2007). Take, for instance, the recommended dietary guidelines published by United States Department of Agriculture. Whereas the current nutrition guide, "My Plate" (2011), marks an improvement from the Basic Four (1956–1992), the Food Guide Pyramid (1992-2005), and MyPyramid (2005–2011), it still promotes too much carbohydrate intake in the form of refined carbohydrates (including foods made from flour and sugars) (Marantz, 2010; Taubes, 2007). If the current nutrition guide is inadequate, imagine how problematic the past models were. One has to wonder what influence, if any, the food industry had on these recommendations, given the number of studies they funded over the years. The food industry represents a billion dollar business and has a lot of money to lose if Americans change their diets. It is more difficult to market fruits and vegetables because they tend not to come in fancy packages, in contrast with cereal, for example.

The Hippocratic Oath[4] states to do no harm; did public health authorities and health educators send a maleficent message by promoting a low fat, high carbohydrate diet? Maybe the government made recommendations from a resource perspective, based on the relatively limited supply of fresh fruit, vegetable and meat sources to feed the American public, let

---

[4] The Hippocratic Oath is a promise made by doctors on graduation that they will practise medicine honestly and ethically.

alone the rest of the world. Conversely, what if the government subsidized fresh fruits and vegetables rather than field corn 230 (in contrast to sweet corn or popcorn), which represents over 90 percent of corn grown today in the U.S. (USDA, 2010)? Consider the environmental impact of a landscape rich with fruits and vegetables 235 rather than the same crop, depleting the topsoil year after year. To offset expenses further, elected officials could pass legislation taxing sugar. The United States is currently considering a penny-per-ounce 240 soda tax, which would only increase the cost of a can of soda by about 12 cents but would provide $14 billion in revenue a year (Lustig, et al., 2012). Farmers could also use these resources and subsidies to provide 245 free-range farms, which preserve the land and are more humane to the animals.

It is difficult to imagine a more important topic than nutrition based on the environmental, fiscal and health outcomes 250 associated with obesity. Similar to tobacco and alcohol prevention efforts, improvements to the obesity epidemic warrant the implementation of traditional public health measures. Using environmental 255 management strategies such as restricting advertising and access to unhealthy foods, as well as incorporating taxes on certain food products, merits serious consideration. This is the first time in history that the poor 260 suffer from obesity at higher rates than the wealthy; often-unhealthy foods (e.g., processed foods) tend to be cheaper and more aggressively marketed than healthier options. The government needs to ensure 265 that school lunches, WIC (Special Supplemental Nutrition Program for Women, Infants and Children) services and food stamp programs eliminate or at least minimize the distribution of foods with high 270 levels of sugar. Providing the poor with unhealthy food constitutes not only poor

public policy based on the long-term medical costs associated with dietary comorbidities, it also raises serious ethical 275 considerations.

The terminology used in discussing obesity causes all sorts of confusion, leading to *learned helplessness* for some. As previously noted, contrary to popular belief, 280 the consumption of dietary fat does not cause the accumulation of adipose tissue (body fat) per se. It also turns out that not all carbohydrates are created equal. Many diet recommendations call for a low 285 proportion of carbohydrates without delineating which type and source of carbohydrate to avoid. For example, fruits and vegetables are classified as carbohydrates, yet most people do not consume 290 enough of either. Thus, endorsing a low carbohydrate diet exemplifies a gross oversimplification, as does the law of thermodynamics, when applied to nutrition. For example, the mantra "a calorie is a 295 calorie" has dominated dietary rhetoric for at least the last half century. Intuitively, the formula makes sense, because people need to burn more calories than they consume. However, the hormonal influence certain 300 foods (e.g., sugar) have on weight gain may be a more critical, or at least an underemphasized, variable.

In conclusion, the obesity epidemic is on par, from a public health perspective, with 305 water treatment, sewage regulations, the advent of food refrigeration, seat belt regulations and tobacco prevention, among others, representing the iconic challenge of this era. As with any public health issue, the 310 foundation for remedying any problem begins with research. Scientists need to conduct rigorous research free from overt bias, reporting on the results of hypotheses and alternative hypotheses, a failure of 315 earlier research in this area. Researchers then need to disseminate the results in a ⇒

clear and comprehensible fashion, to shape individual behaviour and inform public policy, even if the results counter con-
320 ventional wisdom. With courage, conviction and persistence, the prevalence of obesity will decrease, in turn, lowering the rates of diabetes, heart disease and other co-morbidities. Ultimately, these health
325 improvements will lead to increased quantity and quality of life while reducing the financial burden to families and communities. Given the ever-escalating expenditures concurrent with health care
330 costs, prevention efforts cannot wait.

Glassman, T., Glassman, J., & Diehr, A. J. (2013). Obesity: A Public Health Failure? *American Journal of Health Studies, 28*(4), 8–11.

References

Bray, G. A. (2007). How bad is fructose? American *Journal of Clinical Nutrition*, 86(4), 895-896.

Centers for Disease Control and Prevention (2004). Trends in intake of energy and macronutrients— United States, 1971–2000, *MMWR Morbidity Mortality Weekly Report 53*(04) 80–82. Retrieved February 20, 2013 from http://www.cdc.gov/mmwr/preview/mmwrhtml/mm5304a3.htm

Centers for Disease Control and Prevention. (2012). *Prevalence of obesity among persons Aged 12–19 years, by race/ethnicity and sex—National Health and Nutrition Examination Survey, United States, 2009–2010.* Retrieved February 20, 2013 from http://www.cdc.gov/mmwr/preview/mmwrhtml/mm6109a7.htm

Davis, C., Patte, K., Levitan, R., Reid, C., Tweed, S., & Curtis, C. (2007). From motivation to behaviour: A model of reward sensitivity, overeating, and food preferences in the risk profile for obesity. *Appetite, 48*(1), 12–19.

Ebbeling, C. B., Swain, J. F., Feldman, H. A., Wong, W. W., Hachey, D. L., Garcia-Lago, E., & Ludwig, D. S. (2012). Effects of dietary composition on energy expenditure during weight-loss maintenance. *JAMA, 307*(24), 2627–2634.

Lustig, R. H., Schmidt, L. A., & Brindis, C. D. (2012). Public health: The toxic truth about sugar. *Nature, 482*(7383), 27–29.

Marantz, P. R. (2010). Rethinking dietary guidelines. *Critical Reviews in Food Science & Nutrition, 50,* 17–18.

Marshall, R. O., Kooi, E. R., & Moffett, G. M. (1957). Enzymatic conversion of d-glucose to d-fructose. *Science, 125*(3249), 648–649.

Ogden, C. L., Carroll, M. D., Kit, B. K., & Flegal, K. M. (2012). Prevalence of obesity in the United States, 2009–2010. *NCHS Data Brief, 82,* 1–8.

Popkin, B. M., & Gordon-Larsen, P. (2004). The nutrition transition: worldwide obesity dynamics and their determinants. *International Journal of Obesity & Related Metabolic Disorders, 28,* S2–S9.

Ribeiro, A. C., Ceccarini, G., Dupré, C., Friedman J. M., Pfaff, D. W., & Mark, A. L. (2011). Contrasting effects of leptin on food anticipatory and total locomotor activity. *PLoS ONE, 6*(8), 1–8.

Sacks, F. M., Bray, G. A., Carey, V. J., Smith, S. R., Ryan, D. H., Anton, S. D., . . . Williamson, D.A. (2009). Comparison of Weight-Loss Diets with Different Compositions of Fat, Protein, and Carbohydrates. *New England Journal of Medicine, 360*(9), 859–873.

Sartor, F., Donaldson, L. F., Markland, D. A., Loveday, H., Jackson, M. J., & Kubis, H.-P. (2011). Taste perception and implicit attitude toward sweet related to body mass index and soft drink supplementation. *Appetite, 57*(1), 237–246.

Shelton, A. M., Zhao, J. Z., & Roush, R. T. (2002). Economic, ecological, food safety, and social consequences of the deployment of Bt transgenic plants. *Annual Review of Entomology, 47,* 845–881.

Taubes, G. (2007). Good calories, bad calories: *Challenging the conventional wisdom on diet, weight control, and disease.* New York: Anchor Books.

Tyner, W. E., & Quear, J. (2006). Comparison of a fixed and variable corn ethanol subsidy. *Choices: The Magazine of Food, Farm & Resource Issues, 21*(3), 199–202.

U.S. Department of Health and Human Services. (2010a). *Healthy People 2020.* Retrieved February 20, 2013 from http://www.healthpeople.gov/2020/topicsobjectives2020/objectiveslist.aspx?topicId=29.

U.S. Department of Health and Human Services. (2010b). *Overweight and Obesity Statistics.* Retrieved February 20, 2013 from http://win.niddk.nih.gov/publications/PDFs/stat904z.pdf.

USDA. (2002). *Agriculture Fact Book* Government Printing Office.

USDA. (2010). *Economic Research Service.* Retrieved August 10, 2012, from http://www.ers.usda.gov/topics/farm-economy/bioenergy/findings.aspx.

2144 words (excluding references)

Werkö, L. (2008). End of the road for the dietheart theory? *Scandinavian CardiovascularJournal*, 42(4), 250–255.

Check Your Understanding

A. Which statement best summarizes the arguments presented by the authors of this paper?

    a) Many people who want to lose weight try to limit the amount of fat they consume. However, a more effective way to maintain a healthy weight would be to limit the number of carbohydrates in your diet, especially carbohydrates in the form of sugar.

    b) A calorie is a calorie. It doesn't matter what you eat, as long as you don't consume an excessive number of calories. Dietary trends come and go, but the difference between a low-fat and a low-carbohydrate diet is very small.

    c) The best way to lose weight is to eat a low-fat diet. This was proven in the 1950s by Ancel Keys and his colleagues. People who want to lose weight need to reduce their consumption of animal fats, such as butter and milk.

B. Choose the best ending for each of the following sentences.

1 According to the authors, the obesity problem in the United States is caused by the fact that

    a) Americans eat too much fat.

    b) Americans eat too much sugar.

2 In the 1950s, doctors concluded that for optimal health, people should eat

    a) less fat.

    b) fewer carbohydrates.

3 It is often hard to know that a food product contains sugar because

    a) it is not always easy to taste the sugar in food.

    b) sugar is often given other names, such as "sucrose."

4 The introduction of high-fructose corn syrup has caused sugar consumption to

    a) increase.

    b) decrease.

5 The more sugar a person eats, the more that person feels

    a) hungry.

    b) full.

6 The "Big Study" of 2009 showed that

    a) most people eat too much sugar to lose weight.

    b) the best way to lose a lot of weight is to limit calories.

7 A healthy diet should include

    a) less fruit, because fruit contains carbohydrates, which cause weight gain.

    b) more fruit, because not all carbohydrates act in the same way.

8 Poor people are more likely to be obese than wealthy people because

    a) they lack education about good eating habits.

    b) unhealthy food is often cheaper than fresh, healthy food.

Key Vocabulary

Find the following words and expressions in the text. Choose the best synonym for the word or expression.

1 associated with (line 18)

　　a) related to　　　　　　　　　　　　b) responsible for

2 life expectancy (line 30)

　　a) goals in life　　　　　　　　　　　b) predicted length of life

3 prove a hypothesis (line 40)

　　a) show that a theory is correct　　　b) show that someone is wrong

4 euphemism (line 76)

　　a) polite way of saying something negative　　b) definition of a word

5 complicate matters (line 94)

　　a) show the importance of something　　b) make a difficult situation more confusing

6 work in conjunction with (line 111)

　　a) work against　　　　　　　　　　b) work together with

7 sabotage (line 187)

　　a) improve　　　　　　　　　　　　b) damage or obstruct

8 fiscal (line 249)

　　a) related to the body　　　　　　　b) related to money

9 merit serious consideration (line 258)

　　a) deserve careful thought　　　　　b) be seen as negative

10 conventional wisdom (lines 319 to 320)

　　a) general knowledge　　　　　　　b) common way of thinking

Analysis and Discussion

A. Work in pairs. Complete the chart below with information about all three articles in this chapter. What differences do you see?

	THE CAVEMAN DIET	THERE'S NO REASON TO EAT ANIMALS	OBESITY: A PUBLIC HEALTH FAILURE?
Is there an abstract?			
How long are the paragraphs?			

	THE CAVEMAN DIET	THERE'S NO REASON TO EAT ANIMALS	OBESITY: A PUBLIC HEALTH FAILURE?
How complex are the sentences?			
How technical or specialized is the vocabulary?			
How many references are given?			
What, if any, other differences can you see?			

Based on your answers, in what kind of publication do you think this article appeared? Who do you think this article was written for?

B. Discuss the following questions with your group.

1. The authors suggest in the title obesity is "a public health failure." Who do they blame for the rise in obesity? Do you agree with their analysis?

2. How do you think the authors of this text would respond to the readings on the paleodiet and the vegetarian diet? Would they agree or disagree with proponents of each of these diets?

3. Do you think the solutions put forward by the authors are the best ones? Are they realistic? Could there be any drawbacks to these solutions?

4. Has this text convinced you of the need to limit sugar in your diet? Why, or why not?

Going Further
Focus on Language

A. The following chart contains ten words from the readings. Complete the chart with related words in the other categories, and, where possible, in the same category. (There may not be a word for each category.)

➡

	NOUN	VERB	ADJECTIVE	ADVERB
1	argument			
2		complicate		
3		consume		
4		decide		
5	development			
6			optimal	
7			personal	
8			popular	
9			stable	
10		theorize		

B. The word *paleodiet* is a combination of the words *paleolithic* + *diet*. When two words are combined to make a new word, this is called a "blended" word. Blended words often come and go in and out of fashion. Look at the following examples and decide which words they are made from. Can you think of any others?

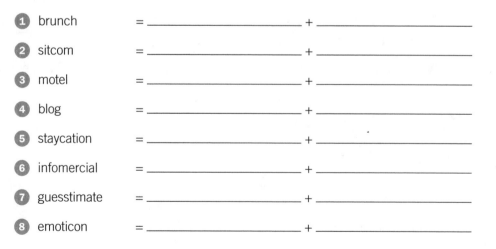

1 brunch = _____ + _____

2 sitcom = _____ + _____

3 motel = _____ + _____

4 blog = _____ + _____

5 staycation = _____ + _____

6 infomercial = _____ + _____

7 guesstimate = _____ + _____

8 emoticon = _____ + _____

Independent Research

Choose one of the following diets and carry out some online research about this approach to eating. You will present your findings to your class.

> Atkins Diet

> Mediterranean

> Beverly Hills Diet

> South Beach Diet

> Macrobiotic diet

> Raw foods diet

Synthesis and Written Response

Based on your reading of the texts in this chapter as well as your own research into dietary trends, write a short response to the following question:

> Meat is an essential part of a healthy diet. Do you agree or disagree?

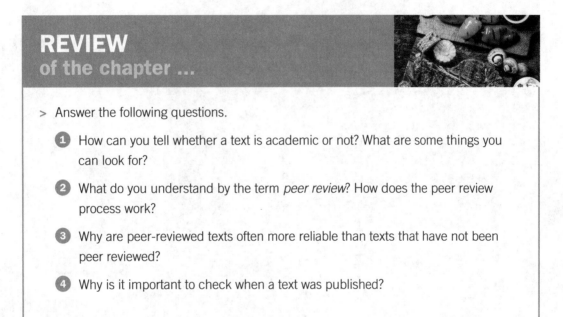

REVIEW
of the chapter ...

> Answer the following questions.

1 How can you tell whether a text is academic or not? What are some things you can look for?

2 What do you understand by the term *peer review*? How does the peer review process work?

3 Why are peer-reviewed texts often more reliable than texts that have not been peer reviewed?

4 Why is it important to check when a text was published?

Sources of text excerpts pages 24–25:

1. Martin, D. S., Williams, J.L., Breitkopf, N. P., Eyster, K. M. (2002). Pressor responsiveness to angiotensin in soy-fed spontaneously hypertensive rats. *Canadian Journal of Physiology and Pharmacology, 80*(12), 1180–1186.

2. Barnes, E. (2008, Sept. 8). The tofu trap: our soy habit has environmental consequences. *Our Planet.* Retrieved from http://www.thefreelibrary.com/The+tofu+trap%3a+our+soy+habit+has+environmental+consequences.-a0187427198

3. Macedo, M. N., DeFries, R. S., Morton, D. C., Stickler, C. M., Galford, G. L., & Shimabukuro, Y. E. (2012). Decoupling of deforestation and soy production in the southern Amazon during the late 2000s. *Proceedings of the National Academy of Sciences, 109*(4), 1341–1346.

4. Navazio, J. (2002, June–July). The joys of edamame. *Mother Earth News*, online edition. Retrieved from http://www.motherearthnews.com/organic-gardening/growing-and-harvesting-edamame-zmaz02jjzgoe.aspx#axzz2zex9juMZ.

The Values of Sports

FOCUS **AUTHOR CREDENTIALS AND BIAS**

Who is the author of the text you are reading? How about the people being quoted or referred to in the article—who are they? What do we know about these people? What are their backgrounds, professions and credentials? Does it matter? What biases might the author or people referred to bring to the text?

In this chapter
YOU WILL LEARN ...

> why it is important to know something about the author of a text and the people quoted by the author;

> what bias is and how to recognize it; and

> why an author may be biased.

Warm-up

Discuss the following questions with your group.

> What sports have you been involved in? What have you learned from taking part in these sports?

> What values do you think are associated with sports activities?

> Think of some controversial issues in sports. Have you heard different opinions about these topics? If so, whose opinions are you familiar with? Whose opinions do you agree with?

Who Is the Author?

> Sports are about more than just winning and losing; issues related to values and ethics also need consideration. Discuss with reference to one sport or sporting event.

Imagine you have been given this essay topic in a course entitled *Introduction to Sports Science*. Like any controversial topic, this topic will generate many different opinions. It is always helpful to find out something about the author of a text and to determine a) whether the author is qualified to write with authority on a particular topic and b) what biases an author might bring to a text. This is especially true for a text that presents a strong opinion or that urges you to follow a particular course of action.

Credentials

First, evaluate the author's **credentials**. Find out who the author is and what expertise he or she has in the subject. What educational background does the author have? What is the author's job? Has he or she published previously on this topic? Is the author considered an authority on the topic? An Internet search can be helpful here.

Bias

Next, consider whether the text is influenced by the personal background or beliefs of the author. In these cases, the text may not be **objective**, or balanced, in the information and opinion it presents; it may support one point of view over another. This is known as **bias**.

In other cases, the *author* does not take a stance, but the *people quoted in the article* present one-sided arguments. Their opinions are biased.

Bias is found in books, articles, newspaper columns, website materials and other print and online sources. Consider where the article was published: some academic journals support specific schools of thought, while many newspapers are aligned with the opinions of specific political parties.

How can I recognize bias?

These are some of the things you can look for:

> Only one side of the argument is presented. Positive factors supporting the opposing side are missing. Instead, the author or person quoted by the author gives supporting information only about his or her own stance on the topic.

> Generalizations are common. The author or person quoted may make sweeping statements without any real support. It could be that statistical evidence does not support the conclusion presented, so it is omitted.

> Extreme statements are used; these are designed to have an emotional effect on the reader.

Where does bias come from?

Bias can originate from a number of different sources. A person's opinion can be influenced or determined by various factors including the following:

> age
> cultural background
> educational background
> gender
> political beliefs
> profession
> religious background
> social status
> upbringing

Find out, too, what financial interests are present. For example, if the author is presenting research results, was the research sponsored by a particular company? Was the author paid to promote a particular point of view? In the case of a website, are you being encouraged to buy something? Commercial websites may give you a one-sided view of their product or service.

Be careful!

Be aware of who the author is and what biases the author may bring to the text, but don't fall into the trap of stereotyping. Don't assume that you can automatically guess someone's opinion on a topic just because that person is a certain age or gender or has a certain job or education. You might be surprised!

Put It into Practice

A. The following chart shows some examples of texts in which author bias may appear. Give examples to show how specific authors *may* be biased in their stance toward these topics.

TOPIC OF TEXT	WHO MIGHT SAY YES? WHAT REASON(S) MIGHT THEY GIVE?	WHO MIGHT SAY NO? WHAT REASON(S) MIGHT THEY GIVE?	WHAT DO YOU THINK? WHY?
Should professional athletes be allowed to compete in the Olympic Games?			
Do well-known soccer players deserve the enormous salaries they receive?			
Should girls younger than fourteen be permitted to compete in international adult gymnastics competitions?			

TOPIC OF TEXT	WHO MIGHT SAY YES? WHAT REASON(S) MIGHT THEY GIVE?	WHO MIGHT SAY NO? WHAT REASON(S) MIGHT THEY GIVE?	WHAT DO YOU THINK? WHY?
Should countries with weak human rights records be permitted to host the Olympic Games?			
Should clothing or jewellery with religious significance be permitted during international sports competitions?			

B. Read the following story from a city's daily newspaper.

Olympic bid launched

Today, the mayor announced that the city will bid to host the 2028 Olympic Games. The announcement was made at a press conference at City Hall early this morning.

Initial reaction to the announcement has been mixed. Many local people greeted the announcement with excitement and optimism. Local business owners praised the decision, saying the boost to revenue, should the city be successful, will benefit the city. "The tourists who come here for the Olympics will not only bring millions of dollars to the city, they will also put us on the map as a world-class city," said hotel owner Ashley Romero.

Other reactions have been less enthusiastic. Some city residents have expressed concerns about whether the city can afford to host an event of this magnitude; the possibility of increased taxes has also been raised, as have suggestions that city councillors should prioritize spending on social programs. "How can we even think about this, when we have people living on the streets and sleeping in shelters?" asked Pete McBride, manager of a shelter for the homeless.

More details on the bid will be announced in the next two weeks, City Hall promises.

Answer the following questions.

1. Is this text objective or biased? Explain your answer.

_____

_____

2. Write a paragraph of five or six sentences from the point of view of either Ashley Romero or Pete McBride, giving her or his opinion on the Olympic bid.

_____

_____

_____

_____

_____

_____

_____

_____

_____

3 Ask yourself: is your own paragraph biased or unbiased? Why?

_____

_____

_____

_____

C. Find a published text on ONE of these sports controversies. Then answer the questions that follow about the text you find.

> Cyclist Lance Armstrong admits winning races with the help of illegal drugs.

> Soccer star Zinedine Zidane head-butts his opponent in the World Cup final.

> Runner Caster Semenya's gender is called into question.

1 Who is the author? What can you find out about his or her credentials?

2 Is the text objective, or is it biased? How do you know?

3 If the text is biased, what stance does the author take?

MMA for Kids: Teaching Violence, or Values?

Can sports generally considered dangerous teach positive values to children? See what various people think about this question.

 As you read, consider the credentials of each person quoted by the author and consider how each may be biased.

Before You Read

Work in groups of three or four. Discuss the following questions.

1 Do an Internet search for videos of mixed martial arts (MMA). Watch two or three videos together and share your opinions on the sport.

2 Do you think MMA is a suitable sport for children? Why, or why not?

3 What groups or individuals might support the involvement of children in MMA? Why? What groups or individuals might oppose it? Why?

Key Vocabulary

The words below are all in the reading. Fill in the space in each sentence with the correct word. Some words are used twice in the same sentence.

NOUNS	evolution	maturation	perseverance
	precedent	self-esteem	validation
VERB	embrace		
ADJECTIVES	incapacitated	mainstream	vulnerable

1 If someone tries very hard to overcome obstacles to accomplish a difficult task, that person shows _____.

2 People with high _____ recognize their positive qualities and are generally happy with themselves. People with low _____, on the other hand, feel unworthy of love or appreciation.

3 A person who is _____ is not able to carry on a normal life, usually because of injury or illness.

4 A/An _____ is set when a decision is made that will influence future decisions.

5 If you _____ something, you accept it eagerly; this word also means to hug someone.

6 If you are _____, you are in a risky situation; for example, if you don't get enough sleep, you may be _____ to illness.

7 The _____ of something is its development and change over a period of time. This term is commonly used to describe the development of animals, but it is also used with political or cultural movements.

8 _____ is the process of becoming older or more established.

9 Something that is _____ is enjoyed by a majority of people; it is not considered strange or unusual. Examples might be fashion, music and movies.

10 When something is given _____, it becomes accepted by society.

MMA for Kids:
Teaching Violence, or Values?

By Paul Hunter

The petite girl, long brown hair pulled back into a ponytail, dimples flashing, lifts one leg and steadies herself on the other as she steals a glimpse of how she looks in the wall-length mirror.

It's a scene you'd see in any dance studio.

5 But suddenly, with a staccato *thwack-thwack-thwack*, she snaps her elevated leg at the kicking pad with speed and precision. The blows land so hard the boy holding the pad is pushed back a step before bracing himself for another onslaught.

This is no ballet class. Gesenia Abenoja-Barrios tried that more traditional activity and dismissed it as "a little boring."

10 Instead, at nine, she is in her fifth year at Lanna MMA, a martial arts school in an industrial complex. On this day she is working on Muay Thai, a combat sport that involves striking with feet, shins, knees, elbows and fists. It is one of the disciplines used in the mixed martial-arts promotion known as the Ultimate Fighting Championship (UFC).

One day Gesenia hopes to fight in the UFC.

15 "There are girls in UFC, and I'd like to be like one of them. One day I feel I'll be better than I am right now," she says during a break. "I'm not afraid of getting hurt—well, maybe a little."

Call it an **evolution** or a **validation** but UFC—the almost-anything-goes, often bloody brawling in a cage once famously decried as "human cockfighting"[1] by US Senator 20 John McCain—has become so **mainstream** that significant numbers of parents encourage their children to get involved in mixed martial arts.

Children who, a generation ago, might have dreamed of being the next Wendel Clark or Joe Carter,[2] are now looking to the likes of Georges St. Pierre and Anderson Silva from the UFC's Octagon as their role models, heroes of a sport that was banned in 25 Ontario until 2010.

"MMA has now been around for twenty years. The next generation has already accepted it and **embraced** it for the values it provides and the excitement that it shows," says Tom Wright, director of operations for UFC Canada. "They're making those decisions for their children. It's a natural evolution and **maturation** of a sport 30 and its acceptance."

The UFC has toned down some of the unseemly gore that characterized its early days by introducing weight classes and clarifying rules—"It's evolved from spectacle to sport," says Wright—and taken strides to ensure better health for its fighters. The UFC rule book lists thirty-one fouls—including eye gouging, biting, hair pulling and groin attacks

---

[1] *Cockfighting* is an activity, illegal in many places, in which two male chickens—cocks, or cockerels—are forced to fight until one of them dies; cockfighting is often associated with gambling.
[2] Wendel Clark is a former player with the Toronto Maple Leafs hockey team. Joe Carter played for the Toronto Blue Jays baseball team.

35 of any kind—that result in penalties. Even McCain conceded in 2007 that he no longer considered it human cockfighting.

Still there are vocal critics of a sport in which opponents are allowed to, for example, use choke holds or knees to the face.

The Canadian Medical Association (CMA) has called for an outright ban on mixed
40 martial arts in [Canada] and current CMA president Dr. Louis Francescutti says it's a "no-brainer" to hold steady on that stance.

"The last thing we want is for any activity that will increase the likelihood that somebody is going to be hurt. When the whole purpose of mixed martial arts is to kick, punch or otherwise pummel your opponent to the point where they are **incapacitated**,
45 then it's obvious that somebody is going to get injured," he says. "The goal is go out and replicate the days of gladiators, beat up your opponent and win the prize money."

Paul Dennis is a high-performance coach at York University who has lectured extensively on concussions[3] on behalf of Hockey Canada. Dennis says he admires and endorses all the benefits that flow from martial arts training, including discipline, **self-**
50 **esteem** and **perseverance**.

"But I think all that is neutralized once they go into the ring to compete and their brain becomes **vulnerable** to serious injury," he says. "I love the concept for training, but I don't understand why anyone would put themselves in a position where they could suffer serious brain damage."

55 Dennis says he would like to see UFC banned and is particularly troubled when young people regard the fighters as role models.

"If [the children are] in there for all the benefits I mentioned, it's positive and its healthy, but if they're in it because mom and dad want them to become the next alpha male, I think it could be a serious problem," he says. "I know it's incredibly popular,
60 but I think it sets a **precedent** for nothing but future catastrophic injuries amongst our youth."

Bellissimo challenges those who are critical of teaching MMA to children to visit a gym. The vast majority of his students, he says, have no intention of competing. They are there for fitness, confidence and self-growth. The gym's motto, posted in large
65 letters, is "Respect, Hard Work, Honour."

"Don't look at fifteen seconds (of UFC) on television and then make a judgment," he says. "Come to a place like Lanna MMA and watch what the kids do. And you tell me whether or not this is about violence or whether this is about learning and making words like respect, honour and hard work not just words but words to live by."

70 The gym does stage martial arts exhibitions, but the contact is light and competitors wear head guards, mouthguards, pads on the body and shins, and sixteen-ounce gloves he says are "like pillows."

---

[3] A *concussion* is a brain injury caused by a blow to the head. Concussions have been linked to a number of physical and mental problems, including headaches and memory loss.

"They might as well be wearing bubble wrap," says instructor Dave Mirabelli, noting that those competitions are strictly voluntary. "We get parents who come in, and one of the first thing they'll say is, 'Is my child going to have to fight?' Absolutely not. Never. That's something later on in your martial arts career if you choose to pursue it."

A day at the gym

On a typical late afternoon at the gym, parents sit along the walls watching while their children take part in exercises or listen to instructors talk about paying attention or leadership.

Any striking is against pads, they are told. Walk away from an altercation if you're being bullied. Anyone who is found to be using their combat skills outside the gym is suspended for a week or banned.

There is lots of laughter here. The kids work hard, but the environment is calm and relaxed.

But what about the small percentage of kids who want to doff the protective gear one day and step into the UFC's Octagon? Are they, as Dennis says, making themselves vulnerable to catastrophic injuries?

The medical association's Francescutti says there is no accurate reporting of injuries relative to each sport, but "if you're going to get repeatedly punched to the head and kicked to the head, it doesn't take a rocket scientist to figure out that the likelihood of concussion is great."

Dana White, who heads the UFC, counters by saying, "We've never had a death or serious injury in the twenty-year history of the UFC."

The British Journal of Sports Medicine reviewed five years of sanctioned MMA fights in Nevada from 2002 to 2007—635 fights—and found 300 of the 1,270 participants suffered injuries, mostly lacerations and injuries to the upper limbs. It found that 3 percent of matches resulted in a concussion and concluded "the overall risk of critical sports-related injury seems to be low."

White says if a UFC fighter suffers a concussion, he or she must sit out ninety days and then be cleared by an independent doctor before returning to competition.

"Could you imagine the NFL[4] doing that?" asks White, adding that it is hard to make the argument that UFC fighting is "barbaric" and dangerous.

As for kids pursuing mixed martial arts, White says its popularity is understandable because children have grown up watching it with their parents.

"People are used to it," he said. "The kids that are growing up now are growing up with the UFC."

Francescutti believes that by getting the kids involved, UFC is "trying to normalize something that's not normal."

---

[4] The NFL is the National Football League in the United States. The NFL comprises thirty-two American football teams from across the US.

110 "It's pretty amazing that a big segment of our society thinks it's OK to have activities like this," he says.

Gesenia is at Lanna MMA most evenings after school. So is her seven-year-old brother, Isaiah, and her sister, Precious, who is four. Their parents, after seeing the benefits of the workouts, have started training here.

115 Denisse Barrios, the children's mother, says Gesenia was once so shy that part of the reason she quit ballet was that she was afraid of performing at the end of the session. Now she bubbles with confidence. Isaiah, who had a speech impediment, used to take out his frustrations by hitting himself when he couldn't pronounce words. Now he is channelling those energies into martial arts. Like his sister, he now carries himself with 120 confidence. His speech issues have disappeared, and he no longer hits himself.

"It gives them patience, it gives them listening skills, respect for others and a better understanding of the importance of hard work," says Barrios.

"They've also become more responsible, especially at home, cleaning up after themselves. It helped them to express themselves, even toward new people. They don't 125 hide behind me anymore. They have big-time confidence."

Barrios says she would "love" to see her kids compete in the UFC one day.

"I told my kids, whatever you want to be, I'm behind you 100 percent. And if you want to be in the UFC one day, I'm there. Your No. 1 fan, I told them. It's very violent, yes, but if it is something my kids have decided on when they're older, I will give them 100-percent 130 support."

"You make your choice. If you want to be a professional, you have to work hard, and if you really want it, if that's what you really love, you should go for it."

(1634 words)

(Hunter, P. (2013, Sept. 21). MMA for kids: Teaching violence, or values? *Toronto Star*. Retrieved from http://www.thestar.com/news/insight/2013/09/21/kids_getting_involved_in_mixed_martial_arts.html

Check Your Understanding

A. Without referring to the reading, make notes on what you remember about the following.

1 The popularity of MMA

_____

_____

_____

2 Arguments in favour of MMA for children

_____

_____

_____

3 Arguments against MMA for children

_____

_____

_____

B. Are the following statements true (T) or false (F)?

	T	F
1 MMA are becoming increasingly popular among children and their parents.	○	○
2 Aggressive behaviour, such as biting and hair pulling, is encouraged in MMA.	○	○
3 Martial arts are admired for teaching discipline, self-esteem and perseverance.	○	○
4 Children must wear protective equipment when practising MMA.	○	○
5 Children are encouraged to use their MMA skills outside the gym.	○	○
6 No one has died while practising MMA.	○	○
7 _The British Journal of Sports Medicine_ thinks MMA are very dangerous.	○	○
8 MMA may have psychological as well as physical benefits.	○	○

C. Now, we'll look at paraphrasing a section of the text. A paraphrase is similar to a summary in that you are rewriting the text in your own words; however, while a summary contains only the main ideas, a paraphrase is _the same length_ as the original. For this reason, longer texts are usually summarized and short segments are often paraphrased.

How to Write a Paraphrase

1 Read the text carefully. Look up any important vocabulary (main ideas, definitions or repeated words).

2 Write down the key points of the text. It may be easier to state the main ideas orally; this is a good way of checking your understanding.

3 Write the meaning of the original in your own words. Don't be afraid to change the sentence structure; a good paraphrase is not just the original text with a few words changed.

4 Edit your paraphrase; check for grammatical accuracy, and check to see that you have included all the key points of the original.

Paraphrase the following statements. Then, share your paraphrases with your class. How are they similar or different?

1. MMA has now been around for twenty years. The next generation has already accepted it and embraced it for the values it provides and the excitement that it shows. They're making those decisions for their children. It's a natural evolution and maturation of a sport and its acceptance.

Tom Wright

2. The last thing we want is for any activity that will increase the likelihood that somebody is going to be hurt. When the whole purpose of mixed martial arts is to kick, punch or otherwise pummel your opponent to the point where they are incapacitated, then it's obvious that somebody is going to get injured. The goal is go out and replicate the days of gladiators, beat up your opponent and win the prize money.

Louis Francescutti

3. If [the children are] in there for all the benefits I mentioned, it's positive and it's healthy, but if they're in it because mom and dad want them to become the next alpha male, I think it could be a serious problem. I know it's incredibly popular, but I think it sets a precedent for nothing but future catastrophic injuries amongst our youth.

Paul Dennis

4. It gives them patience, it gives them listening skills, respect for others and a better understanding of the importance of hard work. They've also become more responsible, especially at home, cleaning up after themselves. It helped them to express themselves, even toward new people. They don't hide behind me anymore. They have big-time confidence.

Denisse Barrios

Analysis and Discussion

Discuss these questions with your group.

1. Look at the people quoted in the previous exercise. Fill in the chart below with information about each person, along with his or her opinion on MMA. Discuss how each person might be biased.

NAME	WHO IS THIS PERSON (CREDENTIALS, JOB, BACKGROUND)?	DOES THIS PERSON THINK MMA IS SUITABLE FOR CHILDREN? WHY?
Tom Wright		
Louis Francescutti		
Paul Dennis		
Mel Bellissimo		

NAME	WHO IS THIS PERSON (CREDENTIALS, JOB, BACKGROUND)?	DOES THIS PERSON THINK MMA IS SUITABLE FOR CHILDREN? WHY?
Dana White		
Denisse Barrios		

2 Find a reference in the text to a peer-reviewed study of MMA. What conclusions are reached by the academic study? Which opinion put forward in the text is best supported by the results of the academic study?

3 Do you think the article itself is biased? Has the writer adequately presented both sides of the argument, or does he favour one side? Explain your answer.

4 Choose one of the people in the chart above. If you met this person, what would you say to him or her?

5 What is your personal opinion about this topic? Do you think MMA are dangerous, or do you think there is no real difference between MMA and other martial arts such as karate or tae kwon do?

READING 2

Sports Doping Should Be Legal and Controlled

The author of this article discusses another controversial topic in sports: doping.

 As you read, think about who the author might be, what biases might be present here and who might agree or disagree with him.

Before You Read

Work in groups of three or four. Discuss the following questions.

1 What do you understand by the term "doping"? Can you think of any famous cases of doping in sports?

2 How do you think the sports world should deal with doping?

3 Which of the following statements do you most agree with?

> Doping is a serious problem. Athletes caught doping should be banned for a long period of time, or even for life.

> Doping may be dangerous, but it's too hard to control. We need to accept its presence in sports.

> Doping should be the choice of the individual athletes. If they want to risk their health, that's their decision.

Key Vocabulary

The words below are all in the reading. Match each word with the correct definition.

1. anabolic steroids (n. line 60) _____ a) key or necessary aspect of something

2. doping (n. line 1) _____ b) sensible; based on reason, not emotion

3. dose (n. line 67) _____ c) platform where gold, silver and bronze medals are presented

4. integral (adj. line 18) _____ d) carry out checks at regular intervals

5. monitor (v. line 31) _____ e) amount of medicine that should be taken at any given time

6. naivety (n. line 74) _____ f) use of illegal substances to improve performance in sports events

7. performance-enhancing drugs (n. line 46) _____ g) substances taken to help an athlete to achieve better results in sports competitions

8. podium (n. line 9) _____ h) drugs designed to support the development of stronger muscles

9. rational (adj. line 35) _____ i) approach whereby no amount of any illegal substance is permitted, no matter how small

10. zero-tolerance (n. line 73) _____ j) state of being inexperienced and too trusting

Sports Doping Should Be Legal and Controlled

By Julian Savulescu

Lance Armstrong is the arch-villain of the allegedly extinct era of doping in cycling. The cancer survivor, philanthropist and seven-time winner of the Tour de France[1] has been burned at the stake, both figuratively and literally. (Well, in effigy.)

The king is dead, and so, the logic goes, is his kingdom of doping. "So ends one of
5 the most sordid chapters in sporting history," wrote the US Anti-Doping Agency in its dismissal of Armstrong.

Yet the idea that the cycling world has been purged of drugs cheats is almost certainly wrong. The investigation into Armstrong's cheating revealed the practice was ➡

---
[1] The Tour de France is an annual 23-day cycling race around France.

widespread. Of twenty-one podium
10 finishers in the Tour between 1995 and
2005, twenty have been directly linked
to doping.

Armstrong has been stripped of his
titles, but his medals will not be real-
15 located because virtually all the second-
place holders have been found doping
at some point in their careers. Doping
has for decades been an integral part
of cycling, and despite a claim in 2001
20 by cycling's governing body that the
practice had been eradicated, cyclists
continue to be caught. (The US Anti-
Doping Agency has also admitted that
difficult-to-detect drug products mean "it is not possible to equate a 'negative test' with
25 the absence of doping at the current time.")

So is it still cheating if everyone is cheating? Well, yes: it is against the rules. But rather
than excoriating Armstrong, wouldn't it be better to ask why everyone is cheating, and
why the rules are failing?

I have long argued that doping bans should be relaxed. The present broad-based ban
30 is unenforceable. And it has three perverse effects.

First, it is unsafe. There is no monitoring of the nature, dosing or administration of
doping agents. The only pressure is not to get caught. Second, it is unfair to those
perhaps few athletes who don't dope. Third, it is ruining the spectacle of sport and the
lives of sportsmen, such as Armstrong.

35 What would a rational doping policy look like? First, we need to stop all investigations
into past doping. We can never fully and fairly investigate who was doping in the past.

Second, we should relax the ban on doping. Much of the fuss in the Tour is related
to the use of erythropoietin (EPO—a hormone that controls red blood cell production)
and pure human blood.

40 But we could eliminate this whole problem with the stroke of a pen. If we allowed riders
to blood-dope up to a haematocrit level of 50 percent, where half their blood would be
red blood cells, we could administer a cheap, reliable test on all riders. Those over 50
percent would be out. There would be no more blood doping scandals. Such a level is
already accepted by the governing body, the Union Cycliste Internationale, as safe.

45 What about other drugs, such as steroids and growth hormone?

Three reasons are commonly given for prohibiting performance-enhancing drugs:
they are unsafe; pervert the nature and spirit of sport; and they should be banned simply
because they enhance performances.

The last reason ought to be dismissed immediately. Modern athletic sport is entirely
50 focused on finding new ways to break old records, and most of the effective methods
are legal—and far from "natural."

Hypoxic training tents, which simulate the effect of training at high altitude by allowing
the blood to carry more oxygen, are legal. Caffeine, which improves reaction time and
fights fatigue, is legal.

55 The first two arguments provide good reason for banning drugs in certain situations.
Some drugs do change the nature of a sport. For example, one of the most interesting
things about boxing is that boxers need to overcome their fear of being hit to perform
well. If they took a drug that eliminated their ability to feel fear, or pain, this aspect of
the performance would be eliminated.

60 Do anabolic steroids and growth hormone make cycling and athletic sports such
as running less interesting or challenging? No. Steroids allow athletes to train longer
and recover more quickly. Athletes on steroids still have to train hard. If every Olympic
sprinter or cyclist were using steroids, it would still be the same sport, just slightly
faster.

65 Finally, there is the argument that drugs are too dangerous. The biggest problem
with steroids is that they are obtained illegally and then administered in secret by athletes
who are not trained to identify overuse, or to scale their dose appropriately.

We should put enhancers in the hands of the prescription system.

The moral and legal responsibility for the athlete's health would be passed from the
70 athlete to the doctor.

Armstrong is not the disease. He is a symptom, and the disease hasn't been cured.
But it is not a disease, it's a condition: the human condition. To try to be better.

The zero-tolerance ban on drugs is an example of the victory of ideology, wishful
thinking, moralism and naivety over ethics and common sense. Human beings have
75 limitations. Lance Armstrong is no god, but he is also no devil. We should change the
rules, and take Armstrong off the bonfire. There will, after all, be more like him.

(855 words)

Savulescu, J. (2013, January 19). Sports doping should be legal and controlled. *The Sydney Morning Herald*. Retrieved from
http://www.smh.com.au/federal-politics/society-and-culture/sports-doping-should-be-legal-and-controlled-20130118-2cyrs.html

Check Your Understanding

A. Which statement best summarizes the arguments presented by the author in this paper?

    a) Doping is terrible. People who use drugs are putting themselves at risk and making
       their sports look bad. We need zero tolerance!

    b) Doping is not good. However, the human body cannot improve any more without it.
       Let's accept that there will always be doping. Instead of banning it, let's work with it.

    c) Doping is fine. People who watch sports want to see records broken and races won
       in fast times. The more things people can do to increase their speed, the better!

B. Answer the following questions in your own words using information from the reading.

1. What prompted the author to write this text?

_____

_____

2. Why could Lance Armstrong's medals not be given to those who had placed second?

_____

_____

3. What seems to be the author's opinion of the US Anti-Doping Agency?

_____

_____

4. What is meant by the statement that "it is not possible to equate a 'negative test' with the absence of doping at the current time"? Paraphrase this statement.

_____

_____

5. What three problems does the author identify with the present ban on doping?

> _____

> _____

> _____

6. In your own words, summarize the "rational" policy that the author proposes to replace the current ban.

_____

_____

_____

_____

7. In what circumstances does the author agree that doping should be banned?

_____

_____

8. How does the author respond to the argument that drugs are too dangerous?

_____

_____

Analysis and Discussion

Discuss the following questions with your group.

1. Is this text objective, or is it biased? Explain your answer.

2. Which readers might agree with the author's opinion? Why?

3 Which readers might disagree? Why?

4 Do an Internet search for the author of this text, Julian Savulescu. What do you learn about the following?

> His academic credentials

> His current profession

5 Which of the following statements do you most agree with?

a) Savulescu knows nothing about sports. He shouldn't get involved with this topic. He should leave this discussion to the people who organize and play these sports.

b) Savulescu gives a valuable opinion. He is not involved with sports, so he can look at this issue objectively and without bias. We should listen to his opinion.

c) I have another opinion: _____

_____

_____

6 Julian Savulescu has written many other controversial texts. Here are some of his other beliefs:

> It is our duty to have genetically engineered ("designer") babies.

> Cloning should be encouraged.

> Human embryos should be tested for intelligence.

Would you like to take a course with Professor Savulescu? Why, or why not?

7 Write a response to the author, stating your own stance on this topic.

READING 3

Why the Olympics Are a Lot Like *The Hunger Games*

The author of this text is a past Olympic competitor.

 FOCUS **As you read her story, think about the points she is making and the extent to which her past experiences have shaped her views.**

Before You Read

Work in groups of three or four. Discuss the following questions.

1 Do you enjoy watching the Olympics on television? Why, or why not?

2 What do you think the long-term effects of participating in the Olympics might be for the athletes? Think about both positive and negative effects.

3 Have you read *The Hunger Games*? Have you seen the movies? Can you imagine why the author might think the Olympics are like *The Hunger Games*?

Why the Olympics Are a Lot Like *The Hunger Games*

By Samantha Retrosi

As a former Olympic athlete, I can tell you from experience that the Olympic Games have much more in common with *The Hunger Games*[1] than anyone would want to admit.

I connect with the inhumanity of *The Hunger Games* because I've been there, as a luge[2] competitor at the 2006 Winter Olympics in Turin, Italy. No, I didn't get sucked into
5 the depths of an artificial lake, like the character played by Jennifer Lawrence. But I did get sucked into the rafters of an artificially manufactured tube of glare ice, only to come crashing down in the second run of my Olympic moment.

The grandeur of the opening ceremonies of *The Hunger Games* is designed to mask the cruelty of the competition itself. The Olympic opening ceremonies serve a similar
10 purpose. Like the kids representing the districts of Panem, each nation's athletes are trotted around a massive arena like prize ponies, shrouded in the patriotic glory of their particular flag. The carefully orchestrated pageantry is misleading, telling us that the Olympics are a celebration of the human capacity to achieve, to overcome obstacles, and that the world's best athletes represent something bigger than themselves.

15 But make no mistake: for the global elite, the Olympics are an investment—and one with a rapidly growing price tag. At the London Games, the cost of the opening ceremonies alone was a whopping $42.3 million. This year, Russia will shell out more than $51 billion for the two-week event, making these Games more expensive than all previous Winter Olympics combined.

20 In *The Hunger Games*, Jennifer Lawrence is the sacrificial lamb of District 12. As one of the prize ponies of the US team, I served a similar purpose for the Turin Games. Groomed from the tender age of eleven, I spent my childhood pursuing Olympic glory, which epitomizes the American dream of merit-based success.

Looking back now, I finally understand an experience I couldn't quite grasp as a child.
25 I see that the beautiful illusion I once searched for is a fabrication, the creation of ingenious marketing mechanisms by those who run the Olympic show. I once hoped that the patriotic glory I was told so much about would give meaning to the physical and emotional pain of my athletic struggle. I grew accustomed to gritting my teeth under the strain of various forms of pain: the daily grind of hours of elite-level training,
30 and the toll it exacted on my developing body; the pain I felt upon slamming into a wall of ice at eighty miles per hour; the biting winter cold that whipped across my thinly protected, spandex[3]-clad form while sitting atop a frozen winter landscape. Then there was the emotional pain and fear, which took on various forms: the constant fear of bodily harm that scarred my mind, just as my body was scarred by more than a hundred
35 stitches; the fear that I would disappoint those I loved and those who had invested time

---

[1] *The Hunger Games* is a trilogy of books set in a future world in a country called Panem. Teenagers are selected from each District to compete to the death in an arena in front of a television audience. In the movies based on the books, the main character, Katniss Everdeen, is played by actress Jennifer Lawrence.

[2] *Luge* is an Olympic event in which competitors ride a sled feet-first down an ice-covered track at very high speeds.

[3] *Spandex* is a thin, stretchy fabric that is used in the manufacture of sports clothing.

and money in my athletic career. There was the pain of failure, of hope swallowed by frequent defeat. Then there was the gendered pain: that of an adolescent female standing in underwear in the glass cube of sport science, each area of fat accumulation clinically pinched by a man with metal tongs. I once hoped that by withstanding all this pain, 40 there would one day be a payoff, even if only an emotional one.

Now I understand my failure to connect to the pomp of the opening ceremonies, the confused emptiness that consumed me as I stood in the cold of a Turin winter, wrapped in the American flag, wincing under the cruel glare of a thousand flashbulbs. The real function of the Olympic athlete in the world of corporatized sports is clear 45 to me now.

Amateur status is mandatory for any Olympic hopeful, but athletic training at the elite level is a full-time job. Most nations get around the problem by 50 giving their Olympic athletes significant government support, but our best athletes are almost entirely dependent on corporate sponsorship. For the athletes, the consequences of this 55 addiction can be disastrous.

The socialization of my allegiance to Verizon began the moment I was selected—as an eleven-year-old—for the US development team. The culture 60 within the US Luge Association

Luge.

viewed brand loyalty as integral to the survival of the organization. All of my clothing was plastered with the Verizon logo. I was not allowed near any camera without giving a visual and verbal statement of thanks to Verizon for making all of my dreams come true. I went through intensive media training each year to reinforce this 65 allegiance—to learn how to be a better spokesperson for Verizon. During my Olympic year, I signed away my rights to use media time for just about anything other than gratitude to sponsors. It was a condition for entrance into the Olympic Village.

In the wake of the 2008 recession, Verizon found itself on rocky terrain, so it began breaking many of its sponsorship contracts with amateur sports organizations. One of 70 those was with the US Luge Association, to which it gave millions of dollars a year. USA Luge, which spent decades cultivating this relationship at the expense of all other sources of funding, has been unable to replace Verizon. Today's luge athletes have had to look elsewhere for support, with many having little choice but to join the US Army World Class Athlete Program (not surprising, given the similarity in value systems: both the armed 75 forces and elite-level sports cultivate extreme discipline, patriotism and victory at all costs). Apparently, one must be willing to enlist—and possibly fight and die for one's country— in order to cover the expenses of international competition. Many of those who haven't gone this route hold down outside jobs in addition to full-time training schedules. ➡

There's a lot of money to be made in Olympic sports, a huge global media event
80 that rolls around every two years. Corporate-sponsor bottom lines are merely one
indicator of the vast sums involved. To see just who is generating this wealth,
one has to look no further than the act of sponsorship itself, with individual athletes
and entire teams purchased and traded among the corporate elite like valuable
additions to bursting stock portfolios. As an athlete in a sport as insignificant in the
85 United States as luge, I could never hope to see my face plastered on a Wheaties
box. However, I wasn't too obscure to escape the eye of the masterminds of gender
commodification at *Maxim*.[4] Apparently, spandex uniforms make the women of USA
Luge hot commodities. Lucky me.

For sponsors, the way to cash in is clear. Athletes are put up for sale in a variety of ways.
90 Olympic event coverage, elaborate marketing devices and product placement, branding
rights and exclusive access to the use of athlete images and identities are used not only
in the sale of media products but in the gamut of other commodities attached to the
Olympic brand during the course of an Olympic year. The Olympic rings themselves have
been copyrighted by the IOC,[5] reserved exclusively for use by corporate sponsors.

95 As those who generate super-profits for sponsors, today's Olympic athletes are
workers. Like any other workers, athletes are limited by their economic vulnerability—
in this case, control by the sporting hierarchy. Iron-clad corporate control enforces
social discipline over the athletes themselves, but also over the economy of the
Olympics as a whole. The IOC, the USOC[5] and each sport's national governing body
100 are mere intermediaries between athletes and corporate sponsors, solidifying the
relationship of exploitation.

Corporate domination of the Olympic economy is supreme. Yet as any good
capitalist knows, the best way to ensure the continuation of top-down control is
successful psychological manipulation. All too often, athletes' perspectives on the
105 nature of their social position are shaped by the same PR campaigns that further
the exploitation of their labour. To sponsors, athlete value is about how much money
can be made off an individual not just in the act of competition but, more importantly,
in victory. It's no surprise that the indicators of athlete success are also those that
drive market success, and that both are products of the same ideology: competition,
110 individualism, domination. When these values are combined with the athletes'
tenuous economic identity as an exploited labour pool, the competition for resources
cements a divide-and-conquer relationship that undermines their ability to think
and act in terms of solidarity with their fellow athlete-workers. Throw in a teaspoon
of patriotism and a dash of nationalism, and the recipe for divide and conquer is
115 complete. The result is a subservient class that plays by the rules of the corporate
sponsors and the sporting managerial class—the IOC, USOC and other national
governing bodies.

The economics of the Olympic movement mirror the global picture. Privatization,
deregulation and austerity politics have overtaken the world of sports, just as they have

---

[4] *Maxim* is a men's magazine that features pictures of attractive women.
[5] The IOC is the International Olympic Committee; the USOC is the United States Olympic Committee.

120 all other aspects of the global economy. But every cloud has a silver lining, right? Privatization may appear to lead us toward a dystopian future, but the potential remains for a uniquely explosive, and possibly transformative, resistance. Corporate supremacy in the Olympic movement has brought under its control the world's best athletes. In previous epochs of working-class growth, class consciousness has inevitably blossomed.

125 As the austerity agenda advances, governments will likely continue slashing their budgetary allocations for "unnecessary spending." Clearly, the well-being of the sporting world's prize ponies is on the chopping block. The likelihood is that the privatization of sports will continue on a global scale. Will the creation of an internationalized resistance follow? That's up to the athletes—and those in solidarity with them.   (1616 words)

Retrosi, S. (2014, Feb. 10). Why the Olympics are a lot like *The Hunger Games*. *The Nation*. Retrieved from http://www.thenation.com/article/178048/why-olympics-are-lot-hunger-games

Check Your Understanding

A. Work in groups. Find sections in the text where the author talks about the following topics. Then take notes on her opinions in your own words.

1 Samantha Retrosi's Olympic experience

_____

_____

2 Why she thinks the Olympic Games are like *The Hunger Games*

_____

_____

3 How she felt at the opening ceremony, and why

_____

_____

_____

4 The kinds of pain she experienced as a young athlete in training

_____

_____

5 How she felt about being supported financially by a company

_____

_____

_____

6 What happens to athletes who do not receive corporate support

_____

_____

7 How the ideology of corporate sponsors prevents athletes from working as a team

_____

_____

_____

8 Whether there will be international resistance to the situation she outlines

_____

_____

B. Now use the information you have collected above and write a summary of the article in 250 words or fewer.

Key Vocabulary

Find the following sentences in the text. <u>Underline</u> the word in the sentence that matches the definition below.

1 But make no mistake: for the global elite, the Olympics are an investment—and one with a rapidly growing price tag. (lines 15 to 16)

> a group of people with exceptional wealth or talent

2 Groomed from the tender age of eleven, I spent my childhood pursuing Olympic glory, which epitomizes the American dream of merit-based success. (lines 22 to 23)

> provide a perfect example of something

3 I see that the beautiful illusion I once searched for is a fabrication, the creation of ingenious marketing mechanisms by those who run the Olympic show. (lines 25 to 26)

> something invented, often to mislead people

4 Amateur status is mandatory for any Olympic hopeful, but athletic training at the elite level is a full-time job. (lines 46 to 48)

> obligatory, not optional

5 The socialization of my allegiance to Verizon began the moment I was selected—as an eleven-year-old—for the US development team. (lines 56 to 59)

> loyalty

6 Apparently, spandex uniforms make the women of USA Luge hot commodities. (lines 87 to 88)

> items that can be bought and sold

7 Like any other workers, athletes are limited by their economic vulnerability—in this case, control by the sporting hierarchy. (lines 96 to 97)

> a system in which people are organized into levels, from top to bottom

8 The IOC, the USOC and each sport's national governing body are mere intermediaries between athletes and corporate sponsors, solidifying the relationship of exploitation. (lines 99 to 101)

> a situation in which someone receives very little in return for his or her work

9 It's no surprise that the indicators of athlete success are also those that drive market success, and that both are products of the same ideology: competition, individualism, domination. (lines 108 to 110)

> a set of beliefs, often political or economic

10 Privatization, deregulation and austerity politics have overtaken the world of sports, just as they have all other aspects of the global economy. (lines 118 to 120)

> a situation in which there is little money available to spend

Analysis and Discussion

Discuss these questions with your group.

1 Does the author present an objective view of the Olympics, or is her article one-sided? Explain your answer.

2 Which of the following do you think might have influenced the author's opinions? How?
> her gender
> her age
> her nationality
> her political views
> other: _____

3 The author crashed in her Olympic event. Do you think her opinions might be different if her outcome had been different (for example, if she had won a medal)?

4 The author makes a number of comparisons in this text:
> She compares the Olympic Games to *The Hunger Games*.
> She compares athletes at the opening ceremony to ponies in an arena.
> She compares women in sports clothing to commodities for sale.

To what extent do you think these comparisons are fair and reasonable?
Explain your opinion.

5 A report published by the International Olympic Committee (IOC) defines the concept of "Olympism" in the following way:

> Olympism is a philosophy of life which places sport at the service of humanity. This philosophy is based on the interaction of the qualities of the body, will and mind. Olympism is expressed through actions which link sport to culture and education. (IOC, The Olympic Museum, 2013.[1])

How do you think the author would respond to this statement?

6 If a young friend or relative of yours showed promise as a future Olympic athlete, would you encourage that person to pursue his or her dreams? Why, or why not?

[1] *Olympism and the Olympic Movement.* (2013) The Olympic Museum. Lausanne. 3rd ed. Retrieved from http://www.olympic.org/documents/reports/en/en_report_670.pdf

Going Further

Focus on Language

A. The following chart contains ten words from the readings. Complete the chart with related words in the other categories, and, where possible, in the same category. (There may not be a word for each category.)

	NOUN	VERB	ADJECTIVE	ADVERB
1		administer		
2	domination			
3	evolution			
4			exclusive	
5	maturation			
6		normalize		
7			patriotic	
8	privatization			
9	tolerance			
10			voluntary	

B. This chapter contains a number of abbreviations: MMA, UFC, CMA, EPO, IOC and USOC. Here are some other common abbreviations. Do you know what each one stands for?

1 UN _____

2 ASEAN _____

3 OPEC _____

4 BRICS _____

5 FIFA _____

6 NGO _____

7 IMF _____

8 NATO   _____

9 OECD   _____

10 WHO   _____

Can you think of any others?

Independent Research

Choose a sport and carry out some online research. Find out about its history, its famous teams and participants, its popularity with young athletes, the risk of injury accompanying this sport and any scandals (doping or other) it may have experienced. You will present your findings to your class.

Synthesis and Written Response

Based on your reading of the texts in this chapter as well as your own research into sports-related topics, write a short response to the following prompt.

> Sports are about more than just winning and losing; issues related to values and ethics also need consideration. Discuss with reference to one sport or sporting event.

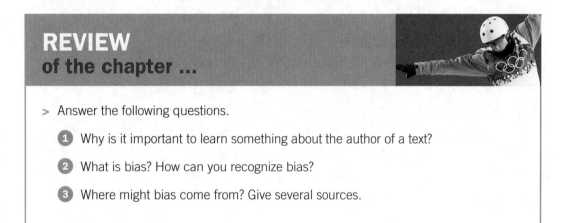

REVIEW
of the chapter ...

> Answer the following questions.

1 Why is it important to learn something about the author of a text?

2 What is bias? How can you recognize bias?

3 Where might bias come from? Give several sources.

CHAPTER 4

Approaches to the Global Energy Crisis

 FOCUS **STANCE, AUDIENCE AND PURPOSE**

What opinion is being expressed in the text? Who was the text written for—a general audience or an academic audience? Why was the text written? Does the author want to convince us, educate us, entertain us, sell something to us or simply share knowledge with us? What does the author want us to do after reading the text? You will consider these questions as you read several texts on alternative forms of energy.

In this chapter
YOU WILL LEARN ...

> how to identify the author's stance;

> how the author's intended audience influences the text; and

> why the author's purpose is important.

Warm-up

Discuss these questions with your group.

> What do you understand by the term *global energy crisis*?

> What are *fossil fuels*? What are *alternative* forms of energy? Which alternative forms of energy are you familiar with?

> Do you think authors who say the solution to the energy crisis lies in alternative forms of energy are correct? Why, or why not?

Stance

> How can we solve the energy crisis? Compare and evaluate two or more possible solutions.

Imagine you have been given this essay topic in a course entitled *Introduction to Environmental Engineering*. This is a controversial topic, and different authors will have different perspectives on the topic. The opinion put forward by an author is called his or her **stance**. It could also be called the author's "position" or "point of view."

How can you identify an author's stance? Here are some clues.

The author expresses his or her opinion with words and expressions like this:

> nouns: *advantage, disadvantage, benefit, threat, danger* or *risk*

> verbs: *I think …,* or *I believe …; this study demonstrates …,* or *this research confirms …; it seems …,* or *it appears …*

> adjectives: *crucial, important, promising, significant, worthwhile* or *(ir)relevant*

> adverbs: *clearly, definitely* or *obviously*

Note that authors of research papers are usually reluctant to express their conclusions too strongly. Often expressions like *The results prove …* or *It is obvious that …* are too strong and need to be softened. The author might prefer to use expressions like *It seems that …* or *There is evidence to suggest that …* This shows caution, and it shows politeness on the part of the author. This use of language is known as **hedging**.

Implication and Inference

Sometimes, the author's stance is not stated explicitly. An opinion or attitude may be **implied**; in other words, it may be suggested indirectly. You may need to **infer** what is being said—you may need to take the author's words and figure out the intended meaning.

Audience

Who was the text written for? Was it written for an academic audience or a general audience? The type of language used will be a clue; as shown in Chapter 2, texts written for the academic community will use technical or specialized vocabulary, while texts written for a general audience will avoid terms that may be unfamiliar to readers.

Purpose

Having considered your author's stance and audience, your final task is to consider the author's purpose, i.e., *why* the text was written. What was the author's goal? Here are some possible reasons for writing a text.

WHAT IS THE ARTICLE?	THE AUTHOR'S PURPOSE
An academic article from a journal	• To make a contribution to his or her field and to add to the bank of knowledge available on a topic
A non-academic text from a magazine, a newspaper or a commercial website	• To report on new information using language accessible to a general audience • To persuade/convince the reader to adopt a certain belief or to act in a certain way • To warn the reader about something • To give advice or suggest a course of action • To reassure the reader about something • To entertain or amuse the reader • To advertise a product or service

Put It into Practice

A. Look at the following statements about the use of the earth's tides as a source of energy. For each one, decide whether the author is a) in favour of tidal power, b) against it or c) undecided. Explain your answers.

1 66 There is no doubt that tidal power is one potential source of energy, but the threat to aquatic life is too great. Tidal energy stations need to be located in estuaries, which are home to many species of fish and marine creatures. These would be vulnerable to injury and death from the machines as well as to disruption to their natural habitats. There must be a kinder approach to energy than this. 99

_____

_____

2 66 The sustainable energy produced by the tides holds great promise. Certainly, there may be ecological effects, but in this case the benefits clearly outweigh any possible disadvantages. Tidal energy is a renewable source of energy, it produces no harmful greenhouse gases, and it requires little maintenance. The way forward is obvious! 99

_____

_____

3   66 Although the earth's oceans seem to be the source of limitless amounts of energy, far more research needs to be carried out into the ecological risks posed by the harnessing of tidal energy. I am not convinced tidal energy is the answer. It is important that governments explore this option carefully before investing massive amounts of money in tidal energy schemes. 99

_____

_____

4   66 The development of tidal energy plants would be a colossal waste of resources. It is an illusion to think the oceans hold the solution to the energy crisis. In most parts of the world, tides are simply not powerful enough to generate energy. In fact, there are fewer than fifty suitable sites for tidal energy schemes in the world. Anyone who thinks tidal energy is the answer is seriously misguided. 99

_____

_____

B. Read the following text from the website of the Centre for Research on Globalization and answer the questions on the next page.

Some advocates of nuclear power have long argued that a major accident is about as likely as being hit by a meteorite. In 1975, the nuclear industry asked Professor Norman Rasmussen to produce a report that would reassure the public about the safety of nuclear energy. The report concluded that the probability of a complete core meltdown is about 1 in 20,000 per reactor per year.

Reality has shown this to be a gross underestimation. The three best known serious nuclear power accidents are those of Three Mile Island in 1979, Chernobyl 1986 and Fukushima 2011. But there have been many more accidents and partial core meltdowns releasing radioactivity.

A study commissioned by Greenpeace concluded that the Chernobyl accident may have resulted in an estimated 200,000 additional deaths in Belarus, Russia and Ukraine alone between 1990 and 2004. The nuclear power plants in Fukushima have about thirty times as much radioactive material as the reactor that exploded in Chernobyl, and Japan is much more densely populated.

Even if there were no accidents, no solution has yet been found in over fifty years for the safe storage of the radioactive waste produced by nuclear power plants. One of the by-products, plutonium 239, has a half-life of 24,100 years. That means, after 24,100 years, the intensity of radiation has declined by only 50 percent. It will take 241,000 years until the radiation has declined by a factor of 1000, which is considered a safe level. How can we guarantee that our descendants will not be exposed to those wastes for 10,000 generations?

The "precautionary principle" urges us to avoid the worst possible outcome of any decision. This implies that we should dismantle all nuclear power plants.

D. Fischer. (2011). How Safe Is Nuclear Power? *Global Research*. Retrieved from http://www.globalresearch.ca/how-safe-is-nuclear-power/23967.

1. Why do you think this text was written?

   a) To educate the public about nuclear power

   b) To reassure people that nuclear power is safe

   c) To persuade people to support the installation of nuclear power stations

   d) To warn people about the dangers of nuclear power

2. Who do you think is the intended audience for this text? Why?

   a) Experts in nuclear power

   b) Non-experts in nuclear power

   _____

   _____

3. Do you find the text convincing? If so, why? If not, why not?

   _____

   _____

   _____

C. Find two other published texts on the topic of nuclear power:

> Your first text should be published by an organization or individual that is in favour of nuclear power.

> Your second text should be published by an organization or individual that is opposed to nuclear power.

Your texts may be from local, national or international sources. For each text, answer the following questions.

1. What stance does the author take? What language is used to show the author's stance?

2. Who is the intended audience?

3. Why was the text written?

4. Do you find the text convincing? If so, why? If not, why not?

Share your findings with your class.

READING 1

Panda Poop Power Promising for Biofuel Production

Learn how a cute but endangered animal may hold a key to the development of sustainable energy.

 FOCUS As you read, think about the author's stance and audience.

Before You Read

Work in groups of three or four. Discuss the following questions.

1 Are you familiar with the word *biofuel*? Share your thoughts on what biofuels might be.

2 What do you think might be the connection between pandas and biofuel?

3 Do you think biofuels hold the answer to the energy crisis? What advantages and disadvantages of biofuels can you think of?

Key Vocabulary

The words below are all in the reading. Fill in the space in each sentence with the correct word.

NOUNS	bacteria enzyme	boon microbe	conservation shortage
VERBS	ferment		
ADJECTIVES	endangered	sustainable	widespread

1 A/An _____ of something occurs when there is not enough of a particular item for everyone. At this time, the price of the item often increases.

2 _____ animals in the world include the mountain gorilla and the green turtle. Their numbers are decreasing, and their survival is threatened.

3 The process of _____ refers to the protection of animals and plants. Don't confuse this word with a word spelled *almost* the same, which means "talking"!

4 A/An _____ is an organism too small to see with the human eye. This group includes bacteria, viruses and fungi.

5 A/An _____ is a chemical substance found in an animal or plant. These substances allow changes to take place within the animal or plant.

6 If a form of energy is _____, it can be replaced as it is used.

7 Something that is _____ is commonly found or is popular.

8 When a food product is allowed to _____, it undergoes a chemical change; for example, when this happens to fruit, it turns into alcohol.

9 _____ are organisms that are very small and that may cause disease.

10 A/An _____ is something that brings a positive change to someone's life.

Panda Poop Power Promising for Biofuel Production

By James A. Foley

Ya Ya and Le Le, two giant pandas at the Memphis Zoo, are making regular contributions to research into more **sustainable** biofuel production by providing plenty of panda poop.

5 As odd as it may sound, researchers say using panda poop to develop biofuels could become a great **boon** to the industry, which often faces criticism for using perfectly good food, namely corn and soy beans, to make fuel.

Presenting at the 246th National Meeting & Exposition of the American Chemical Society (ACS), researcher Ashli Brown of Mississippi State University said that if further research into panda poop power proves successful, she will reach out for "contributions" 10 from other pandas.

"The giant pandas are contributing their feces," Brown said. "We have discovered **microbes** in panda feces might actually be a solution to the search for sustainable new sources of energy. It's amazing that here we have an **endangered** species that's almost gone from the planet, yet there's still so much we have yet to learn from it. That 15 underscores the importance of saving endangered and threatened animals."

Brown and her colleagues identified more than forty gut microbes that could make biofuel production from plant waste easier and cheaper. Those microbes, naturally, make their way into the panda's excrement as well.

Researching the poop microbes may also lead to the discovery of new information 20 that can be used to keep pandas healthy.

In the US, ethanol made from corn is the most abundant alternative fuel. But common criticisms over biofuels includes that the **widespread** use of corn, 25 soybeans and other food crops to make biofuels could contribute to increased food prices or lead to **shortages** of food.

One alternative researchers are exploring is using inedible food parts and 30 other plant material, such as corn stalks and corn cobs, as sources of ethanol. But doing so on a large scale is costly and difficult because of the tough-to-breakdown lignocellulose in plant waste and 35 other crops grown for ethanol production.

But the **bacteria** in the panda poop have proven to be prime candidates for a novel way of breaking down the rough

plant matter. Pandas' digestive tracts are short, and their diet of bamboo requires their
40 bodies to break down significant amounts of lignocellulose.

"The time from eating to defecation is comparatively short in the panda, so their microbes have to be very efficient to get nutritional value out of the bamboo," Brown said. "And efficiency is key when it comes to biofuel production—that's why we focused on the microbes in the giant panda."

45 Brown's team identified the bacteria that break down the lignocellulose into simple sugars, which can be **fermented** into bioethanol. Moreover, they found that they can transform those sugars into oils and fats for biodiesel production, which led the researchers to believe that the bacteria or the **enzymes** in the panda poop could be worked into the industrial process of biofuel production.

50 "These studies also help us learn more about this endangered animal's digestive system and the microbes that live in it, which is important because most of the diseases pandas get affect their guts," Brown said. "Understanding the relationships between the microbes and the pandas, as well as how they get their energy and nutrition, is extremely important from a **conservation** standpoint, as fewer than 2,500 giant pandas
55 are left in the wild and only 200 are in captivity." (561 words)

Foley, J.A. (2013, Sept. 11). Panda poop power promising for biofuel production. Retrieved from *Nature World News*, http://www.natureworldnews.com/articles/3927/20130911/panda-poop-power-promising-biofuel-production.htm

Check Your Understanding

A. Choose the best ending for the following sentence.

The main reason for studying panda excrement is

a) because pandas' digestive tracts contain a microbe that breaks down plant matter easily; this microbe could be used to improve the process of biofuel manufacture.

b) because panda excrement is a sustainable form of energy; if we collect enough panda excrement, we might be able to burn it and use it to power homes and businesses.

B. Answer the following questions in your own words using information from the reading.

1 Why is the biofuel industry often criticized?

_____

_____

2 What discovery has been made in the examination of panda excrement?

_____

_____

3 What point is Ashli Brown making in lines 13 to 15?

_____

_____

4 What is the most common biofuel in the United States? What is it made from? Why is this a problem?

_____

_____

_____

5 What is special about the microbes found in the digestive tracts of pandas?

_____

_____

6 How might the bacteria and enzymes in panda excrement be used in the development of alternative energy resources?

_____

_____

7 What secondary advantage does this research have for pandas?

_____

_____

_____

Analysis and Discussion

Discuss the following questions with your group.

1 What stance is taken in this article?

2 Do you think this article was written for a general audience or an academic audience? Explain your answer.

3 Which of the following responses to this research do you most agree with? Explain your own stance on this topic.

a) 66 I think this is fascinating research. The earth has a limited supply of fossil fuels, and we need to develop various sources of energy. This kind of research should be supported and adequately funded. 99

b) 66 Sure, it's interesting, but we already have several alternative forms of energy available to us: wind power, solar power, tidal energy…. Let's put our resources into developing those instead of trying to create new forms of energy. 99

c) 66 I think this is the wrong approach. Instead of looking for alternative sources of energy, why don't governments invest more money in trying to reduce energy consumption? For example, they could fund campaigns to encourage people to use less power. 99

d) 66 We're on dangerous ground when we start experimenting with microbes. What happens if the microbes mutate, for example? We need to experiment with non-organic forms of energy, such as geothermal energy. 99

4 If you were asked to write a paper on the potential benefits of biofuels, would you refer to this article? Why, or why not?

Living Off-Grid

Living off-grid means living without access to energy from power companies. Read about the lifestyles and energy choices of people who choose to live off-grid.

 As you read, think about the author's audience and purpose.

Before You Read

Work in groups of three or four. Discuss the following questions.

1 This reading is about a couple who decided to live off-grid. What would you like to find out about them and about their decision? Write five questions below.

a) _____

b) _____

c) _____

d) _____

e) _____

2 In addition to saving energy, what advantages to off-grid living can you think of? What disadvantages might there be?

Key Vocabulary

The words below are all in the reading. Match each word with the correct definition.

1 conveniences (n. line 40)   _____
a) equipment that collects and stores energy from the sun

2 downsize (v. line 16)   _____
b) decrease dramatically

3 epiphany (n. line 2)   _____
c) moment of sudden realization or understanding

4 have a thing for something (idiom line 23)   _____
d) equipment that produces energy from the wind

5 liberation (n. line 18)   _____
e) eliminate some to leave a reduced number

6 plummet (v. line 63)   _____
f) model behaviour to other people

7 set an example (phrase line 75)   _____
g) something needs to change

8 solar panel (n. line 26)   _____
h) have an emotional attraction to something

9 something's got to give (idiom line 13)   _____
i) freedom

10 wind turbine (n. line 30)   _____
j) items that make our lives easier

Living Off-Grid

By Deborah Carr

Debbie Cameron was enjoying the good life—wind in her hair, sun in her face, salt spray at her back—when she experienced an epiphany. In hindsight, an epiphany—at the time, it was a good old-fashioned meltdown.

In the spring of 2008, she and her husband Mike were sailing with his relatives off
5 British Columbia's Gulf Coast. The couple lived full-time on their boat and Debbie enjoyed the freedom.

At home in Nova Scotia, the Camerons owned a beautiful log home they had designed and built themselves. They also had an off-grid, 600-square-foot beachfront cottage on family land.

10 But the emotional cost of maintaining two properties wore thin. Not prone to envy, Debbie was surprised at the intensity of emotion she experienced when considering the confines of the life she had built. "I was overwhelmed," she recalls. "I thought, something's got to give."

She and Mike discussed options. Despite being half the size of their log home, a
15 kilometre from a serviced highway and requiring a major change in their lifestyle, the cottage won out. They put their cherished home up for sale, downsized their possessions and joined the ranks of folk who have adopted off-grid living.

"The liberation of letting go of something you held so dear far surpasses the feeling of loss," says Debbie, who admits their home had been their identity. "A friend said that
20 we have done what a lot of people want to do, but never will be able to do." She delights in the idea that she is not beholden to a power utility.

People choose off-grid living for two reasons, says Robert MacKean, owner of Nova Sun Power. "Some have a thing for being off-grid," he says. "They don't like the utilities and want to live differently. For others, it is necessity or a cost issue because they are
25 too far from utility lines."

The main source of energy for off-grid living is the sun. Solar panels mounted on a roof or on the ground feed into deep-cycle batteries that store the energy until it is needed. An inverter modifies the current for household use.

The Camerons maintain four deep-cycle batteries charged by solar panels and a small
30 wind turbine. This provides enough power to run a satellite TV, washing machine, refrigerator, deep freeze, water pump and various small appliances. Their main heat source is a wood stove. They use a propane range and hot-water heater and also have a backup RV[1] furnace and a gas-powered generator.

In our climate, you need an alternate energy source. "Most solar installations are
35 backed up by a fossil-fuel generator," says MacKean, "or some people may use wind turbines as a complement. Solar should be considered as your primary source and then wind as a secondary, along with a generator. It is cheaper per unit of energy and there

---

[1] RV stands for "recreational vehicle"; this is a mobile home, a large trailer that you can live in.

is no maintenance required with solar. With wind turbines, there are multiple moving parts, so that would require some maintenance over time and use."

40   Many people think that living off-grid means giving up modern conveniences. But MacKean has installed solar on everything from a one-room camp to a 3,000-square-foot home.

"Whatever you have in a regular house, you can have in an off-grid house—even air 45 conditioning," he says. "Solar works best in summer and that's when you need the cooling."

For Rob Elias, the choice wasn't a moral issue, it was necessity. The power lines 50 stopped 1.5 km from his property. He began homesteading on the land seven years ago with a log cabin, one solar panel, one battery and two vehicle fog lights. "I didn't know anything about solar power until I actually 55 tried to do it," he says with a laugh.

He has improved on the power structure and home design over time. Now he sources all his electrical needs from solar panels and his heat from wood and propane. He uses a propane stove and a hot-water heater and has in-floor heat using wood-fired hot water.

Annually, for his 1,100-square-foot home, Elias burns about four cords[2] of wood that 60 he cuts himself and spends about $900 for propane and gas. Overall, he estimates the solar panels and batteries would have cost about $10,000 to $15,000, which is equal to the original quote to bring utility power to his home.

"The price of solar has plummeted in the last five years," notes MacKean. "It's now a third of what it used to be, largely due to the US dollar being on par, and the demand 65 and production worldwide."

MacKean actually does not recommend converting to full off-grid living if electricity is financially feasible and available. "I encourage people to install solar panels but remain tied into the power grid."

With this set-up, batteries are not required, so costs are less. The homeowner generates 70 and uses solar energy as required, but when extra electricity is needed, it is supplied through the grid. The power utility's distribution system absorbs the surplus solar and applies a credit against the customer's account. This is called "net metering." With this arrangement, the homeowner has a steady and reliable supply of energy.

Debbie Cameron remains grateful for the epiphany that led her to a better way of 75 living. "For us, it's about setting an example and becoming more aware about how we live," she says.

(929 words)

---

[2] A *cord* is a unit of measurement for firewood. One cord equals 128 cubic feet or 3.62 cubic metres.

Carr, D. (2013, Nov. 25). Living off grid. *East Coast Living*. Retrieved from http://eastcoastliving.ca/2013/11/living-off-grid/

Check Your Understanding

A. How many of your questions from "Before You Read" were answered in the article? Go back to your questions and fill in the answers where you can.

Did you ask any question that was not answered? What answer might you infer from the reading?

_____

_____

_____

_____

B. Answer the following questions in your own words using information from the reading.

1 What properties did the Camerons own before they moved off-grid?

_____

_____

2 How did Debbie Cameron feel about her lifestyle before she moved off-grid?

_____

_____

3 Give two reasons why people might choose to live off-grid.

_____

_____

4 What energy sources do the Camerons now use? Check all that apply.
- ○ gas
- ○ power grid
- ○ propane
- ○ solar power
- ○ wind power

5 Why does Robert MacKean recommend having a back-up energy source?

_____

_____

6 In what way was Rob Elias' decision to live off-grid different from the Camerons' decision?

_____

_____

7 How does Debbie Cameron feel now about her family's decision to move off-grid?

_____

_____

C. What inferences can you make from the way the author has described the off-grid lifestyle? Check all that apply.

- ○ a) The Camerons are a financially secure couple.
- ○ b) Alternative energy can be cheaper than energy from power companies.
- ○ c) Power from the sun or the wind is not reliable.
- ○ d) It is possible to live off-grid with no previous experience of this lifestyle.
- ○ e) Living off-grid means giving up all luxuries.
- ○ f) The author thinks the Camerons' choice to move off-grid was strange.

Analysis and Discussion

Discuss the following questions with your group.

1 Where do you think this article appeared?

a) In a magazine about the lives of ordinary people

b) In an advertising brochure for solar energy

c) In an academic journal about energy conservation

What features of the article led you to your conclusion?

2 What was the author's purpose in writing this text?

a) To encourage people to move off-grid

b) To compare the cost of on-grid and off-grid living

c) To point out the hardships of living off-grid

d) To tell a story that would interest readers of the publication

3 How you think someone from the local utilities company might respond to this article?

4 Many people around the world, especially in developing countries, live off-grid out of necessity, not by choice. How do think they would respond to this article?

5 How do you personally respond to the Camerons' story?

a) I envy their simple, back-to-nature lifestyle; I admire people like this.

b) I think it's interesting, but I couldn't do it myself. I'm a city person.

c) I think they were crazy to sell a big house and move to an off-grid cottage.

d) Other: _____

_____

6 What question(s) would you like to ask the Camerons or Rob Elias?

7 Do you think off-grid living is an effective solution to the world energy crisis? Explain your answer.

Adverse Health Effects of Industrial Wind Turbines

Read about one alternative source of energy which seems to have negative effects on the health of nearby residents.

 As you read, think about the authors' stance, audience and purpose.

Before You Read

Work in groups of three or four. Discuss the following questions.

1. In Reading 2, the use of wind turbines was discussed as a source of energy. What do you know about wind turbines? Share your information with your group.

2. One of the authors of this article is a doctor. What might you expect a doctor to think about alternative energy?

3. How might an academic paper address the topic of alternative energy differently from a newspaper or magazine article?

Adverse Health Effects of Industrial Wind Turbines

Roy D. Jeffery, MD FCFP, Carmen Krogh and Brett Horner, CMA

Canadian family physicians can expect to see increasing numbers of rural patients reporting adverse effects from exposure to industrial wind turbines (IWTs). People
5 who live or work in close proximity to IWTs have experienced symptoms that include decreased quality of life, annoyance, stress, sleep disturbance, headache, anxiety, depression and cognitive dysfunction.
10 Some have also felt anger, grief or a sense of injustice. Suggested causes of symptoms include a combination of wind turbine noise, infrasound, dirty electricity, ground current and shadow flicker.[1] Family phy-
15 sicians should be aware that patients reporting adverse effects from IWTs might experience symptoms that are intense and pervasive and might feel further victimized by a lack of caregiver understanding.

20 **Background**
There is increasing concern that energy generation from fossil fuels contributes to climate change and air pollution. In response to these concerns, governments
25 around the world are encouraging the installation of renewable energy projects, including IWTs. In Ontario, the Green Energy Act was designed, in part, to remove barriers to the installation of IWTs.[2]

30 Noise regulations can be a considerable barrier to IWT development, as they can have a substantial effect on wind turbine spacing, and therefore the cost of wind-generated electricity.[3] Industrial wind
35 turbines are being placed in close proximity to family homes in order to have access to transmission infrastructure.[4]

In Ontario and elsewhere,[5] some individuals have reported experiencing
40 adverse health effects resulting from living near IWTs. Reports of IWT-induced adverse health effects have been dismissed by some commentators, including government authorities and other organizations.
45 Physicians have been exposed to efforts to convince the public of the benefits of IWTs while minimizing the health risks. Those concerned about adverse effects of IWTs have been stereotyped as "NIMBYs" (not
50 in my backyard).[6,7]

Global reports of effects

During the past few years there have been case reports of adverse effects. A 2006 Académie nationale de médecine working
55 group report notes that noise is the most frequent complaint. The noise is described as piercing, preoccupying and continually surprising, as it is irregular in intensity. The noise includes grating and incongruous
60 sounds that distract the attention or disturb rest. The spontaneous recurrence of these noises disturbs the sleep, suddenly awakening the subject when the wind rises and preventing the subject from going back to
65 sleep. Wind turbines have been blamed for other problems experienced by people living nearby. These are less precise and less well described and consist of subjective (headaches, fatigue, temporary feelings of
70 dizziness, nausea) and some-times objective (vomiting, insomnia, palpitations) manifestations.[8]

A 2009 literature review prepared by the Minnesota Department of Health[9]
75 summarized case reports by Harry (2007),[10] Phipps et al (2007),[11] the Large Wind Turbine Citizens Committee for the Town of Union (2008)[12] and Pierpont (2009).[13] These case studies catalogued complaints
80 of annoyance, reduced quality of life and health effects associated with IWTs, such as sleeplessness and headaches.[9]

In 2010, Nissenbaum et al used validated questionnaires in a controlled study of two
85 Maine wind energy projects. They concluded that "the noise emissions of IWTs disturbed the sleep and caused daytime sleepiness and impaired mental health in residents living within 1.4 km of
90 the two IWT installations studied."[14]

Reports of adverse health effects[15] and reduced quality of life[16] are also documented in IWT projects in Australia and New Zealand.

95 A 2012 board of health resolution in Brown County in Wisconsin formally requested financial relocation assistance for "families that are suffering adverse health effects and undue hardships caused by the
100 irrespon-sible placement of industrial wind turbines around their homes and property."[17]

An Ontario community-based self-reporting health survey, WindVOiCe, identified the most commonly reported
105 IWT-induced symptoms as altered quality of life, sleep disturbance, excessive tiredness, headache, stress and distress. Other reported effects include migraines, hearing problems, tinnitus, heart palpitations,
110 anxiety and depression.[18] In addition, degraded living conditions and adverse socioeconomic effects have been reported. In some cases the effects were severe enough that individuals in Ontario aban-
115 doned their homes or reached financial agreements with wind energy developers.[19]

After considering the evidence and testimony presented by twenty-six witnesses, →

a 2011 Ontario environmental review tribunal decision acknowledged IWTs can harm human health:

> This case has successfully shown that the debate should not be simplified to one about whether wind turbines can cause harm to humans. The evidence presented to the Tribunal demonstrates that they can, if facilities are placed too close to residents. The debate has now evolved to one of degree.[20]

Indirect effects and annoyance

When assessing the adverse effects of IWTs, it is important to consider what constitutes human health. The World Health Organization (WHO) defines health as "a state of complete physical, mental and social well-being and not merely the absence of disease or infirmity."[21]

Despite being widely accepted, the WHO definition of health is frequently overlooked when assessing the health effects of IWTs. Literature reviews commenting on the health effects of IWTs have been produced with varying degrees of completeness, accuracy and objectivity.[22] Some of these commentators accept the plausibility of the reported IWT health effects and acknowledge that IWT noise and visual effects might cause annoyance, stress or sleep disturbance, which can have other consequences. However, these IWT health effects are often discounted because "direct pathological effects" or a "direct causal link" have not been established. In 2010, the Ontario Chief Medical Officer of Health released *The Potential Health Impact of Wind Turbines*, which acknowledged that some people living near wind turbines report symptoms such as dizziness, headaches and sleep disturbance but concluded "the scientific evidence available to date does not demonstrate a direct causal link between wind turbine noise and adverse health effects."[23] The lead author of the report,[23] Dr Gloria Rachamin, acknowledged under oath that the literature review looked only at direct links to human health.[24]

Focusing on "direct" causal links limits the discussion to a small slice of the potential health effects of IWTs. The 2011 environmental review tribunal decision found that *serious harm to human health* includes "indirect impacts (e.g., a person being exposed to noise and then exhibiting stress and developing other related symptoms)."[20]

According to the night noise guidelines for Europe:

> Physiological experiments on humans have shown that noise of a moderate level acts via an indirect pathway and has health outcomes similar to those caused by high noise exposures on the direct pathway. The indirect pathway starts with noise-induced disturbances of activities such as communication or sleep.[25]

Pierpont documented symptoms reported by individuals exposed to wind turbines, which include sleep disturbance, headache, tinnitus, ear pressure, dizziness, vertigo, nausea, visual blurring, tachycardia, irritability, problems with concentration and memory, and panic episodes associated with sensations of internal pulsation or quivering when awake or asleep.[13] The American Wind Energy Association and the Canadian Wind Energy Association convened a panel literature review that determined these symptoms are the "well-known stress effects of exposure to noise," or in other words, are "a subset of annoyance reactions."[26]

Noise-induced annoyance is acknowledged to be an adverse health effect.[27-30] Chronic severe noise annoyance should be classified as a serious health risk.[31] According to the WHO guidelines for community noise, "[t]he capacity of a noise to induce annoyance depends upon many of its physical characteristics, including its sound pressure level and spectral characteristics, as well as the variations of these properties over time."[32] Industrial wind turbine noise is perceived to be more annoying than transportation noise or industrial noise at comparable sound pressure levels.[33] Industrial wind turbine amplitude modulation,[34] audible low frequency noise,[35] tonal noise, infrasound[36] and lack of nighttime abatement have been identified as plausible noise characteristics that could cause annoyance and other health effects.

Health effects in Ontario expected

Evidence-based health studies were not conducted to determine adequate setbacks and noise levels for the siting of IWTs before the implementation of the Ontario renewable energy policy. In addition, provision for vigilance monitoring was not made. It is now clear that the regulations are not adequate to protect the health of all exposed individuals.

A 2010 report commissioned by the Ontario Ministry of the Environment concludes:

> The audible sound from wind turbines, at the levels experienced at typical receptor distances in Ontario, is nonethe-less expected to result in a non-trivial percentage of persons being highly annoyed .... [R]esearch has shown that annoyance associated with sound from wind turbines can be expected to contribute to stress-related health impacts in some persons.[37]

Consequently, physicians will likely be presented with patients reporting health effects.

Family physicians should be aware that patients reporting adverse effects from IWTs might experience symptoms that are intense and pervasive and that they might feel further victimized by a lack of caregiver understanding. Those adversely affected by IWTs might have already pursued other avenues to mitigate the health effects with little or no success. It will be important to identify the possibility of exposure to IWTs in patients presenting with appropriate clinical symptoms.[38]

Conclusion

Industrial wind turbines can harm human health if sited too close to residents. Harm can be avoided if IWTs are situated at an appropriate distance from humans. Owing to the lack of adequately protective siting guidelines, people exposed to IWTs can be expected to present to their family physicians in increasing numbers. The documented symptoms are usually stress-disorder–type diseases acting via indirect pathways and can represent serious harm to human health. Family physicians are in a position to effectively recognize the ailments and provide an empathetic response. In addition, their contributions to clinical studies are urgently needed to clarify the relationship between IWT exposure and human health and to inform regulations that will protect physical, mental and social well-being.

Footnotes

This article has been peer reviewed.

Dr. Jeffery is a family physician in the Northeastern Manitoulin Family Health Team in Little Current, Ont. Ms. Krogh is a retired pharmacist and a former Editor-in-Chief of the *Compendium of Pharmaceuticals and Specialties*. Mr. Horner is a Certified Management Accountant.

Competing interests

Dr. Jeffery, Ms. Krogh and Mr. Horner are on the Board of Directors for the Society for Wind Vigilance, an international federation of physicians, acousticians, engineers and other professionals who share scientific research on the topic of health and wind turbines.

References

1. Havas M, Colling D. Wind turbines make waves: why some residents near wind turbines become ill. Bull Sci Technol Soc 2011;31(5):414-26.

2. Government of Ontario [website]. *Chapter 12. An act to enact the Green Energy Act, 2009 and to build a green economy, to repeal the Energy Conservation Leadership Act, 2006 and the Energy Efficiency Act and to amend other statutes.* Toronto, ON: Government of Ontario; 2009. Available from: www.e-laws.gov.on.ca/html/source/statutes/english/2009/elaws_src_s09012_e.htm#. Accessed 2013 Mar 26.

3. Canadian Wind Energy Association [website]. *Letter to Neil Parish re: sound level limits for wind farms.* Ottawa, ON: Canadian Wind Energy Association; 2004. Available from: www.canwea.ca/images/uploads/File/Wind_Energy_Policy/Environmental_Issues/SoundLevels.pdf. Accessed 2013 Mar 26.

4. Hornung R. *Business of green: wind energy and budget expectations [video].* Toronto, ON: Business News Network; 2010. Available from: http://watch.bnn.ca/clip272347. Accessed 2013 Apr 4.

5. Hanning CD, Evans A. Wind turbine noise. *BMJ* 2012;344:e1527.

6. Martin C. NIMBY mentality unacceptable when it comes to green-energy projects, McGuinty says. *London Free Press.* 2009 Feb 12.

7. Schliesmann P. Wind turbine debate swirls. *Kingston Whig-Standard* 2010 Jan 2. Available from: www.thewhig.com/ArticleDisplay.aspx?e=2244137&archive=true. Accessed 2013 Mar 26.

8. Académie Nationale de Médecine Groupe de Travail. *Le retentissement du fonctionnement des éoliennes sur la santé de l'homme.* Paris, France: Académie Nationale de Médecine; 2006. Available from:www.academie-medecine.fr/sites_thematiques/EOLIENNES/chouard_rapp_14mars_2006.htm. Accessed 2013 Mar 26.

9. Minnesota Department of Health [website]. *Public health impacts of wind turbines.* St Paul, MN: Minnesota Department of Health; 2009. Available from: www.health.state.mn.us/divs/eh/hazardous/topics/windturbines.pdf. Accessed 2013 Mar 26.

10. Harry A. *Wind turbines, noise and health.* Rowe, MA: National Wind Watch; 2007. Available from: http://docs.wind-watch.org/wtnoise_health_2007_a_harry.pdf. Accessed 2013 Mar 26.

11. Phipps R, Amati M, McCoard S, Fisher R. *Visual and noise effects reported by residents living close to Manawatu wind farms: preliminary survey results.* Rowe, MA: National Wind Watch; 2007. Available from: http://docs.wind-watch.org/phippsvisualnoiseeffects.pdf. Accessed 2013 Mar 26.

12. Large Wind Turbine Citizens Committee for the Town of Union. *Setback recommendations report.* Rowe, MA: National Wind Watch; 2008. Available from: http://docs.wind-watch.org/LWTCC-Town-of-Union_FinalReport_01-14-08.pdf. Accessed 2013 Mar 26.

13. Pierpont N. *Wind turbine syndrome: a report on a natural experiment.* Santa Fe, NM: K-Selected Books; 2009.

14. Nissenbaum MA, Aramini JJ, Hanning CD. Effects of industrial wind turbine noise on sleep and health. *Noise Health* 2012; 14(60):237-43.

15. Thorne B. The problems with "noise numbers" for wind farm noise assessment. *Bull Sci Technol Soc* 2011;31(4):262-90.

16. Shepherd D, McBride D, Welch D, Dirks KN, Hill EM. Evaluating the impact of wind turbine noise on health-related quality of life. *Noise Health* 2011;13(54):333-9.

17. *Brown County board of health resolution requesting emergency state aid for families suffering around industrial wind turbines.* Rowe, MA:National Wind Watch; 2012. Available from: http://docs.wind-watch.org/Brown%20County%20Board%20of%20Health%20Resolution%20011012.pdf. Accessed 2013 Mar 28.

18. Krogh CME, Gillis L, Kouwen N, Aramini J. WindVOiCe, a self-reporting survey: adverse health effects, industrial wind turbines, and the need for vigilance monitoring. *Bull Sci Technol Soc* 2011;31(4):334-45.

19. Krogh CME. Industrial wind turbine development and loss of social justice? *Bull Sci Technol Soc* 2011;31(4):321-33.

20. *Erickson v. Director, Ministry of the Environment.* 2011. Environmental Review Tribunal Nos. 10-121 and 10-122. Available from:www.ert.gov.on.ca/files/201108/00000300-AKT5757C7C0026-BHH51C7A7S0026.pdf. Accessed 2013 Mar 28.

21. World Health Organization. *Preamble to the Constitution of the World Health Organization.* Geneva, Switz: World Health Organization; 1948.Definition of health. Available from: www.who.int/about/definition/en/print.html. Accessed 2013 Mar 28.

22. Horner B, Jeffery RD, Krogh CME. Literature reviews on wind turbines and health: are they enough? *Bull Sci Technol Soc* 2011;31(5):399-413.

23. Chief Medical Officer of Health. *The potential health impact of wind turbines.* Toronto, ON: Ministry of Health and Long-Term Care; 2010. Available from: http://health.gov.on.ca/en/common/ministry/publications/reports/wind_turbine/wind_turbine.pdf. Accessed 2013 Mar 27.

24. *Erickson v. Director, Ministry of the Environment.* Environmental Review Tribunal Nos. 10-121 and 10-122. Transcript of Dr G. Rachamin. 2011 Mar 4.

25. World Health Organization Europe. *Night noise guidelines for Europe*. Copenhagen, Denmark: World Health Organization Europe; 2009. Available from: www.euro.who.int/__data/assets/pdf_file/0017/43316/E92845.pdf. Accessed 2013 Mar 27.

26. Colby WD, Dobie R, Leventhall G, Lipscomb DM, McCunney RJ, Seilo MT, et al. *Wind turbine sound and health effects. An expert panel review*. Washington, DC: American Wind Energy Association, Canadian Wind Energy Association; 2009. Available from: www.canwea.ca/pdf/talkwind/Wind_Turbine_Sound_and_Health_Effects.pdf. Accessed 2013 Mar 27.

27. Health Canada [website]. *Community noise annoyance*. Ottawa, ON: Health Canada; 2005. Available from: www.hc-sc.gc.ca/hl-vs/iyh-vsv/life-vie/community-urbain-eng.php. Accessed 2013 Mar 27.

28. Suter AH. *Noise and its effects*. Washington, DC: Administrative Conference of the United States; 1991. Available from: www.nonoise.org/library/suter/suter.htm. Accessed 2013 Mar 27.

29. Michaud DS, Keith SE, McMurchy D. Noise annoyance in Canada. *Noise Health* 2005;7(27):39-47.

30. Pedersen E, Persson Waye K. Wind turbine noise, annoyance and self-reported health and well-being in different living environments. *Occup Environ Med* 2007;64(7):480-6. Epub 2007 Mar 1.

31. Maschke C, Niemann A. Health effects of annoyance induced by neighbour noise. *Noise Control Eng J* 2007;55(3):348-56.

32. Berglund B, Lindvall T, Schwela DH, editors. *Guidelines for community noise*. Geneva, Switz: World Health Organization; 1999.

33. Pedersen E, van den Berg F, Bakker R, Bouma J. Response to noise from modern wind farms in the Netherlands. *J Acoust Soc Am* 2009;126(2):634-43.

34. Leventhall G. Infrasound from wind turbines—fact, fiction or deception. *Can Acoust* 2006;34(2):29-36.

35. Møller H, Pedersen CS. Low-frequency noise from large wind turbines. *J Acoust Soc Am* 2011;129(6):3727-44.

36. Salt AN, Kaltenbach JA. Infrasound from wind turbines could affect humans. *Bull Sci Technol Soc* 2011;31(4):296-302.

37. Howe Gastmeier Chapnik Limited. *Low frequency noise and infrasound associated with wind turbine generator systems. A literature review.* Toronto, ON: Ontario Ministry of the Environment; 2010. Available from:www.ene.gov.on.ca/stdprodconsume/groups/lr/@ene/@resources/documents/resource/stdprod_092086.pdf. Accessed 2013 Mar 27.

38. McMurtry RY. Toward a case definition of adverse health effects in the environs of industrial wind turbines: facilitatin a clinical diagnosis. *Bull Sci Technol Soc* 2011;31(4):316-20.

1592 words (excluding references)

Jeffery, R. D., Krogh, C., and Horner, B. (2013, May). Adverse health effects of industrial wind turbines. *Canadian Family Physician, 59*(5), 473–475.

Check Your Understanding

A. What stance is taken by the three authors of this paper? Summarize their argument in two or three sentences.

_____

_____

_____

_____

_____

_____

_____

B. Answer the following questions, in your own words where possible, using information from the reading.

1. The effects experienced by people who live near industrial wind turbines (IWTs) are

a) physiological.

b) psychological.

c) both physiological and psychological.

2. What did the Green Energy Act do?

_____

③ Name three *physiological* symptoms reported by patients who live near IWTs.

_____

④ Name three *psychological* symptoms reported by patients who live near IWTs.

_____

⑤ Negative effects of IWTs are reported only by people who live in Ontario: true or false?

_____

_____

⑥ What did a 2011 Ontario environmental review tribunal decision establish?

a) IWTs have negative effects on the health of people living close to them.

b) IWTs have been located too close to people's homes and should be moved.

⑦ How does the World Health Organization define "health"?

_____

_____

_____

⑧ What should doctors living in areas with IWTs expect to see in the future?

_____

_____

C. What inferences can you make from the article? Check all that apply.

○ a) People who complain about IWTs need to be taken more seriously.

○ b) IWTs do not produce enough energy for daily use.

○ c) The authors are frustrated about the lack of acceptance of people's complaints.

○ d) IWTs are linked to cancer and other serious illnesses.

○ e) Health problems caused by noise are not trivial and should be taken seriously.

○ f) Psychological complaints are just as serious as physiological complaints.

Key Vocabulary

Find the following sentences in the text. Which of the words and expressions below is NOT a synonym for the word in **bold**?

① Canadian family physicians can expect to see increasing numbers of rural patients reporting **adverse** effects from exposure to industrial wind turbines (IWTs). (lines 1 to 4)

a) beneficial   c) detrimental

b) negative   d) harmful

② Some have also felt anger, grief or a sense of **injustice**. (lines 10 to 11)

a) unfairness   c) inequality

b) wrongdoing   d) respect

3 Reports of IWT-induced adverse health effects have been **dismissed** by some commentators including government authorities and other organizations. (lines 41 to 44)

a) denied

b) not taken seriously

c) recognized

d) disregarded

4 The **spontaneous** recurrence of these noises disturbs the sleep, suddenly awakening the subject when the wind rises and preventing the subject from going back to sleep. (lines 61 to 65)

a) scheduled

b) unpredictable

c) irregular

d) unplanned

5 The debate has now **evolved** to one of degree. (lines 128 to 129)

a) developed

b) deteriorated

c) progressed

d) advanced

6 Despite being widely accepted, the WHO definition of health is frequently **overlooked** when assessing the health effects of IWTs. (lines 138 to 140)

a) ignored

b) neglected

c) remembered

d) forgotten

7 However, these IWT health effects are often **discounted** because "direct pathological effects" or a "direct causal link" have not been established. (lines 150 to 153)

a) disregarded

b) ignored

c) denied

d) misunderstood

8 The lead author of the report, Dr Gloria Rachamin, **acknowledged** under oath that the literature review looked only at direct links to human health. (lines 163 to 167)

a) admitted

b) disputed

c) accepted

d) agreed

9 It is now clear that the regulations are not **adequate** to protect the health of all exposed individuals. (lines 231 to 233)

a) lacking

b) sufficient

c) good enough

d) satisfactory

10 Family physicians are in a position to effectively recognize the ailments and provide an **empathetic** response. (lines 274 to 277)

a) understanding

b) compassionate

c) sensitive

d) uncaring

Analysis and Discussion

Discuss the following questions with your group.

1 This article appeared in a publication called *Canadian Family Physician*. Who do you think the article was written for?

a) doctors

b) the general public

c) scientists

d) wind turbine experts

② Why do you think the authors wrote this article?

③ What do you think the authors would like readers to do after they read this article?

④ Why do you think the authors give so many references in this paper?

⑤ How do you think Debbie Cameron (Reading 2) might respond to this article?

⑥ Are *you* convinced about the dangers of wind turbines? Why, or why not?

Going Further
Focus on Language

A. The following chart contains ten words from the readings. Complete the chart with related words in the other categories and, where possible, in the same category. (There may not be a word for each category.)

	NOUN	VERB	ADJECTIVE	ADVERB
1			adverse	
2				comparatively
3			endangered	
4	envy			
5	identity			
6		perceive		
7	possession			
8	production			
9		recognize		
10		simplify		

B. The following sentences, all taken from the three readings, use language commonly found in descriptions of research or experiments. Choose the best verb from the list below for each sentence. Each verb should be used only once.

conducted	documented	estimates	exploring
focused	identified	notes	presented

1. Brown and her colleagues _____ more than forty gut microbes that could make biofuel production from plant waste easier and cheaper.

2. One alternative researchers are _____ is using inedible food parts and other plant material, such as corn stalks and corn cobs, as sources of ethanol.

3. "And efficiency is key when it comes to biofuel production—that's why we _____ on the microbes in the giant panda."

4. Overall, he _____ the solar panels and batteries would have cost about $10,000 to $15,000, which is equal to the original quote to bring utility power to his home.

5. Reports of adverse health effects and reduced quality of life are also _____ in IWT projects in Australia and New Zealand.

6. The evidence _____ to the Tribunal demonstrates that they can, if facilities are placed too close to residents.

7. Evidence-based health studies were not _____ to determine adequate setbacks and noise levels for the siting of IWTs before the implementation of the Ontario renewable energy policy.

8. A 2006 Académie nationale de médecine working group report _____ that noise is the most frequent complaint.

Independent Research

Choose one of the following energy sources and carry out some online research about this source of energy. You will present your findings to your class.

> solar energy   > geothermal energy   > wave energy

Synthesis and Written Response

Based on your reading of the texts in this chapter as well as your own research into alternative sources of energy, write a short response to the following question:

> How can we solve the energy crisis? Compare and evaluate two or more possible solutions.

REVIEW
of the chapter ...

> Answer the following questions.

1. What is meant by the author's stance?

2. How might an article written for a general audience differ from one written for an academic audience?

3. What purpose might a non-academic author have for writing a text? Name as many as you can.

CHAPTER 5

Leaders and Leadership

 FACT OR OPINION?

Does the text you are reading present facts or opinions, or a mixture of both? How can you tell?

In this chapter
YOU WILL LEARN ...

> how to distinguish facts from opinions.

Warm-up

Discuss these questions with your group.

> What do you think are the essential skills needed to succeed in the business world?

> Think of some people who have been very successful in the business world (for example, Bill Gates, Steve Jobs and Mark Zuckerberg). What personal qualities do you associate them with?

> Name some members of minority groups who have risen to leadership positions in their countries. How does society benefit from having diversity among its leaders?

Fact or Opinion?

> What qualities, skills and personal characteristics should successful leaders have?

Imagine you have been given this essay topic in a course entitled *Introduction to Business Studies*. Different texts will give you different information about this topic. Your role, as a reader, will be to determine whether the text you are reading is presenting facts that you can trust or whether it is presenting the opinions of the individual author. You will read statements that fall into one of the categories below:

> This is a fact; I can't argue with this.

> This could well be a fact, but I need to see some evidence.

> This is the opinion of the author or of someone quoted by the author.

How Can I Distinguish between Facts and Opinions?

Facts are pieces of information that no one can argue with. This could include scientific, historical, biographical, geographical, statistical or other information, as long as it can be confirmed by numerous independent sources. Look at the following information.

> The Tim Hortons chain of doughnut and coffee shops was founded in 1964 by former hockey player Tim Horton. Before going into business, Tim Horton had played hockey for the Toronto Maple Leafs. Tim Horton died in a car accident in 1974.

This is biographical data that can be confirmed by various sources.

Often you will see information presented as fact, but you may wonder whether it is true or whether there is any evidence. Look at the following sentences.

> With twice as many outlets as McDonald's, Tim Hortons is the leading fast-food outlet in Canada.

> Tim Hortons coffee is the most popular brand in Canada.

These statements may or may not be true. You should check to see whether the author has enough evidence to support his or her opinion. Does the author present any statistical evidence? Could the author be biased in some way? Always ask yourself: *How do I know? What evidence is the author giving me to make me believe this?*

Think about where you found your information. Can you trust the article? Is your source peer reviewed? Or is your information from a non-academic source, such as a magazine or website? If your source is a website, consider who is responsible for the website. Is it reliable? If you are in doubt, double-check your information by searching for it in an academic publication.

Opinions are the personal ideas of the author. You can often identify opinions because they contain the following language:

1 *Opinion verbs*: Clearly, if the author states that he or she *thinks* or *believes* something, you can conclude that this is an opinion.

2 *Adjectives*: If the author describes something as *great, terrible, amazing, terrifying* or using other adjectives expressing personal feelings, be careful. This is the author's own opinion. In the same way, if something is described in comparative or superlative terms as *better, more interesting, not as good, the most important* and so on, you should realize that this is the opinion of this particular author. What is important or the best to one author may be considered in a very different way by another author.

3 *Modal verbs*: If the author states that something *should* or *must* happen, this is often an indication that the author is expressing his or her own opinion. Similarly, the verbs *could* or *might* indicate a prediction, which may or may not be accurate.

The following sentences all express opinions.

> I think Tim Horton was a great business leader.

> The coffee at Tim Hortons is better than the coffee at many more expensive places.

> Tim Hortons should focus more on healthy foods and less on sugary doughnuts.

> If Tim Hortons expanded more in Europe, the company could be very successful.

Put It into Practice

A. Look at the statements below. Each contains a mixture of facts and opinions. For each one, do the following:

a) Underline a fact.

b) Circle an opinion expressed by the author.

What are the qualities of a good manager?

1 66 I think a good manager needs to take the time to listen to his or her employees. My current manager is amazing! She always calls team meetings to get our feedback on new developments, and she takes our opinions seriously. I feel respected, and that makes a huge difference. 99

2 66 The most important thing is that the manager is not an egomaniac. I had one manager who was so full of himself that working with him was a nightmare. He thought the company was his own little kingdom, and he was a real bully! I used to go home and cry every night. I no longer work there, thank goodness. 99

3 ❝ My boss spends every day in her office with the door closed. I have no idea what she does in there. I believe a good boss needs to be visible and accessible. A good boss should invite her employees for coffee, talk to them, get to know them. I think office parties are valuable for team building, but I have never been to one. ❞

4 ❝ A good manager should encourage his or her employees to reach their full potential. I develop educational software, and I often have good ideas about new products. My boss always allows me to explore my ideas and to experiment; he never takes the credit for anything I have created. He really allows me to shine. ❞

5 ❝ I once worked for a boss who was so driven to succeed that she hated it when any of her employees took time off for family events. I once took three days off because my child was sick; after that, I was never offered any special projects, and I was never asked for my opinion. She seemed to have decided that I was not a team player. I felt so demoralized that I quit. That's the worst kind of boss. ❞

6 ❝ My manager knows I don't make much money in my job. He never overloads me with extra work; in fact, he tries to make my job as easy as possible. Managers must understand that not everyone makes a six-figure salary with benefits and perks; give us a break sometimes! ❞

B. Read the following short text, taken from a talk given by a career counsellor to a group of graduating high-school students. In groups, discuss whether each of the underlined statements is

a) a fact—we can't argue with this;

b) possibly a fact, but we need to verify this elsewhere; or

c) the speaker's personal opinion.

A lot of people will tell you that you should try to figure out what interests you most and follow that. Well, I'm not going to do that. What if the thing that interests you most won't ever get you a job? How will following that interest benefit you in the long run? You might say playing a certain kind of computer game is the thing that interests you most, but (1) you can't turn playing computer games into some kind of career.

At the same time, it's not enough to just say that you should pursue a career where you know you'll get a job. (2) Right now there's a 100 percent placement rate for people who finish dental programs. Does that mean everyone should try to be a dentist? No. (3) Not everyone can be a dentist. And if there were a huge increase in the number of students in dental programs, would there still be a 100 percent placement rate?

No one expects you to have your career completely mapped out. But you should have some idea of what strengths you have and what courses you can take in your first year. (4) The most important areas are math, chemistry, physics, biology and computers. If you have skills in these subjects, you should plan to take courses in them. If you haven't taken many high-school courses in these areas, you should consider taking some make-up courses this summer so you have that option.

Of course, if you hope to run your own business one day, you will need to take business courses. Did you know that (5) <u>80 percent of new businesses fail?</u> (6) <u>You can't be a successful businessperson without a strong academic background in business studies.</u>

(7) <u>A lot of universities and colleges now have co-op and work placement options.</u> Whatever program you're taking, it's worth your while finding out if you can do some kind of work while you're studying. (8) <u>Graduates with work experience find jobs more quickly than those who have never worked.</u> And make sure you register with your college or university's Career Centre; they provide invaluable advice on career choices.

(9) <u>Your choice of college or university program is the most important decision you will ever make in your life.</u> The program you choose will give you a certain set of skills that will help you establish a career path. (10) <u>In the next five years, 60 percent of all jobs will require a combination of postsecondary education and specialized work experience,</u> so making sure you have the right qualification is essential.

Now decide which of the speaker's opinions you personally agree with. Which do you disagree with?

C. Find a published text about a leader you admire. This could be someone from business, politics, sports or another area. Does your text contain mostly factual information (for example, biographical data), or does it contain opinions about that person's leadership style?

READING 1

Top Ten Qualities that Make a Great Leader

What personal characteristics do successful leaders need?

 As you read this article, consider the opinions expressed by the author and think about whether you agree or disagree.

Before You Read

Work in groups of three or four. Discuss the following questions.

1. Look at the following list. Which do you think are the most important in a leader of a company or organization? Choose the ten qualities and skills that you think are the most important.

A good leader

○ is honest.

○ knows when to pass work to others.

○ stays calm in a crisis.

○ has a business degree.

○ communicates well.

○ has a sense of humour.

○ is confident.

○ has excellent computer skills.

○ is committed to the organization.

○ knows a lot about finance.

○ treats subordinates fairly.

○ has a positive attitude.

○ is polite to others.

○ is creative.

○ works long hours.

○ trusts his/her instincts.

○ got good grades in school.

○ inspires others.

2 Do you personally know anyone who is a leader and who has some of these qualities and skills? How have these helped him or her?

Key Vocabulary

A. The words below are all in the reading. Fill in the space in each sentence with the correct word.

NOUNS	brand morale	crowdfunding setback	entrepreneur startup	intuition
VERBS	delegate	forecast	hone	

1 A/An _____ is a business in its early days of operation.

2 A/An _____ is an unexpected disappointment or problem that can have a negative effect on the development and growth of a business.

3 People who are able to _____ events are skilled in predicting future events such as market changes and demand fluctuations.

4 A/An _____ is a person who has an idea for an independent business and who puts that idea into action.

5 If the workers in a company have high _____, they feel positive and excited about going to work. Where this is low, there is a lack of enthusiasm for the job.

➡

6 If you _____ tasks, you give others the responsibility of carrying out these tasks rather than doing them yourself.

7 If you have strong _____, you have feelings or instinct about something; your decisions are based on feeling rather than on reason or logic.

8 _____ is a means of raising money by appealing online to a large number of individual supporters.

9 A business' _____ is what differentiates that business from others. This includes the business' website, logo, packaging and advertising.

10 To _____ your skills means to improve them until they have reached a high level.

B. Match these business-related idioms with their meanings.

1 break the ice (line 66)   _____   a) deal with sudden crises

2 in the trenches (lines 78 to 79)   _____   b) without any prior planning

3 kick in (line 107)   _____   c) think in a creative way

4 on the fly (line 96)   _____   d) help people get to know each other

5 put out fires (line 70)   _____   e) start; become active

6 raise the bar (line 13)   _____   f) doing the job, rather than supervising it

7 stretch yourself thin (lines 30 to 31) _____   g) increase standards

8 think outside the box (line 99)   _____   h) take on more than you can manage

Top Ten Qualities that Make a Great Leader

By Tanya Prive

Having a great idea and assembling a team to bring that concept to life is the first step in creating a successful business venture. While finding a new and unique idea is rare enough, the ability to successfully execute this idea is what separates the dreamers from the **entrepreneurs**. However you see yourself, whatever your age may be, as soon as
5 you make that exciting first hire, you have taken the first steps in becoming a powerful leader. When money is tight, stress levels are high, and the visions of instant success don't happen like you thought, it's easy to let those emotions get to you, and thereby your team. Take a breath, calm yourself down and remind yourself of the leader you are and would like to become. Here are some key qualities that every good leader should
10 possess and learn to emphasize.

Honesty

Whatever ethical plane you hold yourself to, when you are responsible for a team of people, it's important to raise the bar even higher. Your business and its employees are a reflection of yourself, and if you make
15 honest and ethical behaviour a key value, your team will follow suit.

As we do at RockThePost, the **crowdfunding** platform for entrepreneurs and small businesses I co-founded, try to make a list of values and core beliefs that both you and your **brand** represent and post this in your office. Promote a healthy interoffice lifestyle and encourage your
20 team to live up to these standards. By emphasizing these standards and displaying them yourself, you will hopefully influence the office environment into a friendly and helpful workspace.

Ability to delegate

Finessing your brand vision is essential to creating an organized and
25 efficient business, but if you don't learn to trust your team with that vision, you might never progress to the next stage. It's important to remember that trusting your team with your idea is a sign of strength, not weakness. Delegating tasks to the appropriate departments is one of the most important skills you can develop as your business grows.
30 The e-mails and tasks will begin to pile up, and the more you stretch yourself thin, the lower the quality of your work will become and the less you will produce.

The key to delegation is identifying the strengths of your team and capitalizing on them. Find out what each team member enjoys doing most. Chances are if they find
35 that task more enjoyable, they will likely put more thought and effort behind it. This will not only prove to your team that you trust and believe in them but will also free up your time to focus on the higher-level tasks that should not be delegated. It's a fine balance, but one that will have a huge impact on the productivity of your business.

Communication

40 Knowing what you want accomplished may seem clear in your head, but if you try to explain it to someone else and are met with a blank expression, you know there is a problem. If this has been your experience, then you may want to focus on **honing** your communication skills. Being able to clearly and succinctly describe what you want done is extremely important. If you can't relate your vision to your team, you won't all be
45 working towards the same goal.

Training new members and creating a productive work environment all depend on healthy lines of communication. Whether that stems from an open door policy to your office or making it a point to talk to your staff on a daily basis, making yourself available to discuss interoffice issues is vital. Your team will learn to trust and depend on you and
50 will be less hesitant to work harder.

Sense of humour

If your website crashes, you lose that major client or your funding dries up, guiding your team through the process without panicking is as challenging as it is important.

Morale is linked to productivity, and it's your job as the team leader to instill a positive
energy. That's where your sense of humour will finally pay off. Encourage your team
to laugh at the mistakes instead of crying. If you are constantly learning to find the
humour in the struggles, your work environment will become a happy and healthy
space, where your employees look forward to working rather than dreading it. Make
it a point to crack jokes with your team and encourage personal discussions of weekend
plans and trips. It's these short breaks from the task at hand that help keep productivity
levels high and morale even higher.

At RockThePost, we place a huge emphasis on humour and a light atmosphere. Our
office is dog friendly, and we really believe it is the small, lighthearted moments in the
day that help keep our work creative and fresh. One tradition that we like to do and
brings the team closer is we plan a fun prank on all new employees, on their first day.
It breaks the ice and immediately creates that sense of familiarity.

Confidence

There may be days where the future of your brand is worrisome and things aren't going
according to plan. This is true with any business, large or small, and the most important
thing is not to panic. Part of your job as a leader is to put out fires and maintain the team
morale. Keep up your confidence level and assure everyone that **setbacks** are natural,
and the important thing is to focus on the larger goal. As the leader, by staying calm
and confident, you will help keep the team feeling the same. Remember, your team will
take cues from you, so if you exude a level of calm damage control, your team will pick
up on that feeling. The key objective is to keep everyone working and moving ahead.

Commitment

If you expect your team to work hard and produce quality content, you're going to need
to lead by example. There is no greater motivation than seeing the boss down in the
trenches working alongside everyone else, showing that hard work is being done on
every level. By proving your commitment to the brand and your role, you will not only
earn the respect of your team but will also instill that same hardworking energy among
your staff. It's important to show your commitment not only to the work at hand but
also to your promises. If you pledged to host a holiday party, or uphold summer Fridays,
keep your word. You want to not just create a reputation for working hard but also be
known as a fair leader. Once you have gained the respect of your team, they are more
likely to deliver the peak amount of quality work possible.

Positive attitude

You want to keep your team motivated towards the continued success of the company
and keep the energy levels up. Whether that means providing snacks, coffee, relationship
advice or even just an occasional beer in the office, remember that everyone on your team
is a person. Keep the office mood a fine balance between productivity and playfulness.

If your team is feeling happy and upbeat, chances are they won't mind staying that
extra hour to finish a report or devoting their best work to the brand.

Creativity

Some decisions will not always be so clear-cut. You may be forced at times to deviate
from your set course and make an on-the-fly decision. This is where your creativity will

prove to be vital. It is during these critical situations that your team will look to you for guidance, and you may be forced to make a quick decision. As a leader, it's important to learn to think outside the box and to choose which of two bad choices is the best
100 option. Don't immediately choose the first or easiest possibility; sometimes it's best to give these issues some thought and even turn to your team for guidance. By utilizing all possible options before making a rash decision, you can typically reach the end conclusion you were aiming for.

Intuition

105 When leading a team through uncharted waters, there is no road map on what to do. Everything is uncertain, and the higher the risk, the higher the pressure. That is where your natural intuition has to kick in. Guiding your team through the process of your day-to-day tasks can be honed down to a science. But when something unexpected occurs, or you are thrown into a new scenario, your team will look to you for guidance.
110 Drawing on past experience is a good reflex, as is reaching out to your mentors for support. Eventually though, the tough decisions will be up to you to decide, and you will need to depend on your gut instinct for answers. Learning to trust yourself is as important as your team learning to trust you.

Ability to inspire

115 Creating a business often involves a bit of **forecasting**. Especially in the beginning stages of a **startup**, inspiring your team to see the vision of the successes to come is vital. Make your team feel invested in the accomplishments of the company. Whether everyone owns a piece of equity, or you operate on a bonus system, generating enthusiasm for the hard work you are all putting in is so important. Being able to inspire
120 your team is great for focusing on the future goals, but it is also important for the current issues. When you are all mired deep in work, morale is low and energy levels are fading, recognize that everyone needs a break now and then. Acknowledge the work that everyone has dedicated and commend the team on each of their efforts. It is your job to keep spirits up, and that begins with an appreciation for the hard work.   (1628 words)

Prive, T. (2012, Dec. 19). Top 10 qualities that make a great leader. *Forbes*. Retrieved from http://www.forbes.com/sites/tanyaprive/2012/12/19/top-10-qualities-that-make-a-great-leader/

Check Your Understanding

Answer the following questions using information from the reading.

1 In the author's opinion, what separates a dreamer from an entrepreneur?

_____

_____

2 According to the author, why are the following qualities important? Choose a) or b).

Honesty

a) Your customers will appreciate you more if you don't try to cheat them.

b) Your employees will follow your example and stay honest themselves.   ➔

Ability to delegate

a) You will be able to accomplish more if you delegate tasks to employees.

b) Your employees may have better skills in some areas than you do.

Communication

a) Your team needs to understand your goals for the company.

b) You will have many meetings to attend and e-mails to send.

Sense of humour

a) Laughing at a problem or difficult situation may help you to find a solution to it.

b) If you and your staff share a sense of humour, your staff's morale will be higher.

Confidence

a) You need to assure your team that it is normal to go through difficult times.

b) You need confidence to be able to sell your products to different types of consumers.

Commitment

a) You will not always have easy times, and you may be tempted to give up.

b) Your employees will respect you more if they see that you are part of the team.

Positive attitude

a) Your team will not object to working late if they are happy.

b) Your employees will appreciate it if you bring coffee to the office.

Creativity

a) You will need to think of interesting ways to market your products.

b) You may need to come up with quick or unusual responses to problems.

Intuition

a) Some solutions to problems may come to you in dreams.

b) You need to learn to trust your own feelings.

Ability to inspire

a) You need to keep your employees interested in the company and eager to work.

b) Some of your employees will be lazy and uninterested in coming to work every day.

Analysis and Discussion

Discuss the following questions with your group.

1. Do you think this reading deals mostly with facts or mostly with opinions? Why?

2. To what extent did the ten qualities suggested by the author match the qualities you identified in the "Before You Read" section?

3. Did you identify qualities that the author does not include in her list? If so, how would you convince her of the importance of these other qualities?

4. Imagine you are on the hiring committee for a new manager for your ESL program. Your team has identified four possible candidates. Which one would you choose, and why? Use the information from the reading and your own ideas to help you decide.

> **Selena**, 48, has a Master of Business Administration (MBA) degree and a solid background in student recruiting and student services. She has never been a teacher, but she has worked with students in her role as administrator in a private high school. She is driven to succeed, highly motivated, well organized and a little intimidating.

> **Diego**, 27, makes up for his lack of experience with his confidence and positive attitude. He has been in ESL for only a few years, but he is already making a name for himself as a conference speaker. He is very active on social media and knows many people worldwide; he is ambitious and sees himself as a future leader in the ESL world.

> **Marianne**, 55, has spent her entire career in ESL teaching. She has taught in a college for the last twenty-nine years, and she is ready for a change. She is very creative: she has published teaching materials, and she also writes songs and poems. She is an excellent writer, she is always calm and polite to others, but she can sometimes be shy in a group of people.

> **Chris**, 36, has spent the last twelve years travelling and teaching English around the world. He has worked in China, Nepal, Saudi Arabia and Morocco, but he has never been a manager. His degree is in Sociology, and he has a TESL certificate. He is cheerful, optimistic and outgoing, and he has a great sense of humour.

READING 2

Why We Need Quiet, Introverted Leaders

The following reading presents an unconventional approach to leadership.

 As you read, think about whether the author's statements can be considered facts or opinions.

Before You Read

Work in groups of three or four. Discuss the following questions.

1. What is the difference between an introvert and an extrovert?

2. Can you think of any leaders who are introverts or extroverts?

3. Why do you think the writer might think we need quiet, introverted leaders? What advantage(s) might introverts have over extroverts in leadership roles?

Key Vocabulary

A. Look at these adjectives, all taken from the reading. Match each adjective with a statement that describes this characteristic.

① aggressive (line 9) _____   a) I do not hesitate to tell people what I need.

② arrogant (line 3) _____   b) I make decisions quickly and easily.

③ assertive (line 26) _____   c) I think only about myself.

④ bold (line 26) _____   d) I don't usually express my emotions.

⑤ charismatic (line 1) _____   e) I don't wait for others to do things.

⑥ decisive (line 3) _____   f) People are always attracted to me.

⑦ dominant (line 27) _____   g) People think I am angry or want to argue.

⑧ egocentric (line 9) _____   h) I think I'm better than everyone else. I am rude.

⑨ proactive (line 31) _____   i) I am not afraid to take risks.

⑩ reserved (line 57) _____   j) I am seen as being more powerful or having more authority than others.

B. Which of these words do you think are positive characteristics? Which are negative?

Why We Need Quiet, Introverted Leaders

By Ray Williams

Our culture, particularly in business and politics, seems to be in love with the charismatic leader—the guns blazing, no-holds barred, centre-of-attention leader, who is a super confident if not arrogant, aggressively decisive leader of a band of star-struck followers. This stereotype of a leader appears to be an integral part of our individualistic society,
5 despite that modern economies and societies are now far from individualistic.

Movies, television and the news media have significantly influenced our popular image of leaders—from Clint Eastwood to Jim Carrey, Larry Ellison and Donald Trump[1]—for the past three decades. This stereotypical view of charismatic, extroverted individuals, often egocentric and aggressive, has been associated with what we want
10 and expect in our leaders.

Extroverted leaders are valued highly regardless of the reality of their performance. The status and reputation of quiet, introverted leadership is undervalued and under-appreciated. Despite decades of research on leadership pointing to other less demonstrative skills that are needed, extroverts are still favoured in recruiting and
15 promoting decisions. Yet recent research reveals that introverted, quiet leaders may be more suited for today's workplace.

---

[1] Clint Eastwood is an American action-movie star; Jim Carrey is a comedy actor; Larry Ellison is CEO of software company Oracle; and Donald Trump is a real-estate entrepreneur and TV star.

You can argue the case that Wall Street financial scandals and even foreign policy and political problems are linked to the dominance of extroverted leaders. In my twenty years of work with senior business leaders, I have found most who got into trouble
20 were extreme extroverts. Rarely did I encounter a highly respected introverted leader who shared the same fate.

Recent research by Francesca Gino of Harvard University and David Hoffman of the University of North Carolina, published in the *Academy of Management Journal*, shows a significant correlation between the types of leadership style needed and the personalities
25 and behaviour of employees.

They argue that extroverted leadership commands attention: being assertive, bold, talkative and dominant, providing a clear authority, structure and direction. However, pairing extroverted leaders with employees who take the initiative, are more independent and speak out can lead to conflict, while pairing the same type of employees with an
30 introverted leader can be more successful. The study also showed when employees are more proactive, introverted managers lead them to higher profits, whereas where employees are not proactive, extroverted managers are more successful. They concluded that introverted and extroverted leadership styles can be equally effective, but with different kinds of employees.

35 The researchers reported that whereas just 50 percent of the general population is extroverted, 96 percent of managers and executives display such personalities. And the higher you go in a corporate hierarchy, the more likely you are to find highly extroverted individuals.

"Introverts are more receptive to people since they tend to listen more than extroverts,"
40 Gino says. "The fact they are more receptive is due primarily to their ability and willingness to listen carefully to what others have to say without being threatened."

Frances B. Kahnweiler, author of *The Introverted Leader: Building on Your Quiet Strength*, offers five key characteristics of introverted leaders:

1. They think first and talk later. They consider what others have to say, then reflect
45 and respond.

2. They focus on depth not superficiality. They like to dig deeply into issues and ideas before considering new ones.

3. They exude calm. In times of crisis in particular, they project reassuring, unflappable confidence.

50 4. They prefer writing to talking. They are more comfortable with the written word, which helps them formulate the spoken word.

5. They embrace solitude. They are energized by spending time alone and often suffer from people exhaustion. They need a retreat, from which they emerge with renewed energy and clarity.

55 So who are the introverted leaders? Warren Buffett[2] was one example cited by Nancy Ancowitz, author of *Self-Promotion for Introverts*, writing in *Psychology Today*.

$\rightarrow$

---

2 Warren Buffett is a very successful businessman, investor and philanthropist.

Despite our culture being biased against quiet and reserved people, says Susan Cain, author of *Quiet: The Power of Introverts in a World that Can't Stop Talking*, "introverts are responsible for some of humanity's greatest achievements—from Steve Wozniak's
60 invention of the Apple computer to J. K. Rowling's Harry Potter. And these introverts did what they did not in spite of their achievements—but because of them." Neither the theory of relativity nor the epic piece of literature *Paradise Lost* was "dashed off by a party animal."

Cain argues that introverts make up one-third to one-half of the population, yet, "our
65 most important institutions, including our schools and our workplaces, are designed for extroverts."

One thing is for sure. The workplace is populated by increasing numbers of intelligent knowledge workers, frequently in self-managing teams, particularly those of Generation Y. Many of these workers don't see themselves as passive employees waiting for orders,
70 nor do they want to be controlled by an egocentric extroverted leader. So the time may be right for us to embrace an introverted leadership style. It's certainly time to have a better balance in leadership style.

(801 words)

Williams, R. (2012, May 30). Why we need quiet, introverted leaders. *Financial Post.* Retrieved from http://business.financialpost.com/2012/05/30/why-we-need-quiet-introverted-leaders/?__lsa=9a2d-238a

Check Your Understanding

Answer the following questions, in your own words where possible, using information from the reading.

1 Who is more likely to

    a) find a job and get promoted—an extrovert or an introvert?

    b) become involved in a scandal—an extrovert or an introvert?

2 Choose the best word in these sentences.

    a) Employees who take the initiative and are proactive often do best with an extroverted / introverted leader.

    b) Employees who do not take the initiative and are less proactive often do best with an extroverted / introverted leader.

What is the reason for this difference?

_____

_____

_____

_____

3 What percentage of managers are extroverted? How does this compare with the general population?

_____

_____

_____

4　Paraphrase Frances B. Kahnweiler's five characteristics of introverted leaders.

Number 1

_____

_____

Number 2

_____

_____

Number 3

_____

_____

Number 4

_____

_____

Number 5

_____

_____

5　What do Harry Potter and the Apple computer have in common?

_____

_____

6　Why, according to the author, do we need to welcome introverts to leadership roles?

_____

_____

Analysis and Discussion

Discuss the following questions with your group.

1　Look again at the title of this reading: "Why We Need Quiet, Introverted Leaders."
Is the author giving a fact here, or is he sharing his opinion?

2　Look at the following ideas expressed in the reading. For each one, choose a), b) or c).

a) This is a fact; I can't argue with this.

b) This could be a fact, but I need to see some evidence.

c) This is the opinion of the author or of someone quoted by the author.

_____ Employers usually value extroverts more than introverts.

_____ Gino and Hoffman's research is about leadership styles.

_____ More scandals are caused by extroverts than by introverts.

_____ Introverts listen more carefully than extroverts.

_____ American culture is biased against introverts.

_____ Today's workplaces have many Generation Y employees.

_____ We need to welcome more introverts to leadership positions.

If you chose b) for a sentence, ask yourself: what evidence do I need to see before I can trust this statement?

3 Do you think the author is biased in favour of one group over another, or is his paper objective? Why?

4 In line 1, the author talks about "our" culture. Whose culture is he referring to? Would the same ideas apply in different cultures?

5 Are you an introvert or an extrovert? How do you personally respond to this article?

READING 3

MIA: Women in the Executive Suite

The following reading explores the question of why men still outnumber women in leadership roles.

 As you read, think about the various statements made by the people quoted in the text. Are their statements based on fact or on opinion?

Before You Read

Work in groups of three or four. Discuss the following questions.

1 What special characteristics can women bring to leadership roles in companies and other organizations?

2 What challenges might women face in pursuing leadership roles?

3 Which professions do you think might be underrepresented by women in leadership roles? Why might this be the case?

MIA: Women in the Executive Suite

Fifty years after the feminist wake-up call, why are women still so vastly outnumbered in key leadership roles in business? Women make up 49 percent of the US workforce, but they account for only 4 percent of corporate CEOs, 14 percent of executive officers and 20 percent of America's government officials.

5 This poor showing is despite evidence that some people perceive women as better leaders than men. In separate recent studies by INSEAD and Zenger Folkman, women outscored men in many categories of leadership. In their study, Jack Zenger and Joseph Folkman[1] found that at every level, women were rated by their peers, bosses, direct reports and other associates as better overall leaders than their male counterparts—and
10 the higher the level, the wider the gap.

---

[1] Jack Zenger and Joseph Folkman run Zenger Folkman, a US leadership development consultancy.

What is standing in the way?

Facebook COO[2] Sheryl Sandberg and Anne-Marie Slaughter, president of the New America Foundation, recently have reanimated the balance-of-power debate by pointing out some hard truths. Sandberg's book, *Lean In: Women, Work, and the Will to Lead*, 15 charges women to take more initiative in getting what they want. Because they don't, she argues, "Men still rule the world."

In the *Atlantic* article "Why Women Still Can't Have It All," Slaughter challenges organizations to do more to support women who want leadership positions 20 without sacrificing the chance to have a family and a balanced life.

Critics contend that these two views set impossible standards for women and organizations. By telling women to look inside themselves and try harder, are 25 we letting corporations off the hook? And is it realistic to expect organizations to support women with family-friendly policies?

Get real

Randy White, co-author of *Breaking the Glass Ceiling:* 30 *Can Women Reach the Top of America's Largest Corporations?*, is as concerned as many professional women about their slow progress to the top. But, he says, "There are still very real issues in the way." He cites a comment attributed to Jack Welch[3] a few years ago. Welch reportedly said, "If someone is worried about work–life 35 balance, I don't have to worry about that person taking my job."

Welch has taken heat for his remarks, but White says, "He's telling the truth. If you have to worry about work–life balance, you're not in the running for top positions in most large organizations today."

White asserts that the job of CEO is like that of a concert pianist or Olympic athlete: 40 It is an all-out commitment. "At the top of fast-moving organizations, there's a tournament model of leadership. You've got to be world-class to play and it's naive to expect an organization to want anything less."

Many structural, social and organizational issues must be resolved before this situation changes, says White. "Organizations aren't going to become less demanding or less 45 complex," he explains. He credits Slaughter for telling the truth about what organizations need to do to support the advancement of women.

White also credits women in organizations with encouraging men to get in touch with their own lives. "I see it in the MBA and corporate classes I teach. Men have permission to question assumptions about leadership behaviour because women are

---

[2] COO stands for Chief Operating Officer.

[3] Jack Welch is a well-known business executive and writer. He was the CEO of General Electric for twenty years and has published books on business management.

50 talking about them." White sees the biggest changes in support for women in companies run by CEOs who have daughters.

Though realistic about the challenges facing women in organizations, White also is irked that they exist. "We waste so much talent," he says.

Avoid the either-or trap

55 There are many theories about what women should do to open the leadership door for themselves. Some of the most on-target advice comes from women executives in HR and training who have climbed the corporate ladder and created programs to develop other leaders in their organizations.

I asked several what it takes. Is it a career plan, a supportive partner, an internal
60 champion or an attitude adjustment? And who needs to make the big changes: women or organizations?

"It's all of the above and more," says Teresa Roche, vice president and CLO[4] at Agilent. She cautions against polarizing the discussion between two extremes: women's responsibility to seek power and others' responsibility to help them get it. "It's the interior
65 experience and the exterior support systems," she says.

Roche's path to the top combines an early rise to power, marriage, a doctorate and a daughter—but not all at once and not all at the same time. After grad school, for example, she took a small-scale executive position so she could still be the mom she wanted to be.

70 "I've learned to modulate parts of my life to make the whole work." Roche adds, "Having it all, whatever that is, will be different for each woman. Know yourself and what you need. Only then will you be able to be conscious about your choices."

According to Lynda McDermott, president of EquiPro International, "I don't think the situation is either-or. The biggest issue facing women is when they decide they want
75 both a family and a C-suite[5] career. The higher up the ladder and the larger the organization, there is a time commitment that can feel unmanageable. And if you are competing for visibility and credibility, and want to spend time with family, that creates tension." She notes that many women don't feel confident to negotiate flexibility and boundaries regarding work.

80 McDermott coaches women seeking leadership positions and finds many who undermine themselves. "Women need to decide if they really want to lead, so I challenge them to define specifically what leadership table they want to be sitting at in two to three years," she says.

McDermott also recommends that women work with coaches and mentors to develop
85 a game plan for building the credibility and visibility they need to get there, and to develop relationships with sponsors. "These are people who will recommend women for assignments and promotions based on the results they've achieved," she explains.

---

[4] CLO stands for Chief Learning Officer. In this role, Teresa Roche is responsible for leadership development.

[5] *C-suite* is a term used to refer to a company's top-level executives. The term comes from the fact that senior executives have titles starting with *Chief*.

Beware the new glass ceiling

Rick Gilkey couldn't agree more. He's a professor of organization and management at
90 the Goizueta Business School and an associate professor of psychiatry at the Emory
University School of Medicine, and he has helped develop women leaders in several
large organizations. From that perspective, Gilkey sees women held back by roles that
stereotype them as not being strategic.

"These are roles that organizations and women's male counterparts assign them and
95 then make attributions and inferences about their not being strategic. The perception
of women as nonstrategic players is the new glass ceiling," says Gilkey.

Start with smarts, then have a plan

"Develop all the skills that are critical to your success," advises Jeanette Winters, vice
president of learning and development at Pitney Bowes. "Ask yourself: What unique
100 set of competencies have I developed to warrant consideration?" Education, skills,
competencies and experience are the common starting points. Then come the
differentiators. Winters singles out having a career plan, a support network and an
internal champion, mentor or coach.

Mary Slaughter, chief talent officer at SunTrust Bank, recommends having a clear
105 business orientation, but understanding that "you're leading people, not machines. As
a leader, you should continuously grow and develop so you are the best you can be,
and then share your expertise in a way that focuses on business outcomes." When
making decisions, Slaughter says, "Seek the facts, but balance that with your instincts
and your experience. Listen to and trust yourself."

110 Slaughter advises women to be purposeful about career moves, neither moving on
too soon nor staying in one role too long. "Over thirty years, that equates to about ten
meaningful assignments."

Her advice to women on overcoming impediments to their advancement is "Don't
wait to be asked to participate or to share your opinion. Step up and be honest about
115 what you think." Slaughter adds that "the higher one goes in a power structure like a
corporation, the less people are willing to speak the truth. You can distinguish yourself
by being candid yet constructive."

Slaughter counsels, "Always be true to yourself and demonstrate kindness to others,
even when you're being incredibly tough on the problem at hand. Consistent, positive
120 behaviour attracts great talent to follow you." (1346 words)

Galagan, P. (2013). MIA: Women in the executive suite. *T + D, 67*(7), 22–24.

Check Your Understanding

A. Are the following statements true (T) or false (F)?

		T	F
1	Women are vastly underrepresented in leadership positions.	○	○
2	There is evidence that women outperform men in leadership positions.	○	○

B. Which of the following business experts expresses each of the following opinions? Use each name only once.

Rick Gilkey	Lynda McDermott	Sheryl Sandberg
Anne-Marie Slaughter	Mary Slaughter	Randy White

1 _____: Women need to be more assertive in stating what they want, otherwise men will continue to dominate.

2 _____: Companies should make it easier for women to combine careers with family responsibilities.

3 _____: One positive result of having women in MBA classes is that they encourage men to consider their lives and leadership styles.

4 _____: It is a good idea for women executives to work with coaches or mentors.

5 _____: Women are hurt by negative stereotypes that show them as not being strategic thinkers.

6 _____: It is important for women to trust their own instincts and experience; they shouldn't just look at the facts.

C. Paraphrase the following opinions, as expressed by people quoted in this article.

1 "At the top of fast-moving organizations, there's a tournament model of leadership. You've got to be world-class to play and it's naive to expect an organization to want anything less."
Randy White

2 "Having it all, whatever that is, will be different for each woman. Know yourself and what you need. Only then will you be able to be conscious about your choices."
Teresa Roche

3 "The biggest issue facing women is when they decide they want both a family and a C-suite career. The higher up the ladder and the larger the organization, there is a time commitment that can feel unmanageable. And if you are competing for visibility and credibility, and want to spend time with family, that creates tension."
Lynda McDermott

4 "Develop all the skills that are critical to your success. Ask yourself: What unique set of competencies have I developed to warrant consideration?" *Jeanette Winters*

5 "The higher one goes in a power structure like a corporation, the less people are willing to speak the truth. You can distinguish yourself by being candid yet constructive."
Mary Slaughter

Key Vocabulary

Find the following sentences in the text. <u>Underline</u> the word or phrase in the sentence that matches the definition below.

1 By telling women to look inside themselves and try harder, are we letting corporations off the hook? (lines 23 to 25)

> saying that someone or something is not responsible

2 "Organizations aren't going to become less demanding or less complex," he explains. (lines 44 to 45)

> having many different parts; not simple

3 "I see it in the MBA and corporate classes I teach. Men have permission to question assumptions about leadership behaviour because women are talking about them." (lines 48 to 50)

> things that people generally believe without any evidence

4 I asked several what it takes. Is it a career plan, a supportive partner, an internal champion or an attitude adjustment? (lines 59 to 60)

> change made in order to improve a situation

5 "I've learned to modulate parts of my life to make the whole work." Roche adds, "Having it all, whatever that is, will be different for each woman ..." (lines 70 to 71)

> change a process to make it slower and more controlled

6 She notes that many women don't feel confident to negotiate flexibility and boundaries regarding work. (lines 78 to 79)

> discuss something to reach an agreement or compromise

7 McDermott also recommends that women work with coaches and mentors to develop a game plan for building the credibility and visibility they need to get there, and to develop relationships with sponsors. (lines 84 to 86)

> people at a higher level in your career who give you advice

8 "These are roles that organizations and women's male counterparts assign them and then make attributions and inferences about their not being strategic." (lines 94 to 95)

> people who do the same job

9 "Ask yourself: What unique set of competencies have I developed to warrant consideration?" (lines 99 to 100)

> special, unlike anyone or anything else

10 "Seek the facts, but balance that with your instincts and your experience. Listen to and trust yourself." (lines 108 to 109)

> judgment based on feeling, not reason

Analysis and Discussion

Discuss these questions with your group.

1. Why was this article written? What statistics make this information necessary?

2. The author of this article quotes many people who all have an opinion on the topic. Why do you think she included so many opinions? Do you find the large number of opinions to be helpful, or do you find it confusing?

3. Does the author state her own opinion on this topic, does she imply (suggest) her own thoughts, or does she remain objective? Explain your answer.

4. Which of the people quoted in the text expresses an opinion that you particularly agree or disagree with? Why?

5. What do you understand by work–life balance? Do you agree that people who are concerned about work–life balance will never achieve high-level positions? What is your opinion on this issue?

6. Lynda McDermott emphasizes the need for a mentor. Have you ever had a mentor for studying, sports or something else? Do you agree with her opinion?

7. Mary Slaughter advises women not to change jobs too quickly, but also not to stay in one role for too long. She suggests having ten significant jobs over a thirty-year period. How does this advice compare to your own career plans? How does it compare to the careers of successful people you know?

8. Based on your reading and on your own opinions, rank the following in importance for women who want to achieve high-level careers.

   _____ a strong educational background

   _____ a supportive spouse and reliable childcare

   _____ a company that understands the needs of women

   _____ confidence and ability to take the initiative

   _____ other? _____

Going Further
Focus on Language

A. The following chart contains ten words from the readings. Complete the chart with related words in the other categories and, where possible, in the same category. (There may not be a word for each category.)

	NOUN	VERB	ADJECTIVE	ADVERB
1	appreciation			
2		create		
3	economy			
4		emphasize		
5			invested	
6	motivation			
7	progress			
8			realistic	
9	society			
10			strategic	

B. In Reading 3, the women quoted all hold positions with gender-neutral titles: Chief Operating Office, Chief Talent Officer and so on. In recent years, many job titles have been changed to promote gender equality. Do you know what the following traditionally male occupations are now called?

> chairman   _____

> fireman   _____

> mailman   _____

> policeman   _____

> garbage man   _____

> salesman   _____

How have these female job titles been changed?

> air stewardess   _____

> waitress   _____

Independent Research

Choose one of the following researchers/writers on business-related topics and do some online research about this person. Find out about the person's theories and think about the applicability of these theories to today's business environment. You will present your findings to your class.

> Abraham Maslow

> Frederick Herzberg

> Laurence J. Peter

> Douglas McGregor

> Bruce Tuckman

> Meredith Belbin

Synthesis and Written Response

Based on your reading of the texts in this chapter as well as your own research into business and leadership, write a short response to the following question:

> What qualities, skills and personal characteristics should successful leaders have?

REVIEW
of the chapter ...

> Answer the following question.

1 How can you distinguish between a fact and an opinion? What are some things you can look for?

CHAPTER ⑥

Technology in Education

 INTERPRETING EVIDENCE 1: CASUAL OBSERVATION AND EMPIRICAL RESEARCH

Does the text present a convincing argument? Has the author done empirical research, and if so, how should you interpret it? Does the research justify the conclusions reached?

In this chapter
YOU WILL LEARN ...

> how to evaluate conclusions drawn from author experience;

> how to recognize the steps of the scientific method; and

> what to consider when reading reports of empirical research.

Warm-up

Discuss these questions with your group.

> How has education changed since the arrival of the computer era? How have your educational experiences been different from those of your parents' generation?

> What are the advantages of using computer technology in education? Are there any disadvantages?

> Have you ever carried out original research in the form of an experiment or survey? What factors did you consider as you designed, performed and wrote up the results of your research?

The Author's Evidence

> Technology is a key component of education in the twenty-first century. Discuss.

Imagine you have been given this essay topic in a course entitled *Introduction to Computer Studies*. As you carry out your research, you will find many papers in which the author formulates an opinion based on his or her experiences and observations; these range from casual observations the author has made to formal academic research projects the author has carried out.

Casual Observation

Where the author presents an argument based on only his or her personal experiences of the subject in question, you need to be careful in analyzing this argument. The author's opinions or conclusion may be influenced by his or her own background and preferences. Ask yourself these questions:

> What do we know about the author?

> How might the author's background affect the conclusions presented? Could the author be biased?

> Who might agree or disagree with the author? On what grounds?

Empirical Research

Empirical research is formal academic research carried out by the author, which involves experimentation or observation. In many cases, empirical research follows the steps of the **scientific method**. The researcher will

> identify a research topic;

> carry out some investigation into what is already known about the topic, for example, what results other researchers have found;

> formulate a **hypothesis**; this is an idea or theory that the researcher will try to prove. The hypothesis is based largely on what previous research has uncovered; it can be called an "educated guess" about what the research will reveal;

> design a piece of research to test the hypothesis. This research can be either **quantitative** (based on data that can be measured) or **qualitative** (based on data that cannot be measured);

> carry out the research project;

> analyze the data;

> formulate one or more conclusions, pointing out limitations of the experiment and the degree to which the results are **reliable** and **generalizable**; and

> share the results and conclusions through publication or other means.

Remember

As shown in Chapter 4, research reports very often use language known as hedging. The author wants to "soften" his or her conclusions. This is done by using expressions such as *It seems that …* or *There is evidence to suggest that …* rather than *The results prove …* or *It has been shown that ….* Note too that, in many cases, conclusions simply state the facts about what was found without adding any "extra" language.

When reading papers of this nature, ask yourself the following questions.

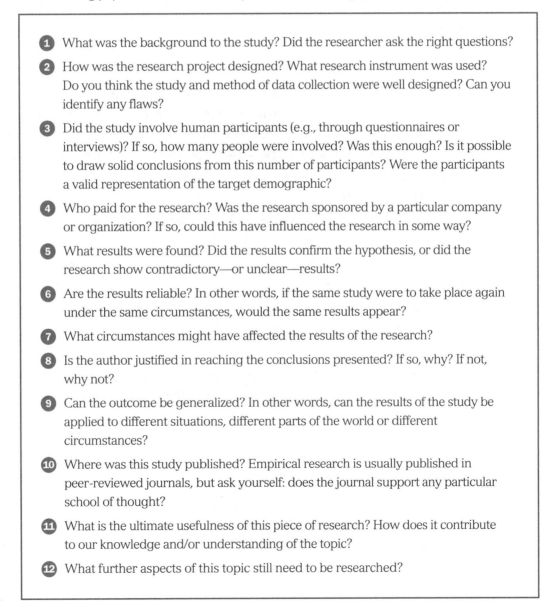

1. What was the background to the study? Did the researcher ask the right questions?

2. How was the research project designed? What research instrument was used? Do you think the study and method of data collection were well designed? Can you identify any flaws?

3. Did the study involve human participants (e.g., through questionnaires or interviews)? If so, how many people were involved? Was this enough? Is it possible to draw solid conclusions from this number of participants? Were the participants a valid representation of the target demographic?

4. Who paid for the research? Was the research sponsored by a particular company or organization? If so, could this have influenced the research in some way?

5. What results were found? Did the results confirm the hypothesis, or did the research show contradictory—or unclear—results?

6. Are the results reliable? In other words, if the same study were to take place again under the same circumstances, would the same results appear?

7. What circumstances might have affected the results of the research?

8. Is the author justified in reaching the conclusions presented? If so, why? If not, why not?

9. Can the outcome be generalized? In other words, can the results of the study be applied to different situations, different parts of the world or different circumstances?

10. Where was this study published? Empirical research is usually published in peer-reviewed journals, but ask yourself: does the journal support any particular school of thought?

11. What is the ultimate usefulness of this piece of research? How does it contribute to our knowledge and/or understanding of the topic?

12. What further aspects of this topic still need to be researched?

Put It into Practice

A. When analyzing papers containing empirical evidence, there are a number of key terms you will need to understand. Match each of the following terms with the correct definition below.

1. A hypothesis is _____.

2. Quantitative research is _____.

3. Qualitative research is _____.

4. A research instrument is _____.

5. The participants (or subjects) in a study are _____.

6. A double-blind test is _____.

7. A control group is _____.

8. Data is _____.

9. Reliability is _____.

10. Generalizability is _____.

a) a study in which one group of participants is given a particular treatment and another is given something different (for example, in testing medicines, one group will take an experimental drug, and another will take a different drug or a placebo). Neither the researchers nor the participants know which group the participants are in

b) a tool used to carry out research; for example, a survey, an experimental technique, a test or an interview

c) the degree to which the conclusions reached by the research can be considered useful or true elsewhere, including in another part of the world

d) the people who take part in the research

e) research based on the collection and analysis of data that is observable but cannot be measured or analyzed with statistics; examples include interviews, observation of behaviour or practices, and descriptions of colours and smells of chemicals

f) a group of participants who do not receive the treatment being studied (for example, in testing medicines, this group does not receive the experimental drug but receives a different drug or a placebo); this group is used as a comparison with those who are given the experimental drug

g) the degree to which the same results will be produced when the research is repeated with another group of participants

h) an idea or theory that the researcher wants to try to prove

i) research that is based on the collection and analysis of measurable data

j) information collected in the course of the research

B. Read the following excerpts from a report on empirical research. Working in groups, discuss the questions below each excerpt.

1 66 The purpose of the study was to determine the extent to which the use of electronic dictionaries in class is helpful in learning and remembering new vocabulary. 99

> Why do you think the researcher chose this topic?

> What practical application might the results have?

2 66 The participants in the study were eight international students ... . Home countries of the students were China (three students), Saudi Arabia (two), Kazakhstan (one), Iran (one) and Mexico (one). Three were male, five were female. The participants ranged in age from eighteen to fifty-two. 99

> Is this number large enough? If so, why? If not, how many participants do you think are needed in order for the conclusions to be meaningful?

> There are different nationalities, different genders and different ages represented. How might this affect the results?

3 66 Participants were given a questionnaire to determine the extent to which they used electronic dictionaries in class. The questionnaire comprised ten questions, which students answered using a Likert scale (i.e., strongly agree / agree / undecided / disagree / strongly disagree). 99

> What are the advantages of using closed questions such as Likert-scale, multiple-choice, true/false or yes/no questions? Could there be any disadvantages?

> It is important in designing questionnaires to avoid "leading" questions. What do you understand by this? Give an example of a leading question to avoid in this study.

> How could open questions (such as those beginning with "Why…?" or "To what extent…?") have been incorporated into the design of this questionnaire?

4 66 At the beginning of the study (i.e., at the beginning of term), students were given a vocabulary quiz using words that would appear in the following weeks. Their scores were recorded. During the term, students were encouraged to use their electronic dictionaries as they normally would. After twelve weeks, they were given another vocabulary quiz, using words that had been introduced and discussed in class during the term. 99

> Is this sound research methodology? Can you see any flaws in the design of this study?

> How could the methodology here be improved?

5 66 The students who reported a high use of electronic dictionaries in class performed better on the end-of-term vocabulary test than those who never or rarely used these devices. 99

> Is this because of their use of electronic dictionaries? Could there be other reasons for these results?

➡

6 ❝ We can conclude, therefore, that students who use electronic dictionaries extensively in class learn and remember vocabulary much more easily than those who do not." ❞

> Is the author justified in reaching this conclusion? If so, why? If not, why not?

> To what extent are these results reliable? In other words, would another group of participants yield different results?

C. Find a published text on a topic related to your own area of specialization. Identify the following:

a) the research question

b) the hypothesis

c) the research methodology

d) the key results

e) the conclusion

f) any limitations of the study

READING 1

Swimming against the Tide of PowerPoint

This reading shows one university professor's attitude toward technology in teaching.

 As you read, consider what his decision is based on and whether he is justified in making this choice.

Before You Read

Work in groups of three or four. Discuss the following questions.

1 Have you ever attended a lecture in college or university? Did the lecturer use any form of technology? If so, what?

2 Do you think PowerPoint is useful for students who want to understand their lectures well? Why, or why not?

3 What is a *tide*? What do you think the title of this reading means?

Key Vocabulary

The words below are all in the reading. Fill in the space in each sentence with the correct word.

NOUNS	kinship	relevance	relic	
VERBS	embellish	eschew	improvise	second-guess
ADJECTIVES	compelling	ignorant	retro	

© **ERPI** Reproduction prohibited

1. When you _____, for example, in a class presentation, you speak without planning what you are going to say.

2. A word often heard in conversation, _____ is used to refer to a style from a period in the past.

3. To _____ something means to deliberately choose not to make use of it.

4. A/An _____ is something that has survived from the past.

5. If you _____ someone, you question that person's judgment.

6. A term often associated with anthropology, _____ refers to relationships, especially family relationships.

7. Someone who is _____ about a topic has no knowledge of that topic; note that this term may also be used to describe a rude person, in which case it may be considered offensive.

8. If you describe something as _____, you are describing it as so interesting that you cannot tear yourself away from it.

9. To _____ means to make something more attractive or interesting by adding details or decorative touches.

10. Something that has _____ to someone is directly connected or related to that person.

Swimming against the Tide of PowerPoint

By Clifford Orwin

Students returning to universities will find them awash in a sea of PowerPoint. Is this what they've thirsted for all summer long? Did they find those lazy days at the cottage boring because the hills weren't alive with Talking Points? If so, those in my courses face severe disappointment.

5   In my lecture hall, however cavernous, the only teaching aid is the book we're reading that you're supposed to have brought with you. This approach is **retro**, I know. My colleagues who teach the other sections of the same large introductory course have all gone techno. Their sections, their call, but I remain to be persuaded.

Another fan of PowerPoint, even dearer to me than my colleagues, is my wife Donna.
10 She teaches Russian literature. Because her students begin by knowing so little of Russian history and society, and to convey the **kinship** between literature and other aspects of an epoch, she showers them with images of various sorts to help the books come alive for them.

→

Occasionally, she'll also project the passage of text under discussion, the better to focus attention on it. I won't **second-guess** her, because she's a wonderful teacher. If I taught her subject or various others—art history, say, or something in science or economics—I, too, might bless the day that PowerPoint came into the world. But I don't and I don't. I like to think that my students recognize that the style of my teaching matches its substance, that the only medium that suits my message is speech.

I teach the history of political thought. The introductory course consists entirely of reading a few old books over the course of the year (in my section, just six, ranging from Plato to John Locke) and discussing their **relevance** to us today. So we practise close reading for part of each lecture and devote the rest to questions and discussion.

It's hard to foster discussion in a class of 250, but we do our best.

Would PowerPoint be helpful in this? Because the books we read are so rich but also so difficult, I'd rather have the students' undivided attention than compete for it with an electronic sideshow. Yes, PowerPoint is useful for conveying information, but students **ignorant** of Socrates' dates can find them in the notes to their edition of *The Republic*. To divert them in class with such factoids wouldn't contribute a thing to their understanding of Plato's argument.

Some of my colleagues project an outline of their argument, but again, I'd rather not dilute the students' attention to what I'm actually saying. It would also inhibit me from **improvising** in class, which is how some of my best points occur to me. Besides, I'd rather devote preparation time to improving my lecture than to making an outline of it.

PowerPoint is great for charts and graphs, but believe it or not, I make no use of charts or graphs. I could **embellish** my teaching of Plato by projecting a picture of the Parthenon[1] on the screen, but even that would leave the wrong impression.

It would suggest that I regard Socrates and Plato, too, as artifacts of the fifth century BCE, as expressions of "Athenian culture." It would imply that they, too, are ruins, dilapidated **relics** of a bygone day, meaningless except within that vanished context.

In fact, the point of my teaching is the opposite, namely that Plato's thought remains as fresh and challenging for us as it was for his contemporaries. While attentive to the historical context, the last thing I want is to encourage the students in their prejudice that since all thought is relative to its time, no old thinker can be of **compelling** interest to us. So I don't want to lump Plato with ancient Athens, I want to rescue him from it.

---

[1] The Parthenon is a temple in Athens, Greece. Now in ruins, it is considered one of the most important remaining structures of ancient Greece.

At the very least, by **eschewing** PowerPoint and other techno bells and whistles,[2]
55 I offer my students an experience that will be as new for many of them as it is old.
Nothing electronic will assault their senses—they get more than enough of that elsewhere
in their lives.

Like students since the time of Plato himself, they'll have to pay close attention to
speech and to arguments conveyed by speech. I'll also refer them again and again
60 to the book open before them. They'll learn that even in classes much bigger than they
should be, less can be more.

Naked came I into the world, and naked will you find me at the lectern, except for a
nice suit, my lecture notes, and (on my good days) Plato or Machiavelli whispering
helpfully over my shoulder. As that famous guy[3] said at the Diet of Worms where the
65 hall wasn't even wired yet, here I stand, I can do no other.   (797 words)

---

[2] *Bells and whistles* is an informal term referring to extra non-essential but attractive features an item may have.
It is often used when describing a car, a computer or another mechanical item.

[3] The famous guy is Martin Luther (1483–1586), a German monk and key figure in the Protestant movement known
as the Reformation. In 1521, Luther was ordered to retract his criticisms of the Roman Catholic Church at an assembly
("Diet") in the German city of Worms. Luther refused to do so, allegedly uttering the famous words, "Here I stand, I can
do no other."

Orwin, C. (2006, Sep. 9). Swimming against the tide of PowerPoint. *The Globe and Mail*, online edition. Retrieved from
http://www.theglobeandmail.com/globe-debate/swimming-against-the-tide-of-powerpoint/article731759/.

Check Your Understanding

Answer the following questions in your own words using information from the reading.

1 In what way does the author's attitude toward technology differ from that of his
colleagues?

_____

_____

_____

2 How does the author's wife use PowerPoint in her classes? Give two techniques she uses.

_____

_____

3 What subject does the author teach? Describe what typically happens in his classes.

_____

_____

4 What good uses of PowerPoint does the author suggest?

_____

_____

_____

5 Paraphrase the argument given by the author in lines 44 to 53.

_____

_____

_____

_____

_____

6 By choosing not to use PowerPoint, what learning skill does the author hope his students will develop?

_____

_____

Analysis and Discussion

Discuss these questions with your group.

1 Where would you place this text on the following continuum?

A report of one person's experiences or casual observations

An academic study involving multiple researchers, many participants, several years and a large research budget

2 On what basis has the author made the decision not to use PowerPoint? Choose one.

a) His own experiences

b) Published research on the effectiveness of PowerPoint

c) His students' feedback

d) His colleagues' recommendation

3 Do you think the author's reasons for eschewing PowerPoint are good ones? Explain your answer.

4 What arguments might his colleagues use to encourage him to use PowerPoint?

5 What do you imagine the author's students might think about his teaching style? Which students might welcome his approach? Which students might disagree with it?

6 How do you respond to the author's statement that he likes to improvise in his lectures? Is improvisation a useful technique in education?

7 What is the value of this kind of personal observation? If you were writing a paper on the effectiveness of PowerPoint in postsecondary education, would you use this paper? Why, or why not?

8 Would you like to take a course with this kind of professor? Why, or why not?

Students Want More Mobile Devices in Classroom

This reading discusses the results of a survey about tablet computers and education.

 As you read, think about the scope and implications of the study.

Before You Read

Work in groups of three or four. Discuss the following questions.

1. Do you own a laptop, smartphone or tablet? If so, have you ever used it for educational purposes? What was the result?

2. Do you think mobile devices help students to learn? If so, which students benefit the most? If not, why not?

3. Which do you personally prefer—learning with a mobile device or learning with a traditional book? Why?

Key Vocabulary

Choose the best definition for each of the words or expressions below.

1. conduct (v. line 7)

    a) carry out   b) take part in

2. device (n. line 1)

    a) tool or gadget   b) small item

3. influx (n. line 1)

    a) popularity   b) large-scale introduction

4. median (adj. line 20)

    a) average   b) typical

5. mobile (adj. line 1)

    a) fixed in one place   b) able to be moved

6. racial (adj. line 18)

    a) related to ethnic background b) related to income

7. rely on (v. line 44)

    a) need   b) enjoy

8. social studies (n. line 16)

    a) study of people in the world b) study of the natural world

9 tally (v. line 7)

   a) comment on   b) calculate

10 unanimously (adv. line 6)

   a) with full agreement   b) infrequently

Students Want More Mobile Devices in Classroom

By Ellis Booker

When it comes to the influx of mobile devices into K–12[1] classrooms, you'll find both proponents and opponents among educators and parents.

But ask kids what they think, and there's no debate: Laptops, smartphones and tablets are the future, they say.

5   Released last week, the Student Mobile Device Survey reveals that students almost unanimously believe mobile technology will change education and make learning more fun. The survey, which tallied the responses of 2,350 US students, was conducted for learning company Pearson by Harris Interactive.

According to the survey, 92% of elementary, middle and high school students believe 10 mobile devices will change the way students learn in the future and make learning more fun (90%). A majority (69%) would like to use mobile devices more in the classroom.

The survey results also contained some surprises. For example, college students in math and science are much more likely to use technology for learning, and researchers expected to see this same pattern in the lower grades.

15   "[We] found that students in grades 4 to 12 use tablets almost equally in math, science, history and social studies, and English/language arts," Pearson's senior VP of market research Seth Reichlin told *InformationWeek* in an e-mail.

Other surprises cut along racial lines. The survey found that Hispanics in grades 4 to 12 are more likely (36%) than white (30%) or black (28%) students to own a tablet. 20 "We expected the opposite based on differences in median family income," Reichlin wrote.

Similarly, black and Hispanic students in grades 4 to 12 were more likely than other students to own a smartphone (51% of black students, 49% of Hispanic, 40% of white).

Overall, the survey found that more than one-third of 4th and 5th graders (36%) and a third of middle school students (34%) currently own a tablet. A quarter of all students 25 intend to purchase a tablet within the next six months, the survey found.

Asked about their use of tablets, one-third of elementary, middle and high school students said they have used one for schoolwork this academic year; another 44% said they have used a smartphone for schoolwork.

---

[1] K–12 means "kindergarten to Grade 12"; in other words, this covers both elementary and secondary education.

Interestingly, among students who use
30 a tablet for schoolwork, more than half
(52%) use a device that they own personally, rather than one borrowed from
the school.

Younger students are more eager to use
35 tablets in class than their older peers,
according to the survey. Also, although
two-thirds of elementary and middle
school students said they would like to use
mobile devices more often in class, only
40 61% of high school students and 43% of
college students said this.

"It is particularly interesting to note
that as students rise to higher levels in
their education, the way that they rely on mobile devices to support learning changes
45 as well," Shawn Mahoney, VP of product design research and evaluation for
assessment and instruction at Pearson, said in a statement. "While smartphones and
tablets are still important tools for high school students, it appears that they are
looking for more full-featured productivity devices, such as laptops, to support their
learning activities."

50 The Student Mobile Device Survey was conducted online by Harris Interactive on
behalf of Pearson between Jan. 28 and Feb. 24 among 2,350 US students, including
500 elementary school (4th–5th grade) students, 750 middle school (6th–8th grade)
students and 1,100 high school (9th–12th grade) students. The survey also included a
national sample of 1,206 college students. (569 words)

Booker, E. (2013, May 6). Students Want More Mobile Devices in Classroom. *Information Week*. Retrieved from http://www.
informationweek.com/mobile/students-want-more-mobile-devices-in-classroom/d/d-id/1109825

Check Your Understanding

A. Which of the following statements best summarizes the results of this study?

a) Now that most students own a mobile device, it is becoming clear that the future
of education lies in digital materials rather than in traditional print materials. Students
are finding that they are now studying more efficiently than ever before; they are also
having more fun with their studies.

b) While mobile device ownership is still quite low, there is excitement and optimism
among students about this new approach to education. Many students expect that
owning a mobile device will enable them to enjoy their studies more than they
do at present.

c) Very few students own a mobile device or are interested in buying one. There is no evidence that smartphones, tablets or laptops will make a difference to students' enjoyment of their studies. From an educational perspective, investment in mobile devices may be a waste of money.

B. Are the following statements true (T) or false (F)?   **T**   **F**

1. Most students think mobile devices will change education. ◯ ◯

2. A lot of students think education will be more fun in the future. ◯ ◯

3. Young children use mobile devices in sciences more than in arts. ◯ ◯

4. The majority of Hispanic students own a tablet. ◯ ◯

5. Black students are more likely than white students to own a smartphone. ◯ ◯

6. Most students plan to buy a tablet within the next six months. ◯ ◯

7. Students usually use mobile devices provided by their school. ◯ ◯

8. The popularity of mobile devices decreases as students get older. ◯ ◯

9. Older students often prefer laptops to tablets. ◯ ◯

10. Most of the students who took part in the study were in high school. ◯ ◯

C. What inferences can you make from this reading? Check all that apply.

◯ a) Students' grades will improve as mobile devices become more popular.

◯ b) Online education will benefit white students more than those from other groups.

◯ c) Smartphones can be used for more than just making phone calls.

◯ d) Tablets are more useful for younger children than for college students.

◯ e) Teachers are excited about the influx of mobile devices into the classroom.

Analysis and Discussion

Discuss the following questions with your group.

1. Where would you place this text on the following continuum?

    ⟵ ─────────────────────────────────── ⟶

A report of one person's experiences or casual observations   An academic study involving multiple researchers, many participants, several years and a large research budget

2. Who were the participants in this study? Do you think this number is large enough to provide reliable data? What does the text tell you about these participants? What other information would you like to know about them?

3. Was this research quantitative or qualitative? What are the advantages of the type of research chosen? What are the disadvantages?

4. Find two surprising results revealed by the study. In each case, ask yourself these questions:

    a) What results did the researchers expect to find?

    b) What results were actually found?

    c) How might the results of the research be useful to the publisher?

5. This survey was commissioned by an international publisher of educational materials.

    a) Why do you think the publisher wanted to carry out this research?

    b) Why do you think the publisher hired an independent research company?

    c) How might the results of the research be useful to the publisher?

6. This research was carried out in the US. To what extent are these results generalizable to other parts of the world?

7. This survey was carried out in 2011. Think back to the section called "The Date of Publication" in Chapter 2. To what extent do you think the results would be the same if the survey were carried out today?

8. Are you surprised by the results of this research? Why, or why not?

READING 3

Facebook as a Formal Instructional Environment

This reading is from an academic journal and describes a research project on the use of social media in education.

 FOCUS Think about the author's methodology, results and conclusions as you read this text.

Before You Read

Work in groups of three or four. Discuss the following questions.

1. Do you use Facebook or other social media? If so, for what purpose(s)? If not, why not?

2. Have you ever used Facebook or other social media for educational purposes? If so, describe your experiences. If not, can you imagine using Facebook as a learning tool?

3. To what extent should university and college professors incorporate social media into their instruction? Explain your opinion.

Facebook as a Formal Instructional Environment

Bahar Baran

Dr. Bahar Baran is Assistant Professor in the Department of Computer Education and Instructional Technologies at Dokuz Eylul University. Her research interests cover design, development and evaluation of social learning environments, e-learning and multimedia environments.

Introduction

It is hypothesized that the use of social networking services such as Facebook will lead the younger generation of learners to more
5 readily embrace e-learning in formal education. Mazer, Murphy and Simonds (2009) have found that students accessing the Facebook website of a teacher with high self-disclosure reported higher levels of
10 teacher credibility, but the research findings on the educational potential of Facebook are limited and are mainly concerned with the conditions of use and users' characteristics. Studies by Selwyn (2009), Greenhow
15 and Robelia (2009), Selwyn and Grant (2009), and Usluel and Mazman (2009) lead to the conclusion suggesting students generally accept Facebook as a social technology rather than a formal teaching tool. Madge,
20 Meek, Wellens and Hooley (2009) characterize Facebook as providing the "social glue" in helping students to settle into university life, but while recognizing its educational potential, express caution about
25 invading a social networking space that students clearly feel is theirs. Bearing these points in mind, I decided to undertake a study with a small sample of undergraduate students at Dokuz Eylul University in Turkey
30 in order to gauge the extent to which they appreciated the formal application of Facebook in their classes. It should be understood that, as in most similar countries, e-learning is still largely underexploited in Turkey, so
35 the students are unfamiliar with many of the tenets on which its adoption is based.

Method

The study was conducted during a twelve-week undergraduate course entitled
40 "Distance Education" in the fall term of 2009. I created a group on Facebook and made the students responsible for building and discussing a library that included videos, links and pictures, advising them
45 that they would be graded on their Facebook-based activities.

There were thirty-two students in this group and the aim of the study was to find out what they thought about the incor-
50 poration of Facebook in their coursework. The data were collected using a questionnaire and face-to-face interviews. The questionnaire consisted of three main parts comprising sixteen Likert-type
55 items. MS Excel (Microsoft Office Excel 2003) was used for analyzing the data gathered from this questionnaire. The frequencies and percentages were calculated with the "COUNTIF" function
60 of Excel. The interviews were used to confirm or enlarge on the responses to the questionnaire items.

Results

Facebook usage before and after
65 the course

Most of the students ($n = 29$; 90.6%) were signed up on Facebook before the course. During the course, just over one-third of the students used Facebook almost every day
70 ($n = 11$; 34.4%). After the course, the students were using it more frequently (one

or more times a day: $n = 13$; 40.63%). One of the students commented:

> Facebook strengthened our
75 communication with one another after the course. I began using it to ask my friends about course assignments (or of course I would ask you) ☺ ... I sent messages or if you were online,
80 I could also instantly write to you using the chat tool.

Student–content dimension

A considerable number of the students stated that they would have preferred a
85 face-to-face course to a Facebook-based course ($n = 14$, 43.6%) and a high percentage of the students indicated that they thought that Facebook should only be one element in the teaching and learning ($n = 24$; 75%).
90 These responses indicated that the majority of the students were neither intrinsically nor positively inclined to information- and communication technology–based study. However, their responses showed that they
95 believed that Facebook could be used for knowledge-sharing in formal education contexts ($n = 27$; 84.4%) and that grading Facebook-based work was a reasonable approach ($n = 20$; 62.5%). Most of the
100 students believed that students could share school-related knowledge on Facebook ($n = 29$; 90.7%), and many of them indicated that communicating with their classmates helped to motivate them in their learning
105 ($n = 21$; 65.7%). However, many of the students were still largely undecided as to whether or not Facebook was of high value to teaching ($n = 23$; 72%), although many agreed that they would be willing to use
110 Facebook on other courses ($n = 19$; 59.4%).

While the students indicated that they liked participating in Facebook activities,

they observed that nearly half of the class did not read all of the messages or examine
115 all of the links. Some of their comments on this matter are as follows:

> I was especially interested in the different links others had sent, not all messages. These links showed me there are so many
120 resources for our field ... many were very beneficial for us.

> Especially, Facebook chat is very problematic. It does not send all messages. Of course, some Facebook tools can be used
125 in education, but not at all. Facebook groups are very beneficial for bringing people who share a common interest together.

> I was bothered by Facebook activities. They should have been voluntary. Especially,
130 grading from it was very stressful. But, if you didn't grade us, some of my friends would not send anything.

Student–teacher dimension

All of the students believed it was quite
135 appropriate for a teacher to use Facebook ($n = 32$; 100%) and for teachers and students to socialize by this means ($n = 29$; 90.6%). Some negative opinions were expressed about teachers sharing personal information
140 and pictures on Facebook ($n = 7$; 21.9%), but most of the students looked upon this favourably ($n = 17$; 53.1%). The findings revealed that the majority of the students felt that Facebook had helped them maintain
145 contact with their teacher ($n = 29$; 90.6%) and that they were excited when the teacher commented on their postings ($n = 20$; 62.5%). By the end of the term, the teacher's Facebook profile showed that half of
150 the students ($n = 16$) had added him to their profile. However, Turkey rates quite highly on Hofstede Dimensions of Power Distance[1]—the extent to which the ⊠

---

[1] Geert Hofstede is a Dutch researcher who specializes in intercultural communication. Hofstede has identified six dimensions according to which cultures can be analyzed. Power Distance refers to the degree to which a culture accepts inequality as the norm within that society.

less powerful members of organizations,
155 institutions, families and other social groups
accept and expect power to be distributed
unequally—therefore, not surprisingly, not
all of the students felt this way. As one of
the students said:

160 > Teachers should be unapproachable and
formal. They should not share their special
pictures in Facebook. This informal sharing
may damage authority and discipline.

Student–student dimension

165 The students believed that Facebook was
valuable for keeping them in contact with
their friends ($n = 24$; 81.3%), and over half
of them felt that Facebook helped them get
to know their classmates better ($n = 18$;
170 56.3%). One student concluded:

> First, I learned about the different sides
of my classmates. I followed their pictures
and comments. Now I know their families
and old friends. In a class, you usually do
175 not know any of your classmates so well.

Discussion

The findings of this small-scale study can
be distilled into the following points:

> Not all students are ready to embrace
180 the use of social networking tools such
as Facebook in formal teaching, learning
and assessment.

> The student–student dimension may be
more important than the student–content
185 and student–teacher dimensions.

> As Madge, Meek, Wellens and Hooley
(2009) suggest, it is important to be aware
of the tensions that may arise between
the formal and the informal uses of social
190 networking tools in education. Mandating
their use with the use of grades will
not necessarily encourage students to
embrace these tools in formal education.
Baran and Cagiltay (2010) observe that
195 the number of students' messages, extent

of their reading each other's messages
and the frequency of their examining
links in depth, etc. are directly related to
the students' intrinsic motivations, so
200 students need to be so motivated that
they voluntarily involve themselves in the
educational applications of these services.

> The students tend to use this tool very
informally, and so not all of the messages,
205 videos, pictures and links will be picked
up by all of the students. Therefore,
if messages, links and resources are
essential to the learning outcomes, the
instructional design and online discussion
210 strategies must be so planned and
managed as to encourage and support
student–student, student–content and
student–teacher interaction.

> In cultures and contexts that uphold
215 traditional social and educational values,
as in Turkish higher education, because
of their longstanding experience with
conventional education, students and
teachers will expect certain patterns
220 of behaviour in the classroom and the
students will still wish to experience
the knowledge, experience and authority
of the teacher, whether face-to-face
or online. Therefore, if the aim of using
225 tools such as Facebook was to contribute to altering the patterns of teaching and learning, time and attention
need to be given to defining and
encouraging the new, different roles of
230 the learners and teachers and the kinds
of communications and collaborations
expected.

> The students may tend to be more inter-
ested in the social than the teaching
235 dimensions of tools such as Facebook.
The technology undoubtedly helped to
emphasize my availability and that of the
other students and helped us feel that we
were part of a group and were sharing

240 the same learning environment. This higher degree of social presence may well be one of the greatest contributions of such tools. However, because of the informal basis of Facebook, the students 245 may not necessarily perceive this as a formally planned element of the teaching and learning.

Conclusions

This study was undertaken with a very 250 small sample and can only be seen as "work in progress." It is also important to note that this study was conducted in a particular cultural setting. Consequently, the findings cannot be generalized, but 255 they may serve to alert fellow practitioners to some of the issues involved in using Facebook in formal teaching and learning and suggest further investigations into the possibilities and limitations of Facebook 260 and the approaches required to ensure its appropriate use.

References

Baran, B. & Cagiltay, K. (2010). The motivators and barriers in the development of online communities of practice. *Egitim Arastirmalari-Eurasian Journal of Educational Research, 39*, 79–96.

Greenhow, C. & Robelia, E. (2009). Informal learning and identity formation in online social networks. *Learning, Media and Technology, 34*, 2, 119–140.

Madge, C., Meek, J., Wellens, J. & Hooley, T. (2009). Facebook, social integration and informal learning at University: it is more for socialising and talking to friends about work than for actually doing work. *Learning, Media and Technology, 34*, 2, 141–155.

Mazer, J. P., Murphy, R. E. & Simonds, C. J. (2009). The effects of teacher self-disclosure via Facebook on teacher credibility. *Learning, Media and Technology, 34*, 2, 175–183.

Selwyn, N. (2009). Faceworking: exploring students' education-related use of Facebook. *Learning, Media and Technology, 34*, 2, 157–174.

Selwyn, N. & Grant, L. (2009). Researching the realities of social software use—an introduction. *Learning,Media and Technology, 34*, 2 79–86.

Usluel, Y. K. & Mazman, S. G. (2009). Adoption of Web 2.0 tools in distance education. *Procedia Social and Behavioral Sciences, 1*, 818–823.

1627 words (excluding references)

Baran, B. (2010). Facebook as a formal instructional environment. *British Journal of Educational Technology, 41*(6), E146–E149.

Check Your Understanding

A. Provide the following information.

1 The author's hypothesis _____

_____

_____

2 The purpose of this study _____

_____

3 Where this study took place _____

4 How Facebook was used _____

_____

_____

_____

5 The number of participants _____

6 The research instrument(s) _____

_____

B. Choose the correct word or expression in **bold**. Then, look back at the reading to check your answers.

1 **Most / Some** of the students were signed up on Facebook before the course.

2 During the course, **just over one third / a high percentage** of the students used Facebook almost every day.

3 **A few / A considerable** number of the students stated that they would have preferred a face-to-face course to a Facebook-based course …

4 … **just over half / many** of the students were still largely undecided as to whether or not Facebook was of high value to teaching …

5 **All / A minority** of the students believed it was quite appropriate for a teacher to use Facebook …

6 … **several / the majority** of the students felt that Facebook had helped them maintain contact with their teacher …

7 By the end of the term, the teacher's Facebook profile showed that only **a few / half** of the students had added him to their profile.

8 … **almost all / over half** of them felt that Facebook helped them get to know their classmates better.

Key Vocabulary

Find each of the nouns or adjectives in **bold** in the text. Find the verb that collocates (= goes with) each word.

1 Madge, Meek, Wellens and Hooley (2009) … _____ **caution** … (lines 19 to 24)

2 … I decided to _____ a **study** … (lines 27 to 28)

3 … in order to _____ the **extent** to which … (line 30)

4 The **data** were _____ … (line 51).

5 The **questionnaire** _____ three main parts … (lines 52 to 54)

6 The **frequencies and percentages** were _____ … (lines 57 to 59)

7 These **responses** _____ … (line 90)

8 Some negative **opinions** were _____ … (line 138)

9 The **findings** _____ … (lines 142 to 143)

10 … the **findings** cannot be _____ … (line 254)

Analysis and Discussion

Discuss the following questions with your group.

1. Where would you place this text on the following continuum?

A report of one person's experiences or casual observations ⟷ An academic study involving multiple researchers, many participants, several years and a large research budget

2. Why did the author decide to carry out this study?

3. Describe the author's research methodology. Would you have done anything differently? How might the author modify the methodology if the study is repeated?

4. The author recognizes that the number of participants in the study is "very small." What do you think would be an optimal number of participants in this type of study?

5. How does the author justify the following conclusions, as expressed in the "Discussion" section? What evidence is given?

   a) Not all students are ready to embrace the use of social networking tools such as Facebook in formal teaching, learning and assessment.

   b) The student–student dimension may be more important than the student–content and student–teacher dimensions.

6. If you have used social media tools for educational purposes, how do the author's conclusions compare with your own experiences?

7. What is the purpose of the author's statement in the "Conclusions" section that "the findings cannot be generalized" (line 254)? Why not?

8. What do you think future research by this author could focus on?

9. Would you personally like to use Facebook in your academic studies, or do you prefer to keep Facebook for personal use only? Explain your answer.

Going Further

Focus on Language

A. The following chart contains ten words from the readings. Complete the chart with related words in the other categories and, where possible, in the same category. (There may not be a word for each category.)

	NOUN	VERB	ADJECTIVE	ADVERB
1			beneficial	
2	contribution			

	NOUN	VERB	ADJECTIVE	ADVERB
3	credibility			
4		expect		
5	expression			
6			introductory	
7			mobile	
8	prejudice			
9	preparation			
10			valuable	

B. This chapter uses the word *research* frequently. Be careful. The word *research* is a non-count noun.

> You cannot say   *a* research, *some* research*es*.

> You need to say   *some* research.

> You can also say   a study, an investigation, a research project.

The following sentences all contain non-count nouns that are used incorrectly. Rewrite each sentence.

1 I carried out three important <u>researches</u> while I was a student.

_____

2 My professor gave me a useful <u>advice</u> on how to interpret my data.

_____

3 The author couldn't find many <u>evidences</u> to support his hypothesis.

_____

4 I found a key <u>information</u> in an academic journal.

_____

5 There are no <u>proofs</u> that this experimental medicine works.

_____

6 We have made many <u>progresses</u> in our understanding of this topic.

_____

Independent Research

Choose one of the following applications of technology and carry out some online research into how it can be used in education. You will present your findings to your class.

> audiobooks

> blogs

> podcasts

> tweets

> wikis

Synthesis and Written Response

Based on your reading of the texts in this chapter as well as your own research into technology in education, write a short response to the following prompt:

> Technology is a key component of education in the twenty-first century. Discuss.

REVIEW
of the chapter ...

> Answer the following questions.

1. What are some questions to ask yourself as you read and evaluate papers based on personal experience?

2. What are the key steps of the scientific method?

3. What are some questions to ask yourself as you read and evaluate papers based on the scientific method?

CHAPTER ⑦
Design and Productivity

 EVIDENCE 2: OTHER FORMS OF SUPPORT

What other types of evidence is the author using: anecdotes, visual items, statistics, quotations? How effective are these? How accurately do they represent the situation they are illustrating? How does the author attempt to convince the reader when no evidence is used? How should you respond to a text that has *no* supporting evidence?

In this chapter
YOU WILL LEARN ...

> how to identify types of evidence not based on author experience: anecdotes, visual items, statistics, and quotations from others;

> how authors try to persuade readers with no evidence at all; and

> how to evaluate these kinds of evidence.

Warm-up

Discuss the following questions with your group.

> Describe your current living space. What do you like and/or dislike about your space? How suitable is it for studying? What would you change if you could?

> What would your ideal work space look like? Think about size, colour, lighting, furniture and decorative items.

> If someone told you that in order to be more productive in your studies or your career you needed to paint your room orange, arrange the furniture in a certain way or buy some tropical fish, would you believe them? What kinds of evidence would you accept before you could trust this advice?

Other Kinds of Evidence

> There is a strong connection between the design of a person's working environment and that person's productivity at work or in school. Discuss.

Imagine you have been given this essay topic in a course entitled *Introduction to Interior Design*. As you saw in Chapter 6, many arguments are based on the author's own experiences, whether these are casual observations or formal investigations. Often, however, the author's arguments are supported by other types of evidence; these include **anecdotes**, **visual items**, **statistics** and **quotations**. Sometimes there is no supporting evidence: the author relies on the skilful use of language to convey his or her opinion.

Anecdotes

What are they?

> Anecdotes are short stories about individual people; they are not based on scientific research. Look at any popular magazine, and you will see that the articles very often begin with an example. A magazine article about weight loss might begin with the story of someone who lost fifty kilograms on a particular diet, or an article about financial planning might begin with the story of someone who retired at forty. These are anecdotes.

Why are they used?

> Anecdotes at the beginning of an article are often used to provide a "hook" for the reader; the example is interesting, so the reader wants to continue reading. Anecdotes throughout the article make the writing "real" for the reader and encourage the reader to pay attention to the argument.

Ask yourself

> To what extent are the anecdotes in the text representative of a larger group? Can the examples of these people be generalized to a larger group? Are they extreme cases, chosen specifically to support a dubious claim?

Visual Items

What are they?

> Examples of visual items are photographs, illustrations, pie charts, bar charts, flow charts, graphs, maps, diagrams and tables.

Why are they used?

> As the saying goes, a picture tells a thousand words. A newspaper story with a graphic photograph will be more compelling than one without; a company report with charts and graphs will be more effective than one without; and an instruction leaflet with diagrams will be easier to understand than one with only words.

Ask yourself

> What purpose does the visual support serve? In the case of an instruction manual, diagrams provide a useful service; in the case of journalistic writing, however, photographs can be used to bring about an emotional reaction in the reader. In such cases, think about why the picture was chosen, what response the writer or photographer is trying to elicit by using the picture and how successful this has been.

> How representational are the visual items? If a photograph is used, for example, does it show the whole scene, or does it show only the part the photographer wishes the reader to see? If a graph is used, does it give a realistic interpretation of the facts? Sometimes a graph is presented in a large scale, so any rise or fall appears more dramatic than it really is.

Statistics

What are they?

> Statistics are numbers; these could come from reliable sources (e.g., large-scale scientific studies) or they could come from very informal surveys and questionnaires. When referring to sources other than his or her own empirical research, the author selects statistics carefully, often choosing only those that support the argument being presented.

Why are they used?

> The use of numbers makes an argument sound more credible; the reader is often impressed by numbers.

Ask yourself

> The same questions that are posed in Chapter 6 also apply here. Would the same statistics be found if the study were carried out elsewhere or under different circumstances? To what extent is evidence from elsewhere, including from another country, useful when considering an issue closer to home?

> Consider the extent to which percentages represent significant numbers. For example, an increase of 50 percent could just mean a rise from 1.0 to 1.5; on the other hand, it could mean a rise from 100,000 to 150,000. Think about a research project in which 75 percent of participants showed a particular response. If the total number of participants is only eight, this simply shows that two people did not react in the same way as the others. The smaller the number, the larger the impact of one or two anomalous results.

Quotations

What are they?

> Quotations are pieces of text copied directly from another source. The writer refers to someone else's writing to support the argument.

Why are they used?

> A quotation from another source will lend credibility to the author's argument. This is especially true if the person quoted is well known as an expert on the topic.

Ask yourself

> Who is being quoted? What do you know about this person? Are you sure this person said the quotation? What was the context in which the quotation was said? As you saw in Chapter 3, it is important to be aware of the potential for bias among people whose words are repeated.

When No Evidence Is Presented

In some texts, the author presents a strong argument but does not support it with any concrete or scientific evidence, or with any reference to other sources. Instead, the author attempts to convince the reader by creating empathy through the skilful use of language. This is particularly common in newspaper columns, blog posts and other texts expressing a personal opinion. There are different ways in which the author tries to get the reader on his or her side:

> The author may choose to use "we" rather than "people"; the author is saying, "You and I have something in common; we both feel the same way about this topic."

> The author may support his or her argument with hypothetical examples that are very close to the lives of the readers and that the readers can identify with.

> The author may describe hypothetical situations that appeal to the reader's emotions; these situations arouse feelings of sadness, anger or frustration on the part of the reader.

> The author may oversimplify a complex topic and present it in black-and-white terms; the reader must either completely agree with the author or completely disagree—there is no middle ground.

> **Keep in mind**
>
> The information above can also be useful as you develop your own writing skills. When you are writing an essay, think about how you are supporting your thesis statement and whether or not the evidence you are providing is convincing.

Put It into Practice

A. Each of the following five paragraphs presents a different type of evidence (and one paragraph uses no evidence). Read each paragraph and decide how the author supports the argument made in the text. Then, with your group, discuss how effective the supporting evidence is.

1 There is no doubt that there is a strong relationship between the colours around us and the way we feel, emotionally and physically. For example, think about the last fast-food restaurant you ate in. What colour scheme was used? Did the restaurant have red trays, orange plates or bright green seats? Were the employees wearing primary colours as opposed to, say, pastels or neutral shades? This is no coincidence. Research carried out by world-renowned colour theorist Natalie Wilson demonstrates the importance for the fast-food industry of using bright colours: "Bright colours, like fire-truck red, lime green or bright orange stimulate the appetite and make us feel hungry," she says. "When our plate is red or our cup is yellow, we want to eat more. Fast-food chains know this, and that's why you'll rarely find a beige burger joint" (2011, p. 459).

2 The colours you surround yourself with at work are also important as they make a difference to how you are perceived by members of the public. Traditional workplaces still use dark colours such as navy blue, forest green and chocolate brown to give clients a sense of seriousness and professionalism. Think about it: which accountant would you choose to prepare your tax return: the one whose office has navy blue drapes and lamps and a maritime scene on the wall or the one whose office is painted in hot pink with a cartoon character on the wall? An online survey of lawyers carried out by *Legal Scene* magazine showed that of 287 respondents, 38 percent chose a navy blue colour scheme for their offices; 32 percent chose brown; 19 percent chose forest green; 7 percent chose burgundy; and only 4 percent chose red, pink or orange (Perkins, 2013).

3 It is unlikely, however, that these sombre colours would be found in a daycare centre or an elementary school. A child's bedroom, too, is most likely to be decorated in light colours, which parents hope will make the child feel happy and secure—and which might help the child to sleep well at night. Research carried out by a chain of paint stores found that parents choosing a paint colour for their children's rooms were most likely to choose a light tone. Results are shown below:

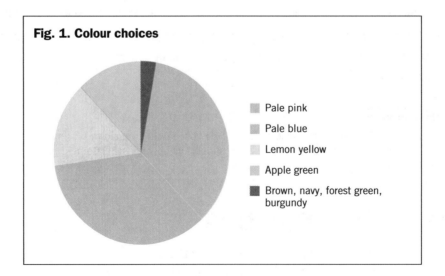

Fig. 1. Colour choices

- Pale pink
- Pale blue
- Lemon yellow
- Apple green
- Brown, navy, forest green, burgundy

4 Now think about a time you went to a hospital, either as a patient or as a visitor. It is unlikely that the walls of the waiting room, operating theatre or patient rooms were painted in bright yellow or hot pink. The preferred colour scheme for medical facilities is often pale blue or pale green. These are calming colours that help to relax nervous patients. Chloë McCrae, a 28-year-old receptionist, remembers when she had to go into the hospital to get her appendix removed. She was terrified, but when she saw how calm the place seemed, she immediately felt more relaxed.

5 As we see, then, we cannot separate colour from the way we feel. Regardless of what shade we choose, let's bring colour into our lives. It's time we embraced colour in our homes. Too many houses and apartments are painted in the same boring whites and beiges. Have you ever visited a friend's house and been amazed by his purple sofa or her turquoise walls? Have you ever noticed how many compliments you get when you wear your favourite red sweatshirt? Do the same in your home! Don't be boring! Don't live in neutral shades! Be colourful!

B. Find a published text on one of the following topics:

> Sick-building syndrome

> Green building design

Identify the type(s) of evidence used in your text:

_____ formal scientific research

_____ author observations

_____ anecdotes

_____ visual items

_____ statistics

_____ quotations

_____ no evidence

Share your thoughts on the effectiveness of the evidence presented in your text.

C. Do an Internet search for photographs of current world events. Choose three or four images that you have a strong reaction to, either positive or negative. With your class, discuss the following:

a) how these images convey messages far more effective than messages conveyed only through words;

b) the extent to which these pictures are reliable; i.e., do they tell the entire story, or do they give a selective view of the event?

Ancient Chinese Wisdom for the Modern Workplace

 FOCUS As you read this text about the Chinese art of *feng shui*, think about what kind of evidence the author uses to support her arguments.

Before You Read

Work in groups of three or four. Discuss the following questions.

1 Have you heard of the Chinese art of *feng shui*? Share your knowledge of feng shui with your group.

2 Do you know any people who have changed their living or working space in some way and experienced improvements in their lives?

3 What do you think a feng shui expert might say in the following situations? Match a problem with its recommended solution.

I want to …		You should …
1. feel powerful.	_____	a) have your office far from the main entrance.
2. make more money.	_____	b) tidy your desk.
3. concentrate better.	_____	c) not sit with your back to a door.
4. be a more effective boss.	_____	d) put a fish tank in your office.

Key Vocabulary

The words below are all in the reading. Fill in the space in each sentence with the correct word.

NOUNS	bottom line	dynamics	grasp	premise
VERBS	assess	contemplate		
ADJECTIVES	auspicious	inspiring	paranoid	
ADVERB	reputedly			

1 An action or event that is _____ encourages people and makes them want to perform a task well.

2 When you _____ something, you judge or evaluate it.

3 When you have a good _____ of a topic or issue, you have a clear understanding of it.

4 The _____ of a business is the amount of money the business gains or loses.

5 People who feel _____ have an irrational fear that someone or something is trying to hurt them.

6 When you _____ an issue, you think carefully about it for a long time.

7 Something that is _____ true is said to be true, but there is no real proof.

8 A _____ is an idea that you accept and that you use as a basis for further investigation or for developing plans.

9 Something that is _____ is considered to be an indication of good luck or future success.

10 The _____ that exist between people are the ways in which people interact and influence each other.

Ancient Chinese Wisdom for the Modern Workplace

By Kirsten Lagatree

Whenever Rose Murray travels on business, she rearranges her hotel room. "I drag the desk around so that I can see the door while I work," she explains. "And if there's unattractive, depressing art on the walls, I take it down and hide it in the closet." As a telecommunications consultant, Murray is hardly an expert on interior design. This
5 thoroughly modern professional woman is actually practising the ancient Chinese art of placement known as feng shui.

Feng shui (pronounced "fung shway") is based on the **premise** that people are affected by their environment—not so far-fetched when you think about it. It unites ancient beliefs with space planning, interior design, ecology, psychology and common
10 sense.

The words *feng shui* mean "wind" and "water"—two natural elements that can pack a lot of energy. The words are shorthand for acknowledging the power of nature and the importance of living in harmony with it. In removing ugly art from hotel room walls, Murray is attempting to make her surroundings feel positive and **inspiring**.

15 When she drags the writing table to face the door, Murray is following one of the most important rules of feng shui: Don't sit with your back to a door. To be powerful, you must feel powerful and sitting with your back to a door makes you vulnerable to anyone who comes in.

→

How it works

20 The first principle of feng shui is *chi*,[1] or energy. Your desk, files, furniture, plants and so forth should allow unobstructed movement of the vital life force throughout your work area. If, for example, you have massive stacks of files or 25 unwieldy piles of journals and magazines on and around your desk, you're blocking the free flow of energy that is essential to your powers of concentration and creativity. Take the time to survey your surroundings and **assess** whether 30 your office arrangement helps or hinders productivity.

Small-business consultant Alice Bredin says that she can tell the difference between the poor feng shui of her cluttered workspace in Maine 35 and the good feng shui of her office in New York City. "There are so many projects stacked up around me in Maine that I literally don't know what to do first," she says. Bredin adds that the energy flow in her carefully arranged New York office makes her feel in control. "I can focus and be highly productive there."

40 Compass directions and their spheres of influence also affect the feng shui of a person's surroundings. Each compass point governs a different aspect of life. Each point has a corresponding colour, natural element and number, which can be combined to create enhancements that engender success in any part of life.

Putting it to work

45 You can also take advantage of feng shui enhancements to promote a bigger and better **bottom line**. Here are some tips.

> Put an aquarium with a water pump in your office. The moving water symbolizes cash flow, and the fish encourage abundance (as in, "there are always more fish in the sea").

50 > Place the aquarium, along with something black, on the north wall. North governs career and business success; water is its element, and black is its corresponding colour.

> To take full advantage of your "money corner," add red or purple touches in groups of four to the southeast direction which governs wealth.

55 > Place your computer or fax machine in a southeast corner says California interior designer Annie Kelly. "The easiest thing to do is put office equipment in a corner anyway, so you might as well put it in the wealth corner!" Or you can place metal equipment on a west wall; west corresponds to the element metal. Experiment and see what works best.

---

[1] *Chi*, or *qi* is the life force inherent in all things. Chi is at the foundation of Chinese philosophy and medicine.

60 > Add plants and flowers. Living things and such enhancements as a bowl
of goldfish or wind chime create a harmonious work environment and impart
the benefits of healthy, smooth-flowing chi.

Desk placement

The location of your desk is the single most important feng shui consideration in the
65 workplace. Generally, your desk should be in a commanding position. That is, arrange
your desk so that you face the entrance door and sit far enough inside your office to see
the whole room from your desk.

Kristin Frederickson, art director at a small New York publishing house, says that she
thinks it's almost impossible for anyone to work well with his or her back to the door.

70 "There's **paranoid** energy in not knowing what's going on behind your back. If you
work that way, your paranoia will be felt by co-workers."

If you sit too close to the entrance door, you won't have control of the room; sitting
farther inside your office will give you a better **grasp** of the business. Facing the door
from well inside the room gives you mastery over all you observe. Therefore, you will
75 think more clearly, your judgment will be sound, and your authority will be respected.

If it isn't possible to arrange your desk so that you face the door, hang a small mirror
over your desk so that you can see the door. If you face the door but are unable to see
the rest of the room, then use a mirror large enough to improve your view.

Lighting

80 Good lighting is important for an office, both for illuminating your work and creating
good feng shui. Bright lights help promote healthy, flowing chi. Glare is distracting
and a source of bad chi, known as *sha*. Be especially careful that glare doesn't hit your
face. Ideally, windows should be to the side of your desk. If glare is unavoidable, hang
a multifaceted crystal at the window to disperse the sha from the glare and create
85 good chi.

The big picture

The location of the manager's or boss's office is the most important factor in determining
the overall success of any business. Check the layout of your workplace to see whether
the location is **auspicious**.

90 The person in charge should have the office farthest from the main door. Away from
the hustle and bustle, a manager can see the big picture and not be distracted by the
minutia of daily transactions. Such distance gives managers time to **contemplate**
decisions that might be made hastily if they are too close to the activity from the street.

The boss's desk should not be close to the office door, or he or she will not have
95 sufficient control over the operation and will not be treated with deference. Similarly,
workers whose desks are farther inside their offices than their bosses are likely to be
insubordinate because they will feel more in command than their superiors.

For a more powerful presence at meetings, sit in the chair facing the door. That will
make you highly sensitive to the **dynamics** of the meeting. Don't sit with your back to
100 a window. A solid wall behind you provides support for your ideas and lends authority
to your presence.

The relationship between feng shui and finance is seen on a grander scale in large multinational corporations. The headquarters of the Hongkong and Shanghai Banking Corporation in Hong Kong is an example.

105 Reputed to be one of the most technologically advanced skyscrapers in the world, the 47-storey building was sited and constructed according to strict feng shui principles.

Many visitors wonder at the odd angle of escalators that lead from the plaza level to the main banking floor. The moving stairs appear to have been placed at random. But, in fact, they are situated in order to disperse chi and wealth evenly throughout the
110 structure. Moreover, it is no accident that the building faces the sea, with Victoria Peak at its back—imbuing the corporation with the benefits of those highly auspicious land formations. The mountain provides support and protection for the firm's business ventures, while the ocean invites wealth to flow into the building.

If you're feeling a bit skeptical about trying out the ancient art of feng shui in your
115 modern office, know that in many parts of the United States—especially in such major metropolitan areas as New York, Los Angeles and Washington, D.C.—business deals **reputedly** can rise or fall on good or bad feng shui.

You might want to take a cue from Donald Trump, who consults a feng shui master before embarking on all new building projects. Trump says that his international clientele
120 prompts him to take the ancient practice seriously. The billionaire real-estate tycoon puts it this way: "If they believe, it's good enough for me."   (1419 words)

Lagatree, K. (1997). Ancient Chinese wisdom for the modern workplace. *Training & Development, 51*(1), 26–30.

Check Your Understanding

A. How many of your guesses from "Before You Read" were correct? Which were not correct?

B. Answer the following questions, in your own words where possible, using information from the reading.

1. What does *feng shui* literally mean? _____

2. What is the underlying premise behind feng shui?

   _____

   _____

3. Why, according to feng shui experts, is it important to keep your workspace free of clutter?

   _____

   _____

4. Which of the following is NOT linked to success in business?

   a) Setting up your computer in the southeast corner of your office

   b) Having plants or flowers in your office

   c) Making sure your lighting is bright enough

   d) Keeping lots of papers and files easily accessible on your desk

5 Why should the manager's office be farthest away from the main entrance?

_____

_____

_____

6 Where should the manager sit in a meeting? Why?

_____

_____

7 In what way(s) were feng shui principles used in the design of the Hongkong and Shanghai Banking Corporation building in Hong Kong?

_____

_____

_____

8 Name one well-known businessman who believes in feng shui.

_____

C. In your own words, summarize why the author believes feng shui is useful in the modern workplace.

Analysis and Discussion

Discuss the following questions with your group.

1 What kind(s) of evidence does the author provide to support her argument in favour of feng shui in the workplace?

a) visual items

b) anecdotes

c) statistics

d) quotations

2 Look at the example of Rose Murray in lines 1 to 18. Answer the following questions.

> Why did the author choose to start the article with this example?

> How does Rose Murray modify her hotel room when she travels on business?

> Is Rose Murray an expert on feng shui or on interior design in general?

> What evidence exists that Rose Murray's actions are effective?

3 Look at the example of Alice Bredin in lines 32 to 39. Answer the following questions.

> What difference does Alice Bredin describe between her two workplaces?

> What evidence exists that feng shui is responsible for her difference in productivity?

4 Who is Donald Trump, and what is his connection to feng shui? What is the value of quoting a well-known person?

5. Look at the following experts quoted by the author. Fill in the table to show a) who this person is, b) what suggestion(s) the expert makes, and c) whether this advice is supported by any data.

PERSON QUOTED	WHO IS THIS PERSON?	SUGGESTION(S) MADE?	SUPPORTING DATA?
Annie Kelly			
Kristin Frederickson			

6. The author provides no concrete evidence that feng shui actually works. Why do you think this kind of evidence is missing from the text?

7. Do you think feng shui can be scientifically proven? If so, how? If not, why not?

8. How do you personally respond to this article? If you were not familiar with feng shui before, has this author convinced you to try it in your study space? Why, or why not?

READING 2

Sitting Too Long Is Bad for You, but a Treadmill Desk Left Me Cold

This reading is a journalistic account of a writer's experience with a treadmill desk.

 FOCUS As you read, look at the evidence the author uses to describe the advantages and disadvantages of this form of workstation.

Before You Read

Work in groups of three or four. Discuss the following questions.

1. How many hours per day do you usually spend sitting at your computer? Have you ever suffered any negative effects from sitting for too long?

2. What workspace features would you recommend in order to improve health and productivity?

3. Do an Internet search for pictures of treadmill desks. What advantages and/or disadvantages do you think these desks might have?

Key Vocabulary

The words below are all in the reading. Match each word with the correct definition.

1. ambivalent (adj. line 55) _____
2. cognition (n. line 46) _____
3. distracted (adj. line 16) _____
4. fidget (v. line 20) _____
5. legitimate (adj. line 61) _____
6. malinger (v. line 52) _____
7. pragmatic (adj. line 40) _____
8. prolific (adj. line 27) _____
9. sedentary (adj. line 11) _____
10. stationary (adj. line 8) _____

a) reasonable, acceptable
b) be unable to keep still, usually out of boredom
c) sensible, practical
d) avoid working, e.g., by pretending to be sick
e) producing many works
f) the process of using the brain to learn and understand information
g) sitting down
h) unable to focus on a task
i) not moving
j) having both positive and negative feelings about something

Sitting Too Long Is Bad for You, but a Treadmill Desk Left Me Cold

By Christie Aschwanden

I don't love my treadmill desk.

I wanted to love my treadmill desk. I've been working at a sit/stand desk for more than ten years, and I stand about 80 percent of the time; it makes me feel more alert, energetic and creative. So when I saw a used treadmill desk for sale, cheap, I grabbed
5 it. Walking at my desk seemed like an even better way to boost my productivity and energy levels when deadlines keep me chained to my workstation.

But what made the treadmill desk most appealing was the growing pile of studies revealing the dangers of time spent stationary. As an avid runner, cyclist and skier, I get plenty of exercise, but the research shows that a five-mile run at the end of the day won't
10 erase the health risks—such as an increased risk of diabetes, hypertension and obesity— wrought by eight hours of sedentary time, says Mayo Clinic physician and researcher James Levine, popularizer of the treadmill desk.

On my first day of desk walking, I set the treadmill to 2.5 mph (or 24 minutes per mile), a rather leisurely pace. Typing and mousing were easy with my adjustable monitor and
15 keyboard tray. The more I raised the speed, the more satisfying the walking felt, but the more distracted I became from details on the screen.

After a day of walking faster and faster, I tried turning the treadmill down to 1.5 mph, which made the walking less distracting—except for my constant runner's urge to go →

faster. I kept experimenting, and I even tried the lowest setting, 0.5 mph, to see if I'd
20 have better luck thinking of this as fidgeting rather than exercise. But that pace felt so
annoyingly slow that I soon quit in frustration.

Eventually, I settled on 1.8 to 2.4 mph as my ideal pace, and found that desk walking
could keep me sane and alert on days when I'm so slammed with deadlines that it's my
only opportunity for exercise. But for me, walking on the desk treadmill is about as
25 satisfying as eating a meal in front of the TV: I'd much rather go out for a run.

I've now had the desk treadmill for more than a year, and I sometimes go weeks
without turning it on. Yet when my writing buddy Paolo Bacigalupi, a prolific novelist,
began using one, he fell in love with his in exactly the way I had expected to love mine.

"I find that I look forward to starting to work in the morning, partly because it's now
30 the moment when I start moving physically," he says. Bacigalupi has always enjoyed
being active and hated that doing good creative work meant becoming inert, "so the
treadmill desk feels like a big win." I'd long ago sold him on the virtues of a standup
desk, but he now prefers the walking one. Even with the standing desk, Bacigalupi
tended to freeze into stationary positions, but the treadmill ensures that he's never static
35 and the back problems that once plagued him have vanished.

What about productivity? A small 2011 study found that transcriptionists'[1] accuracy
did not differ when they switched from sitting to working at a treadmill desk, but their
speed dropped by 16 percent. (They also burned 100 more calories per hour.) A year-long
study of workers at a financial services company found that treadmill desks increased
40 both physical activity and productivity. "This is a pragmatic approach that can work for
almost everybody," says study author Avner Ben-Ner, a professor of human resources
and labour studies at the Carlson School of Management at the University of Minnesota.

Given how many ideas come to me while I'm walking, biking or running outside, I'd
thought the treadmill would increase my creative output, but instead I've found that
45 some tasks, such as editing and taking notes on scientific papers, feel more difficult.

"One thing that's known about walking and cognition is that it needs to be at a
comfortable, self-selected pace to be helpful," says Daniel Schwartz, a professor of
education at the Stanford School of Education, whose research has shown that walking
boosts certain types of creativity. "If you're forced to go too fast or too slow, it's going
50 to siphon off cognitive resources."

Bacigalupi says he's more productive now. "I waste less time," he says. "I tend to focus
in and just get to work, instead of malingering on Facebook and Twitter." He walks two
to four hours per day at 1.8 to 2.6 mph, and he feels energized. "It's sort of pleasant to
finish my day's writing work and have a feeling of my body being a little tired."

55 As for me, I remain ambivalent. After Bacigalupi showed me his setup, I went home
and walked nine miles at my desk. I also developed a blister from walking barefoot, and
felt tired enough at the end of the day that I skipped the higher-quality run I would have
otherwise done.

---

[1] A *transcriptionist* is someone who listens to an audio recording and creates a written document of what is said.

I harbour a gnawing suspicion that treadmill desks are the wrong solution to an
60 important problem: too much time at desks and in front of glowing screens. The treadmill
desk robs office workers of a legitimate reason to leave their workstations once in a
while. Sure, walking at your desk is better than not walking at all, but I wish those
weren't the only two choices. (894 words)

Aschwanden, C. (2014, Sept. 17). Sitting too long is bad for you, but a treadmill desk left me cold. *The Washington Post.*
Retrieved from *Calgary Herald*. http://www.calgaryherald.com/health/diet-fitness/Sitting+long+treadmill+desk+left+co
ld/10211520/story.html.

Check Your Understanding

A. Answer the following questions in your own words using information from the reading.

1 Why did the author decide to buy a treadmill desk?

_____

_____

_____

2 What conclusions have studies reached about the connection between a sedentary
lifestyle and health concerns?

_____

_____

3 What problem did the author experience while using the treadmill desk?

_____

_____

4 What does the author mean by the comparison "walking on the desk treadmill is about
as satisfying as eating a meal in front of the TV"?

_____

_____

5 Why does the author's friend Paolo Bacigalupi enjoy using his treadmill desk?

_____

_____

_____

6 Why does the author think treadmill desks are not the solution to an overly sedentary
lifestyle?

_____

_____

_____

B. The author makes a number of inferences. Which of the following does the author infer?

		Yes	No
1	People with sedentary lives should find more time to exercise.	○	○
2	Running on a treadmill is easier than running outside.	○	○
3	Using a treadmill desk can help some people to concentrate on work.	○	○
4	Treadmill desks work well for some people but not for others.	○	○
5	There is no clear connection between treadmill desks and productivity.	○	○
6	Treadmill desks are a waste of money.	○	○

Analysis and Discussion

Discuss the following questions with your group.

1 What kind(s) of evidence does the author use in this article? Check all that apply.

○ a) visual items   ○ c) statistics

○ b) anecdotes   ○ d) quotations

2 Look at the anecdotal evidence the author uses to support the argument that treadmill desks work well for some people. Answer the following questions.

a) Who is Paolo Bacigalupi? What is his job? What is his connection to the author?

b) Do you think his experience is typical of people who purchase exercise equipment?

Why, or why not?

3 Find one statistic used by the author when talking about productivity. What do you learn from this statistic? Do you think this statistic represents a large change or a small one? Why?

4 Look at the following experts quoted by the author. Fill in the chart to show a) who this person is, b) what the expert says and c) whether this person's views can be trusted.

PERSON QUOTED	WHO IS THIS PERSON?	WHAT DOES HE SAY?	CAN YOU TRUST HIM?
James Levine			
Avner Ben-Ner			
Daniel Schwartz			

5 Based on what you have read, which of the following statements do you most agree with?

    a) I think I spend too much time sitting down. I need to be more active in order to avoid health problems. A treadmill desk might be a good idea; I would like to try this!

    b) I probably do spend too much time sitting down, but I don't think a treadmill desk would be helpful to me. I should look for another way to get more exercise.

    c) I don't have a sedentary lifestyle, so I don't need to worry about this. I find plenty of other ways to get enough exercise.

6 Which piece of evidence in the article are you most convinced by? Why?

READING 3

Workstation Design for Organizational Productivity

The following text contains several examples of visual evidence.

 As you look at these, think about the effectiveness of the different types of visual evidence provided.

Before You Read

Work in groups of three or four. Discuss the following questions.

1 Have you ever worked in an office space? If so, what did you like about the space? What did you dislike about it?

2 What do you understand by an "open-plan" office? What advantages and disadvantages of this kind of design can you think of?

3 Do you have a high tolerance for noise, or does noise bother you? What kind(s) of noise do you find most distracting when you are working?

Workstation Design for Organizational Productivity (Excerpts)

Public Works and Government Services Canada
National Research Council Canada

Part 1

Around 50% of North Americans work in offices, and a large percentage of these work in open-plan offices. Because people spend up to 90% of their time indoors, and much of it in their workplaces, the physical environment in offices should be carefully designed
5 and managed. The physical conditions that occupants experience are important determinants of satisfaction, comfort, well-being and effectiveness.

Employees are greatly influenced by their organization's choices. They produce the goods and services that will be sold and are usually an organization's greatest asset. Employees are also the largest cost. Expenditures such as salaries, benefits, training 10 and recruitment constitute the majority of an organization's costs. Therefore, how the employees think and behave at work—their attitudes and behaviours—can have a significant influence on the organization's input and output. By focusing on employee attitudes and behaviours, we can examine measurable, comparable results that contribute to productivity. This analysis can then support office design choices that are beneficial 15 to employees. We cannot put a dollar value on the effect of one strategy, but we can show that changes that benefit employees also benefit organizations.

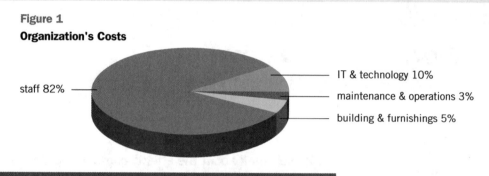

Figure 1

Organization's Costs

staff 82%

IT & technology 10%

maintenance & operations 3%

building & furnishings 5%

Breakdown of an organization's expenditures. Based on Brill et al. (2001).

Employee attitudes and behaviours are affected by numerous different factors, including management practices, employee–employer relations, salary and non-monetary incentives, up-to-date technology, employees' skills and abilities and opportunities for 20 varied and stimulating work. For example, participatory and empowering management styles have a positive influence on job satisfaction, commitment and well-being. Similarly, incentives such as salaries, pension schemes, on-site daycare and gyms, and company cars are factors that employees will consider when choosing to stay with an organization or move to a different company.space to house employees.

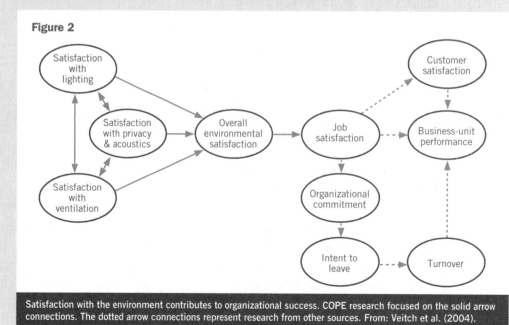

Figure 2

Satisfaction with the environment contributes to organizational success. COPE research focused on the solid arrow connections. The dotted arrow connections represent research from other sources. From: Veitch et al. (2004).

25 Improvements in office design and management are not the only consideration for organizational productivity, but they have an important role to play; offices should be considered as a potential asset rather than just a space to house employees. Office design and maintenance decisions that benefit employees will also benefit organizational productivity.

30 **Part 2**

The acoustic environment in the office comprises all the sounds that occur throughout the day. Some of these sounds may be pleasant, such as music, or carry important information, such as a telephone ring or a fire alarm. However, when sounds are unwanted by the listener, they are perceived as noise: unpleasant, bothersome,
35 distracting or psychologically harmful.

When noise becomes a problem, most people close the door. Unfortunately, in open-plan offices, there are no full-height walls and doors to block noise, and many office sounds are audible at a distance.

A large survey of North American offices found that 54% of office workers were often
40 bothered by noise: ringing phones and conversations were most disruptive. In the COPE[1] field study, conversations and noise from others were the most frequently mentioned complaints about offices.

Figure 3

I am often bothered by ...

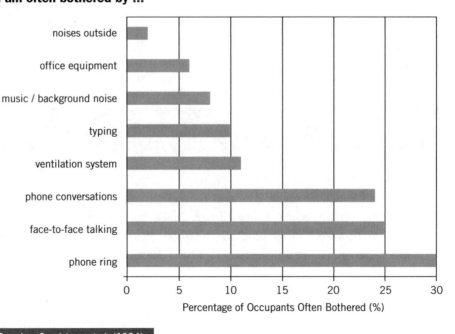

Based on Sundstrom et al. (1994).

---

[1] COPE stands for Cost-effective Open-Plan Environments. This was a four-year study undertaken by the National Research Council of Canada in conjunction with several other governmental and non-governmental organizations.

Good speech privacy allows occupants confidentiality for their actions and conversations while in the office and also limits distractions. To identify good speech privacy, a physical
45 index has been developed. The Speech Intelligibility Index (SII) indicates how well speech can be understood in the presence of noise and ranges from 0 (perfect privacy) to 1 (perfect intelligibility).

Figure 4
Distraction versus SII

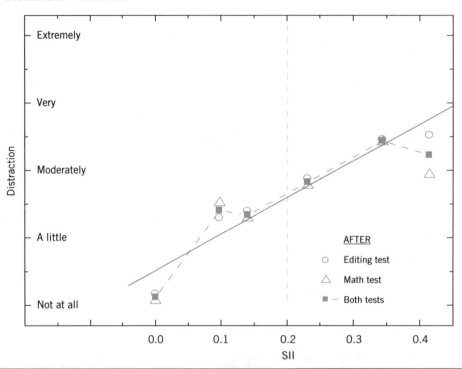

Office occupants rated their level of distraction after math and editing tasks. Their distraction increased beyond acceptable levels when SII was higher than 0.2. (Mean ratings: (a) after an editing task, (b) after a math task, and (c) average of both.) From: Bradley & Gover (2003).

Controlling ambient sound is only one part of creating satisfactory acoustic conditions and speech privacy. Annoying noises, like speech, printer noise, typing and telephone
50 rings, also require control. Noise sources can be isolated and reduced, and travelling sound can be absorbed and blocked with good office design and layout so that noises, such as speech, do not transmit from one workstation to another.

The best way to control noise sources is through office design. The acoustic properties of the office can significantly reduce sound travel by blocking sound
55 transmission and by absorbing reflected sound. Sound Transmission Class (STC) ratings indicate how well a material reduces sound propagating through it (sound transmission). Sound Absorption Average (SAA) ratings indicate how well the material absorbs sound hitting the material. The following table shows material properties recommended for open-plan offices.

Figure 5

ACOUSTIC PROPERTIES	
ELEMENT	**ACOUSTICAL PROPERTIES**
Exterior Walls	STC 50
Windows	STC 35
Ceiling	SAA >0.90
Floors	STC 55 (carpeted)
Partitions	SAA >0.70 STC 20

Based on Canadian Standards Association (2000), and Bradley (2004). Most manufacturers provide the acoustic properties of their products.

(644 words)

Charles, K. E., Danforth, A. J., Veitch, J. A., Zwierzchowski, C., Johnson, B., & Pero, K. (2004). *Workstation design for organizational productivity*. Ottawa: National Research Council of Canada and Public Works & Government Services Canada.

Check Your Understanding

Answer the following questions in your own words using information from the reading.

1 Summarize Part 1 of this text (lines 1 to 29) to show why it is important for companies to make good design choices.

_____

_____

_____

_____

_____

_____

2 What is the main concern of workers in open-plan offices? What percentage of employees expressed this concern?

_____

_____

3 Summarize the information in each of the figures in four or five sentences.

a) Figure 1

_____

_____

_____

_____

_____

b) Figure 2

_____

_____

_____

_____

_____

c) Figure 3

_____

_____

_____

_____

_____

d) Figure 4

_____

_____

_____

_____

_____

e) Figure 5

_____

_____

_____

_____

_____

Key Vocabulary

Find a word or expression in the text that means the same as each of the words and expressions below.

Part 1

1 exciting, motivating   _____

2 extra things given to an employee, e.g.,
a health-care plan   _____

3 things offered as a way of encouraging an employee   _____

4 the way a person thinks or feels about something   _____

5 valuable possession; something helpful or useful   _____

Part 2

6 able to be heard _____

7 of the surrounding area _____

8 related to sound _____

9 secrecy, privacy _____

10 causing a disturbance; preventing someone
from concentrating _____

Analysis and Discussion

Discuss the following questions with your group.

1 Look again at the visual items presented in this reading and answer the following
questions.

Figure 1

a) Why do you think the authors chose to use a pie chart here?

b) Do you think this pie chart gives a realistic picture of the situation?

c) Is this an effective use of a visual item?

Figure 2

a) Why do you think the authors chose to use a flow chart here?

b) Do you think this flow chart gives a realistic picture of the situation?

c) Is this an effective use of a visual item?

Figure 3

a) Why do you think the authors chose to use a bar chart here?

b) Do you think this bar chart gives a realistic picture of the situation?

c) Is this an effective use of a visual item?

Figure 4

a) Why do you think the authors chose to use a line graph here?

b) Do you think this line graph gives a realistic picture of the situation?

c) Is this an effective use of a visual item?

Figure 5

a) Why do you think the authors chose to use a table here?

b) Do you think this table gives a realistic picture of the situation?

c) Is this an effective use of a visual item?

2 What recommendations would you make to anyone responsible for designing a new
office space?

3 What other problems do workers in open-plan offices have? How might these problems
be addressed?

Going Further

Focus on Language

A. The following chart contains ten words from the three readings. Complete the chart with related words in the other categories and, where possible, in the same category. (There may not be a word for each category.)

	NOUN	VERB	ADJECTIVE	ADVERB
1	analysis			
2	creativity			
3			energetic	
4				ideally
5	judgment			
6			satisfying	
7			significant	
8	suspicion			
9		symbolize		
10		unite		

B. The author of Reading 2 uses the following sentence: "Typing and mousing were easy with my adjustable monitor and keyboard tray." By turning the noun *mouse* into a verb, the author is following the current trend of "verbing"—making verbs from nouns. In the following sentences, underline each example of verbing. With your group, discuss the following:

> How might each sentence be expressed in more formal language?

> Is verbing a lazy form of English, or does it represent the natural evolution of language?

1 She friended me on Facebook.

2 Did any athletes from your country medal at the Olympic Games?

3 Can you message me when you hear some news?

4 I'll task John with buying a new office printer.

5 We spent the first half of the class journalling.

6 If you're not sure what something means, you can google it.

7 After a career as an architect, she is transitioning into interior design.

8 As you deplane, please remember to take all hand luggage with you.

Independent Research

Choose a space where you often work or study. This could be an office, a dorm room, a classroom, a lecture theatre, a library or another space. Visit the space and note your observations on the following:

> the colour;

> the lighting;

> the air quality;

> the comfort of the furniture;

> the amount of ambient noise; and

> the proximity to washrooms, sources of food or other necessities.

Then, interview three or four people who also use the space regularly. Ask them about their experiences in the space and how productive they feel when they are trying to work there.

You will present your findings to the class. Include in your presentation any changes you would recommend.

Synthesis and Written Response

Based on your reading of the texts in this chapter as well as your own personal experiences, write a short response to the following prompt:

> There is a strong connection between design of the environment and productivity at work or in school. Discuss.

REVIEW
of the chapter ...

> Answer the following questions.

1 What do you understand by the following kinds of evidence: anecdotes, visual items, statistics and quotations?

2 What are some of the reasons why an author would use each one?

3 In what ways might a) visual evidence and b) statistics be misleading?

4 In what ways might an author try to persuade a reader to support a point of view without using any kind of evidence?

Inequality, Wealth and Happiness

FOCUS THE TEXT IN CONTEXT 1

What is the larger context of this work? Does the text support any particular school of thought? How does the text support or contradict other opinions on this topic? Who might agree with the text? Who might disagree?

In this chapter
YOU WILL LEARN ...

> why it is important to consider the text in its broader context;

> what a school of thought is and why it is important to know the schools of thought in your area of study; and

> how to approach a text that presents an opinion or theory very different from anything else you have read.

Warm-up

Discuss these questions with your group.

> Why do you think some countries are much richer than others? What are some contributing factors to the relative wealth of a country?

> What factors are most important in determining the happiness of a country? Rank the following in order of importance.

_____ accessible education	_____ low taxes
_____ a high GDP	_____ political stability
_____ a mild climate	_____ racial equality
_____ gender equality	_____ strong cultural traditions
_____ health care for everyone	_____ other

> If you read two contradictory texts on this topic, how would you know which one to trust? What are some questions you might ask about the texts?

The Context of a Text

> What is the relationship between the wealth of a country, its economic policies and the happiness of its citizens?

Imagine you have been given this essay topic in a course entitled *Introduction to Economics*. You may find articles on this topic that present different points of view. Texts are not written in isolation; texts, as we have seen, are influenced by the author's personal biases and agenda, by other people in the field as well as by the results of empirical research. It is important to understand something about the **context** in which a text appears. As well as considering why and under what circumstances a text was written, you need to see how it fits in with other texts on the same subject: whether it supports previously published material or whether it presents a new perspective.

Schools of Thought

Academic authors sometimes align themselves with a particular **school of thought** within a discipline. A school of thought refers to the theories put forward by a group of people (for example, researchers or writers) who share the same approach to the subject; they look at issues within the discipline in the same way. Schools of thought are commonly found in the humanities and social sciences. Each of these schools will have a different view of the same phenomena. Here is an example from economics:

Should governments intervene in the economic development of a country, particularly during times of economic difficulty?

> Classical economics: A strong economy is based on free markets with little government intervention; the economy will self-regulate and self-correct.

> Keynsian economics (based on the work of John Maynard Keynes): Government intervention is necessary during economic crises.

> Marxian economics (based on the work of Karl Marx and Friedrich Engels): There is fundamental inequality in the distribution of wealth and a more extreme restructuring of the country's economic system is necessary.

It is necessary to know whether an author whose work you are reading is representative of a particular school of thought. If you are reading a journal article, find out whether the journal supports any particular school of thought. Your text was not written in isolation; don't read it in isolation!

New Perspective or Nonsense?

You may have read several articles on a particular topic that all present the same opinion. Then, you come across a text that presents a very different point of view. How are you going to deal with this?

Don't assume that an article is of no value simply because it contradicts everything else you have read about the topic. Five hundred years ago, people believed the earth was the centre of the universe. When early scientists put forward the theory that the earth revolves around the sun, they were treated with suspicion and hostility. Today, of course, we know the truth.

If you find a text that presents a dramatically different opinion from everything you have read, ask yourself some of the questions that have been addressed in earlier chapters:

> Where was this text published? Is this a reliable source?

> Who is the author? What do you know about this person? Is the author biased in some way?

> Why did the author write this text? What was his or her objective?

> Is the author presenting any facts, or is the entire text based on opinion?

> What evidence does the author present to support his or her stance? Has the author done empirical research? Is the evidence presented based on the work of others? Is there no evidence at all?

What you are reading may be nonsense with no basis in scientific fact—or you may have stumbled upon some ground-breaking new research. Use your critical reading skills to help you to decide.

Put It into Practice

A. What causes inequality in the global economy? Some of the poorest regions on Earth are rich in resources (minerals, gold, diamonds, rubber and even oil) but suffer from poverty and hunger. The following theories have all been put forward to explain why the world's poorest countries are in this situation. For each of the following theories, discuss these questions:

a) Is this theory related to any field of study? Consider, for example, whether an economist, an anthropologist, a geographer, etc. would agree or disagree with this theory.

b) What is your own assessment of this theory?

1. The poorest parts of the world often have difficult terrain (for example, jungles and non-navigable rivers); geographical factors, together with a lack of infrastructure in the form of extensive transportation networks, have meant that these regions have not developed trade relationships and have been isolated from outside influences. Consequently, they have not developed as rapidly as other parts of the world.

2. There is too much fragmentation within societies of poorer nations. There may be many tribes, many languages and many religions. There is often fighting among these groups. In some nations, financial resources are being used for waging civil war, not for developing health or education programs.

3. The legacy of colonization is still hurting the world's poorer nations. For years, large parts of the world were ruled by colonizing powers and used only as a source of raw materials and, in some cases, slave labour. Even today, large amounts of land are still in the hands of descendants of European colonizers; the local population does not have sufficient control over its own resources.

4. When colonized nations gained independence, they did not have the skills to self-govern as they had been exploited for so long. An environment was created in which chaos and corruption flourished; this is still continuing today. It takes a long time to recover from that kind of treatment.

5. Foreign governments think they are helping poorer nations by giving foreign aid. They are wrong; all this does is encourage the governments of these nations to rely on outside help. They have no incentive to develop their own economies.

6. Can you think of any other theories to explain the poverty of the world's poorest countries?

B. Read the following account of a graduate student who challenged a published theory about happiness, with surprising results. Answer the questions below.

Is There a Happiness Number?

Part-time master's degree student Nick Brown caused a stir when he questioned an accepted theory about happiness.

Brown, 53 and a semi-retired IT expert, was taking a part-time graduate course in psychology when he went to a lecture about the psychology of happiness. He was shown a graph that showed in mathematical terms which people would be happy and which people would be unhappy. This was known as the "critical positivity ratio"; anyone with a ratio of 2.9013 positive emotions to one negative emotion would be happy, while anyone with a ratio lower than this would not.

This number first appeared in an academic paper entitled "Positive Affect and the Complex Dynamics of Human Flourishing," written by Barbara Fredrickson and Marcial Losada and published in 2005 in the respected journal *American Psychologist*. →

Frederickson is an award-winning professor of psychology and the author of several books; Losada is a mathematician and business consultant. Until Nick Brown attended his lecture, Frederickson and Losada's theory had barely been questioned by other researchers and had been cited in over 350 other academic articles.

Brown doubted that the complex nature of human happiness could be related to a single number. Despite being only a student in his first term of graduate studies, he studied the mathematics behind this theory and found them to be flawed. With the help of two academics, he published a response in *American Psychologist*. Losada declined to respond, but Frederickson published a response; she stood by her general ideas, but she admitted she did not fully understand Losada's mathematics behind the theory and accepted that the numbers were "questionable." *American Psychologist* published a statement that the mathematical aspects of the theory—including the number 2.9013—were not valid.

It is now generally accepted that Frederickson and Losada's mathematical theory of happiness has been debunked, or discredited, by the field of psychology.

Summarized from Anthony A. (2014, January 19). The British amateur who debunked the mathematics of happiness. *The Guardian*. Retrieved from http://www.theguardian.com/science/2014/jan/19/mathematics-of-happiness-debunked-nick-brown.

1 Explain Frederickson and Losada's theory in your own words.

2 On what grounds did Nick Brown start to question the validity of the theory?

3 Why do you think over 350 other academics cited Frederickson and Losada's theory without questioning it?

4 To what extent do you think *American Psychologist* is responsible for this controversy? What might the journal have done differently?

5 Nick Brown was the first person to question Fredrickson and Losada's theory. He said later, "I'm able to do what I'm doing here because I'm nobody. I don't have to keep any academics happy" (Anthony, 2014). What might Brown be suggesting about the nature of academic discourse?

6 If you were to come across a theory in the course of your research that you consider questionable, how would you attempt to find out whether or not it is valid? What questions would you ask?

C. History is full of researchers whose ideas were rejected or criticized at the time but are known to be true today. Choose one of the following researchers and find some information about this person. Think about how and why the researcher's ideas gained acceptance.

> Rachel Carson

> Charles Darwin

> Galileo Galilei

> Ignaz Semmelweis

> Alfred Wegener

Can Money Buy Happiness?
An Examination of Happiness
Economics

This reading addresses the relationship between economic wealth and happiness.

 As you read, consider how this reading fits in with other things you have read and with your own opinions on this topic.

Before You Read

Work in groups of three or four. Discuss the following questions.

1. What do you understand by the economic term *gross domestic product* (GDP)?

2. What do you think *happiness economics* is? What kind of research might be carried out by happiness economists?

3. The title of this reading asks a question. What do you predict the answer might be?

Key Vocabulary

The words below are all in the reading. Fill in the space in each sentence with the correct word.

NOUNS	implication	paradox	rebuke	welfare state
VERBS	correlate	redistribute		
ADJECTIVES	contentious	intuitive	seminal	subjective

1. A situation in which two apparently contradictory ideas are both true is known as

   a/an _____.

2. An opinion that is _____ is one based on feeling rather than on any presentation of research results.

3. The _____s of a decision or policy are the effects or results of that decision or policy.

4. If you read a/an _____ paper on a topic, you read a paper that has had, or will have, an important effect on future research.

5. When something _____s with something else, there is a close connection between the two things. For example, as A increases, B also increases.

6 A political system in which a country provides a social safety net (for example, health care, unemployment benefits and pensions) for its citizens is known as a/an _____.

7 A/An _____ topic is one that generates a lot of disagreement and argument.

8 If you _____ something—for example, money—you share it out in a different way from the way it was shared before; this is often done to give people a more equal share.

9 A/An _____ is a statement expressing the opinion that something is incorrect.

10 If your opinion is _____, it is based on your own personal evaluation rather than on any external measures. The opposite is *objective*.

Can Money Buy Happiness? An Examination of Happiness Economics

By Tim Mak

Does more money make one happier? A whole field of economics, known as "happiness economics," exists to answer this very question, both on the international level (are 5 richer countries happier than poorer countries?) and the intra-national level (are richer individuals happier than poorer individuals within a given country?).

The answer to this question has serious 10 **implications** for policy makers. If higher standards of living—often measured by average income (GDP)—increase happiness, then any government concerned with the happiness of its citizens should focus on 15 policies that boost the growth of the economy as a whole.

If, as some happiness economists argue, the crucial determinant to happiness is not our absolute income per se, but our income 20 *relative* to others around us, then this suggests the focus should be on **redistributing** wealth and making society more equitable.

The academic literature is—like many topics in the social sciences—**contentious**, 25 but growing evidence supports the GDP notion. Although earlier research suggested that average income had no substantial effect on happiness, more recent research seems to indicate that increasing absolute 30 income does, in fact, buy greater happiness. Such studies also show that there is a strong—perhaps direct—relationship between economic policies and institutions (e.g., economic freedom) that increase 35 average income as well as happiness.

The Easterlin Paradox
Arguably, happiness economics as a field began with the 1974 publication of

University of Southern California Professor Richard Easterlin's **seminal** paper, *Does Economic Growth Improve the Human Lot? Some Empirical Evidence*. Easterlin's paper reaches some fascinating conclusions that prompt inquiries in happiness economics to this day. Within each of the nineteen countries examined, Easterlin finds that individuals with higher incomes report being more happy than those with lower incomes (1974). This makes **intuitive** sense: the richer individuals are, the more they can fulfil their desires, and thus the happier they are.

Paradoxically, however, Easterlin finds also that, as a whole, richer countries do not appear to be happier than poorer countries. In particular, he points out that despite the growth of the American economy between 1946 and 1970, overall happiness had not increased during that period.

What does this mean? Easterlin interprets his results to indicate that it is not absolute income that makes one happy, but one's income in relation to those around him/her (1974).

In other words, if everyone in society made $1,000 more this year than they did last year, under these findings, happiness would not increase because everyone's relative position would remain the same. Individuals would be happier, though, if their income rose while the income of their neighbours did not, thus putting them in a better position in comparison. Although less intuitive, this could make sense: if our expectations depend on the expectations of those around us, then absolute increases in income do not increase our happiness unless our relative income increases as well.

So what are the policy implications of Easterlin's conclusions? Economists who favour this view suggest that if the absolute income of a country is not what makes people happy—and relative income is—then it is incumbent upon the government to promote a more equitable income distribution and to implement a more European-style, socially democratic state (Wilkinson, 2007).

Indeed, this view has traditionally been widely accepted among happiness economists. For instance, *Economist* writer Will Wilkinson noted "that happiness research [which] supports the policies of a more thoroughgoing egalitarian **welfare state** ... appears to have become a sort of conventional wisdom among those who study happiness" in a Cato Institute paper examining the issue (2007:2). However, more recent research with broader data sets now questions Easterlin's findings.

Money does buy happiness

In the 1990s, economists started to revisit and reassess the claims made in Easterlin's paper. Economist Ruut Veenhoven, a professor emeritus[1] at Erasmus University in the Netherlands, wrote papers in 1989 and 1991 concluding that increased GDP per capita **correlates** with greater levels of happiness.

By the time Veenhoven revisited the issue again in a paper with Dr. Michael Hagerty of the University of California, Davis in 2003, a whole host of literature had asserted a relationship between happiness and the absolute income per capita for forty countries, in direct refutation of Easterlin's original study exploring nineteen countries. It found also that, contrary to Easterlin's original findings, happiness in the United States had risen with per capita GDP from 1972 to 1994 (Veenhoven and Hagerty, 2003). The pair do not explain why their results are different from Easterlin's, but their differing methodologies and the different time periods studied probably played a part in their various outcomes.

[1] A *professor emeritus* is a professor who has retired from university teaching.

125 "The results show that increasing national income [GDP per capita] does go with increasing national happiness ... contrary to strict relative utility models," write Veenhoven and Hagerty (2003:2) Among
130 other criticisms, Veenhoven and Hagerty claim that Easterlin made the mistake of only examining middle- and high-income countries, and that including poor countries showed positive correlations between GDP
135 and happiness. It is in poor countries where increasing the average income had the greatest positive effect on happiness.

This is an important revelation, that although absolute GDP growth seems to
140 increase happiness, there is a diminishing marginal return. In other words, increasing GDP among higher-income countries boosted happiness less than increasing the GDP of lower-income countries by the same
145 amount.

The concept of a diminishing marginal return can be illustrated as follows: the more money one has, the less happiness one additional dollar—the marginal
150 dollar—will provide. A destitute man would clamour for a dropped dollar, while a billionaire might not think twice about it. In the same way, an increase of $10 billion for a rich country (assuming same population)
155 may lead to paltry increases of happiness compared to that same increase for an extremely poor country.

Perhaps the most ambitious study on the relationship between average income
160 and happiness, and the most compelling **rebuke** of Easterlin's claims, comes from a 131-country examination of life satisfaction and GDP per capita, written by Betsey Stevenson and Justin Wolfers of the
165 University of Pennsylvania. According to the authors:

Using recent data on a broader array of countries, we establish a clear

170 positive link between average levels of **subjective** well-being [a measure of happiness] and GDP per capita across countries, and find no evidence of a satiation point beyond which
175 wealthier countries have no further increases in subjective well-being (2008:1).

These new and improved works have their own implications: if a growth in the average income increases happiness, then any
180 government hoping to maximize well-being and life satisfaction should promote policies which drive economic growth, rather than focusing merely on the pursuit of income redistribution measures and welfare state
185 programs—in fact income redistribution measures have been shown to have little effect on happiness (Ouweneel, 2002).

Since increasing per capita income increases happiness, then it follows that
190 employing policies and institutions which promote per capita income growth will increase happiness.

Economic freedom makes us happier!

195 There is evidence to show that greater levels of economic freedom—a smaller government, fewer regulations and lower taxes—result in more robust economic growth (Gwartney et al., 2010). This would
200 suggest, based on the case outlined above for GDP growth as a driver of happiness, which freedom would indirectly lead to greater personal satisfaction.

Recent studies suggest that economic
205 freedom may also have a direct and positive effect on happiness. In fact, studies have shown that economic freedom correlates with happiness almost as much as any other factor (Veenhoven, 2005). In fact, the
210 broadest study of the relationship between the two factors show that economic freedom was four times more important than GDP

per capita in directly determining happiness (Ovaska and Takashima, 2006).

215 According to the economists who wrote the study, the positive relationship between economic freedom and happiness may be due to the satisfaction we derive from being able to make our own choices and embrace
220 the opportunities that we desire:

> The results suggest that people unmistakably care about the degree to which the society in which they live provides them opportunities and the
225 freedom to undertake new projects and make choices based on one's personal preferences (Ovaska and Taka-shima, 2006: 210).

Conclusion

230 Although older studies have suggested that relative, rather than absolute, income in a society is the key driver of happiness, more recent work has disputed this by suggesting that absolute growth in income boosts
235 happiness. This, along with increasing evidence that greater economic freedom increases the contentment of individuals, suggests that policymakers who wish to increase overall happiness should focus on
240 economic policies and institutions that boost increases in average income, rather than wealth redistribution.

References

Easterlin, Richard (1974). *Does Economic Growth Improve the Human Lot? Some Empirical Evidence*. In Nations and Households in Economic Growth: Essays in Honor of Moses Abramovitz, Paul A. David and Melvin W. Reder (eds.). Academic Press Inc.

Gwartney, James, Joshua Hall, Robert Lawson et al. (2010). *Economic Freedom of the World: 2010 Annual Report*. The Fraser Institute.

Hagerty, Michael, and Ruut Veerhoven (2003). Wealth And Happiness Revisited – Growing Wealth Of Nations Does Go With Greater Happiness. *Social Indicators Research* 64:2.

Ouweneel, Piet (2002). Social Security and Well-Being of the Unemployed in 42 Nations. *Journal of Happiness Research* 3.

Ovaska, Tomi, and Ryo Takashima (2006). Economic Policy and the Level of Self-Perceived Well-Being: An International Comparison. *Journal of Socio-Economics* 35.

Stevenson, Betsey, and Justin Wolfers (2008). *Economic Growth and Subjective Well-Being: Reassessing the Easterlin Paradox*. Brookings Papers on Economic Activity (Spring).

Veenhoven, Ruut (2005). Apparent Quality-of-Life In Nations: How Long and Happy People Live. *Social Indicators Research* 71.

Wilkinson, Will (2007). In Pursuit of Happiness Research: Is It Reliable? What Does It Imply For Policy? *Cato Policy Analysis:* 590.

1428 words (excluding references)

Mak, T. (2011, Spring). Can money buy happiness? An examination of happiness economics. *Canadian Student Review, the Fraser Institute*. Retrieved from http://www.fraserinstitute.org/uploadedFiles/fraser-ca/Content/research-news/research/articles/can-money-buy-you-happiness.pdf

Check Your Understanding

A. Answer the following questions in your own words using information from the reading.

1 What is "happiness economics"? What do happiness economists study?

_____

_____

2 What is the difference between *absolute* income and *relative* income?

_____

_____

3 Are the following statements true (T) or false (F) according to Easterlin?

	T	F
a) Richer individuals are happier than poorer individuals.	○	○
b) Richer countries are happier than poorer countries.	○	○
c) Increased economic growth leads to increased happiness.	○	○

Why are Easterlin's findings paradoxical?

_____

_____

4 How did results from the following researchers compare to Easterlin's conclusions?

a) Veenhoven and Hagerty, 2003

b) Stevenson and Wolfers, 2008

_____

_____

5 Outline the implications of this research for the economic policy of a country:

a) If governments believe *absolute* income is more important, what should be the goal of their economic policy?

b) If governments believe *relative* income is more important, what should they do instead?

_____

_____

_____

6 What is meant by economic freedom? What is the connection between economic freedom and

a) economic growth?

b) happiness?

_____

_____

_____

_____

B. Using your answers from Part A, summarize the author's answer to the question, "Can money buy happiness?"

_____

_____

_____

_____

_____

_____

Analysis and Discussion

Discuss the following questions with your group.

1. Consider other things you have read or heard about on this topic. Which of these statements is supported by your previous reading?

    a) Richer individuals are happier than those with less money.

    b) The most important thing is your wealth relative to the wealth of others.

2. In your own words, explain what is meant by "diminishing marginal return." Can you think of examples you have heard about?

3. Why do you think different studies on this topic have yielded such contradictory results? What factors might account for these differences?

4. Think about the country where you grew up.

    a) What connections can you make between this country and the article you have just read?

    b) Would citizens of your country agree with the sentiments expressed in this article? Why, or why not?

5. To what extent should governments make economic policies based on results of this kind of research?

6. Based on the information in this article, what recommendation(s) would you personally make

    a) to the government of your country?

    b) to people who you know (friends, family)?

Denmark Is Considered the Happiest Country. You'll Never Guess Why.

 As you read about the world's happiest country, think about how the information provided either supports or refutes the arguments made in Reading 1.

Before You Read

Work in groups of three or four. Discuss the following questions.

1. Think about the country of Denmark. Where is it? What do you know about it?

2. The title of this reading suggests that it is hard to guess why Denmark might be the world's happiest country. Can you predict what the reason(s) might be?

3. Is it realistic to measure the happiness of various countries? What factors do you think should be considered when trying to do so?

Key Vocabulary

Complete each sentence with the best ending to show the meaning of the word in **bold**.

1 (line 9) An organization that shows signs of **corruption**

a) has members who are honest and trustworthy.

b) has members who are dishonest and cannot be trusted.

2 (line 11) Someone known for his or her **generosity**

a) gives freely to others.

b) keeps things to him/herself and does not share.

3 (line 26) A **recipient** of money, an award or a service

a) receives the item.

b) gives the item to someone.

4 (line 36) If someone acts as your **advocate**, he or she

a) supports you and acts on your behalf.

b) is opposed to you and acts as your adversary.

5 (line 43) If you are **uninsured** for medical care and you have an accident,

a) you don't need to pay extra for your medical care.

b) you have to pay your own medical bills.

6 (line 48) When a policy is **prioritized**,

a) it is considered more important than others.

b) it is considered less important than others.

7 (line 53) When two people or things have **parity**,

a) they are equal.

b) they are unequal.

8 (line 67) If you **commute** to work, you

a) work from home on your computer.

b) travel from your home to your workplace.

9 (line 84) Something that **mitigates** a harmful situation

a) reduces the negative effects of the situation.

b) increases the negative effects of the situation.

10 (line 94) **Voluntary** work is work that

a) you get paid for doing.

b) you do not get paid for doing.

Denmark Is Considered the Happiest Country. You'll Never Guess Why.

Last month,[1] Denmark was crowned the happiest country in the world.

"The top countries generally rank higher in all six of the key factors identified in the World Happiness Report," wrote University of British Columbia economics professor John Helliwell, one of the report's contributing authors. "Together, these six factors
5 explain three quarters of differences in life evaluations across hundreds of countries and over the years."

The six factors for a happy nation split evenly between concerns on a government- and on a human-scale. The happiest countries have in common a large GDP per capita, healthy life expectancy at birth and a lack of corruption in leadership. But also essential
10 were three things over which individual citizens have a bit more control over: A sense of social support, freedom to make life choices and a culture of generosity.

"There is now a rising worldwide demand that policy be more closely aligned with what really matters to people as they themselves characterize their well-being," economist Jeffrey Sachs said in a statement at the time of the report's release.

15 But why Denmark over any of the other wealthy, democratic countries with small, educated populations? And can the qualities that make this Nordic country the happiest around apply to other cultures across the globe? Here are a few things Danes do well that any of us can lobby for:

Denmark supports parents
20 While American women scrape by with an average maternal leave of 10.3 weeks, Danish families receive a total of fifty-two weeks of parental leave. Mothers are able to take eighteen weeks and fathers receive their own dedicated two weeks at up to 100 percent salary. The rest of the paid time off is up to the family to use as they see fit.

But the support doesn't stop at the end of this time. Danish children have access to
25 free or low-cost child care. And early childhood education is associated with health and well-being throughout life for its recipients—as well as for mothers. What's more, this frees up young mothers to return to the workforce if they'd like to. The result? In Denmark, 79 percent of mothers return to their previous level of employment, compared to 59 percent of American women. These resources mean that women contribute 34 to
30 38 percent of income in Danish households with children, compared to American women, who contribute 28 percent of income.

Health care is a civil right—and a source of social support
Danish citizens expect and receive health care as a basic right. But what's more, they know how to effectively use their health systems. Danish people are in touch with their
35 primary care physician an average of nearly seven times per year, according to a 2012 survey of family medicine in the country. And that means they have a single advocate who helps them navigate more complicated care.

→

---
[1] This reading is based on a study carried out between 2010 and 2012 and published in 2013.

"This gatekeeping system essentially is designed to support the principle that treatment ought to take place at the lowest effective care level along with the idea of continuity of
40 care provided by a family doctor," wrote the authors of the family medicine survey.

By contrast, Americans seek medical care an average of fewer than four times per year and they don't just visit their general practitioner—this figure includes emergency room visits, where many uninsured Americans must access doctors. This diversity of resources means that many
45 Americans don't have continuity of care—not a single medical professional advocating for them and putting together a comprehensive medical history.

Gender equality is prioritized

It isn't just parents who can expect balanced gender norms.
50 Denmark regularly ranks among the top ten countries in a World Economic Forum's yearly report that measures gender equality. While no country in the world has yet achieved gender parity, Denmark and other Nordic countries are coming close. That is in no small part because of the
55 strong presence of women in leadership positions. Reported the World Economic Forum:

> The Nordic countries were also early starters in providing women with the right to vote (Sweden in 1919, Norway in 1913, Iceland and Denmark in 1915, Finland in 1906). In Denmark, Sweden and Norway, political parties introduced
> 60 voluntary gender quotas in the 1970s, resulting in high numbers of female political representatives over the years. In Denmark, in fact, this quota has since been abandoned as no further stimulus is required.

Indeed, the country currently has its first female prime minister, Helle Thorning-Schmidt (although she has been leader of the Social Democrat party since 2005).

65 Biking is the norm

In Denmark's most populated and largest city, Copenhagen, bikes account for 50 percent of its residents' trips to school or work. *Half.* Half of commuting happens on a bike in Copenhagen, and that doesn't just improve fitness levels and reduce carbon emissions, it also contributes to the wealth of the city, reported *Forbes*:

> 70 Researchers found that for every kilometer travelled by bike instead of by car, taxpayers saved 7.8 cents (DKK 0.45) in avoided air pollution, accidents, congestion, noise and wear and tear on infrastructure. Cyclists in Copenhagen cover an estimated 1.2 million kilometers each day—saving the city a little over $34 million each year.

75 What's more, just thirty minutes of daily biking adds an average of one to two years to the life expectancy of Copenhagen's cyclists.

Danish culture puts a positive spin on its harsh environment

Here's how Danish people turn lemons into spiced mulled wine: Ever heard of the concept of *hygge*? While some would define it as cultivated coziness, hygge is often

80 considered the major weapon in combatting the dreary darkness that befalls the Nordic country over the winter. In a place where the sun shines fewer than seven hours during the height of the winter solstice—a level of darkness that can (and does) stir depression and sad feelings—the concept of a cozy scene, full of love and indulgence, can help to mitigate some of the season's worst psychological effects.

85 After all, both strong social connections and many of the indulgent foods associated with hygge—such as chocolate, coffee and wine—are mood boosters.

Danes feel a responsibility to one another

Danes don't prioritize social security and safety simply so they can *receive* benefits; there's a real sense of collective responsibility and belonging. And this civic duty—
90 combined with the economic security and work-life balance to support it—results in a high rate of volunteerism. According to a government exploration of Danish "responsibility":

> Denmark is a society where citizens participate and contribute to making society
> work. More than 40 percent of all Danes do voluntary work in cultural and
95 > sports associations, NGOs, social organizations, political organizations, etc.
> There is a wealth of associations: in 2006, there were 101,000 Danish
> organizations—worth noting in a population of just 5.5 million.

The economic value of this unpaid work is DKK 35.3 billion. Combined with the value growth from the non-profit sector, public subsidies and membership fees, the total
100 economic impact of the sector represents 9.6 percent of the Danish GDP.

But that sense of stewardship isn't just extra-governmental: Danes also take pride in their involvement with the democratic process. During the last election in September 2011, for example, 87.7 percent of the country voted. It's not surprising, given these statistics, that the University of Zurich and the Social Science Research Center Berlin
105 have given Denmark the very highest rating for democracy among thirty established democracies.

(1236 words)

Denmark is considered the happiest country. You'll never guess why. (2013, Oct 22, updated Nov. 6). *The Huffington Post*. Retrieved from http://www.huffingtonpost.com/2013/10/22/denmark-happiest-country_n_4070761.html.

Check Your Understanding

A. What are the six key factors identified in the World Happiness Report?

1 _____

2 _____

3 _____

4 _____

5 _____

6 _____

B. Which of the following statements are true about Denmark? Check the correct statements.

1 ____ Parents of newborn children are entitled to up to a year's leave from their jobs.

2 ____ Daycare is not a large expense for Danish families with children.

3 ____ Danish citizens rarely visit the doctor or a hospital.

4 ____ Health care is more accessible in Denmark than in the United States.

5 ____ Danish women make the same salaries as Danish men.

6 ____ It is unusual to see female politicians in Denmark.

7 ____ Most Danish workers and students drive cars to work or school.

8 ____ Danish residents are usually sad and depressed in the long, cold winter.

9 ____ There is a strong sense of responsibility to each other among the Danes.

10 ____ Most Danes vote in democratic elections.

Analysis and Discussion

Discuss the following questions with your group.

1 Look again at the factors used in the 2013 study to measure happiness. Are these factors well chosen? Are there any factors you might have added?

2 The ten happiest countries, according to this study, are as follows:

1. Denmark	6. Canada
2. Norway	7. Finland
3. Switzerland	8. Austria
4. Netherlands	9. Iceland
5. Sweden	10. Australia

a) What do these countries have in common?

b) Which of their common features do you think are related to happiness?

3 A 2012 ranking of GDP around the world lists the top ten countries as follows:

1. USA	6. United Kingdom
2. China	7. Brazil
3. Japan	8. Russian Federation
4. Germany	9. Italy
5. France	10. India

a) Why do you think none of these countries appears in the top ten on the happiness list?

b) Denmark places 34th on this list. What does this suggest about theories relating happiness to GDP?

c) How do you think a happiness economist would react to this information?

4 Easterlin's early research into happiness economics suggested that it is not absolute income (i.e., how much money one makes) that determines happiness; instead, it is relative income (i.e., one's income in relation to others).

a) Based on what you have read, do you think Denmark has an equitable distribution of wealth, or does it have a large gap between the richest and poorest members of society?

b) Does the case of Denmark support the notion of absolute income as a predictor of happiness, or does it support the idea that relative income is more important?

5 Denmark has a very high personal income tax rate of 55.6 percent. Other Scandinavian countries also have very high taxes.

a) What do research findings cited in Reading 1 say about the relationship between economic freedom, economic growth and personal happiness?

b) Does the case of Denmark support or refute this?

c) Why do you think people in Denmark are happy despite paying very high taxes?

6 Here are some more facts about Denmark:

> Denmark has a literacy rate of 99 percent.

> Denmark ranks 26th of 194 countries in alcohol consumption. This is somewhat higher than Canada and the USA and significantly higher than China and Japan.

> Denmark has one of the highest divorce rates in Europe, with 46 percent of marriages ending in divorce.

> Denmark is not a religious country; according to one poll, only 28 percent of the population reported that they believed in God.

> Denmark's crime rate is lower than the European average, the OECD average and the G7 average.

a) Which of these facts do you think are related to happiness?

b) Do any of them surprise you?

c) How do you think happiness economists could use this information?

7 What light is shed on the subject of happiness economics by the naming of Denmark as the world's happiest country? Can other countries learn anything from the example of Denmark?

Is Bhutan the Happiest Place in the World?

The Himalayan nation of Bhutan has a unique way of measuring success.

 How does Bhutan's concept of Gross National Happiness compare with other forms of measuring national success?

Before You Read

Work in groups of three or four. Discuss the following questions.

1 Where is Bhutan? What do you know about this country?

2 Do you think Bhutan has a high or low GDP? Why?

3 Do you expect people in Bhutan to be generally happy or unhappy? Why? What might contribute to their happiness, or to their *lack* of happiness?

Is Bhutan the Happiest Place in the World?

By Andrew Buncombe

Within a stone's throw of Bhutan's legendary Tiger's Nest, with lungs burning and heart pounding, misery descends. Smug, grinning hikers are making their way along the narrow, vertiginous path as they return from the monastery set on the side of the cliff, but with vertigo having turned legs and spirit to mush, it appears I am going nowhere.

5   A little while later, with the encouragement of a patient partner and the hand-holding of the tour guide, we are across the gap, beguiled by the majesty of the monastery's location and stunned by the ambition of its architect. I start to feel content, even happy. And then comes the realization: we have to make it back the very same way.

   It is hard not to think about happiness in Bhutan, a Buddhist kingdom set high in the
10 Himalayas between India and China. As the country has gradually opened itself to the West and its tourists' dollars, so it has projected and exported its philosophy of "gross national happiness" (GNH), a belief that a society should be measured not simply by its material indicators but by the health, education and the contentedness of its people. Such is the pervasiveness of the idea that last year, the UN adopted a non-binding
15 resolution that "happiness" should be included among development indicators. The notion sounds fantastic—genuinely radical, even—but is it anything more than a clever piece of global marketing by the Bhutanese, looking to secure their own unique brand amid the multitude of nations?

   "It sounds like a fairytale, but for Bhutan it has not been so. A young king saw the
20 world and saw it for what it was," said Thakur Powdyel, the country's education minister

and one of its most elegant exponents of GNH. "He saw that while the world had achieved economic progress, there were huge gaps and deficiencies. As young as he was, he felt that the ultimate goal of life was to be happy."

On the day I arrived in Bhutan, a high-octane adrenaline flight that weaves its way
25 past stunning mountains, a front-page story in the state-run *Kuensel* newspaper claimed a survey had revealed people from the Haa district in the west of the country were apparently the happiest. By contrast, those from Pemagatshel in the east were the least content. At dinner that evening in the capital, Thimpu, I asked the waitress, Dorji Mo, a cheerful young woman whose family came from Pemagatshel, why that may be so.
30 "It takes three days to reach my grandparents' village. I have to walk across ten rivers," said the nineteen-year-old. "And in the village, there is still no electricity."

One thing that rapidly becomes apparent when you arrive in the country is that it is no Shangri-La,[1] despite the claims of some tourism agencies. People are friendly, but no more so than anywhere else in the region; there is poverty, especially in the rural
35 areas, and in a nation where television arrived only in the late 1990s, there are enduring concerns about the dilution of traditional culture.

This young democracy—the country was an absolute monarchy until four years ago—is confronting a series of challenges, perhaps most pertinently providing meaningful jobs for its young people. Increasing urbanization and a shift away from
40 farming, means there are growing numbers of young adults who do not want to take on work at their family's farm. There are social problems, too; drug abuse and rowdy gangs. Recently, in an unprecedented incident, two police officers in the capital were beaten by a group of youths. Last month, four young men were stabbed in two separate attacks. "What is happening in our GNH nation?" asked one poster on a Facebook page
45 run by social activists.

The idea of gross national happiness was developed by Bhutan's previous monarch, the fourth king, Jigme Singye Wangchuck. Returning from a conference of non-aligned nations in Havana, where he reportedly developed a liking for Cuban cigars, the king's plane stopped in India where a reporter asked the monarch about the
50 economy of the mysterious Himalayan nation. "In Bhutan, we don't just care about gross national product, we care about gross national happiness," the king is said to have retorted.

Three decades on, the philosophy has been expanded into a guiding principle based on four central pillars—equitable social development, cultural preservation, conservation
55 of the environment and promotion of good governance—with up to seventy-two smaller "indices." A GNH commission oversees all government decisions and approves or blocks them depending on whether they fit with these aims. I was told that the commission often steps in and puts a stop to proposals, among them a spa project in the remote town of Gasa that the king had reportedly supported but which local people did not.

60 The grass certainly grows green in Bhutan. There is free health care and free education, and since 1980 life expectancy has increased by twenty years and per capita income →

---

[1] Shangri-La is a mythical country in which everyone is happy. The name comes from the novel *Lost Horizon*, by James Hilton (1933), which is set in an imaginary Himalayan paradise.

by 450 percent. Today, in terms of life expectancy, the amount of education received and income, Bhutan ranks above the average for South Asia. "Bhutan has good results to show for its development over the past thirty years," said Mark LaPrairie, the World
65 Bank's representative.

But as with anywhere, the grass grows more greenly elsewhere, especially when viewed through the prism of the young people who hang out around the handful of streets that make up the centre of Thimpu. One evening, in a bar where a man dressed

in traditional Bhutanese clothes was engaged in a
70 keenly contested game of pool with a friend wearing jeans, and where locals rejected the locally-brewed wheat beer in favour of a drink named in Australia and manufactured in India, a young man told me about the time he had spent in the city of
75 Bangalore.

He had worked in a fast-food outlet in the southern, IT-focused city and enjoyed the people he met. The experience in India had left him satisfied, sated. "Now, whatever happens, I can say
80 I have done that," he said.

The following evening I heard similar wanderlust[2] among the young Bhutanese. Pointed in the direction of a basement karaoke bar that purportedly served as the hub of the city's nightlife, I encountered dozens of youngsters
85 throwing themselves into song and dance routines to a rather disjointed playlist that included Western R&B and traditional Bhutanese songs. The young men wore Western clothes, including baseball caps and bandanas covering their faces, while the young women were sheathed in traditional silk.

Afterwards, in the street outside, one of a group of intoxicated young men stopped
90 me to ask where I was from. "I want to go to the US or the UK, to your country," said the man, who worked in a clothes store. "But I can't. I did not stay in school long enough." I couldn't judge whether the man was happy, sad, or—like many of us—a man whose mood was open to change.

The authorities in Bhutan have received widespread attention for their idea. Delegates
95 and envoys regularly make their way to the nation of 700,000 people to see whether the philosophy of GNH can be borrowed or adapted, and no more so than since the 2007 economic crash. Later this year, a large Bhutanese delegation will take part in a conference on happiness in New York, where Jeffrey Sachs and Joseph Stiglitz[3] will be among the guests. In a sense, Bhutan has become associated with happiness in the
100 same way that the Maldives has entwined itself with the issue of catastrophic climate change.

---

[2] *Wanderlust* is a German word which literally means "desire to travel." The word is widely used in English, as there is no equivalent English word.

[3] Jeffrey Sachs and Joseph Stiglitz are both influential American economists. Sachs is at Harvard University; Stiglitz is at Columbia University.

One evening at dinner, I eavesdropped as a group of Americans from an NGO[4] held an earnest conversation with a Bhutanese politician about their astonishing experiences in the country's rural heartland. One woman said that for the first time in her life she had been content not to be able to constantly check her BlackBerry. In turn, the politician told them of his experience in the US, where he had bought a McDonald's "Happy Meal." The food had been fine, he said, but his children had fought over the free toy.

So do the authorities in Bhutan believe they have built a happier world, a system that is worthy of all this international attention? The matter is currently the subject of intense examination by the Centre for Bhutan Studies, which has been assessing contentment indicators since 2005 to develop a GNH index.

Last year a survey containing more than 750 questions was given out to 8,000 respondents, who took up to three hours to complete it. It asked questions not just about their economic well-being but about their local community, their interaction with their neighbours, their participation in cultural events as well as their psychological well-being.

Tshokey Zangmo, a senior researcher, is currently writing up the results of the survey, but she said variations around the country were actually low. (The front-page story in *Kuensel* had apparently been based purely on the results of question number 12 which asked whether an individual considered themselves to be happy.) "If you look at the GNH index, the differences are very low," said Ms. Zangmo.

It may be that the West has misunderstood the issue of GNH. One evening, in a café located inside a newly built and largely empty shopping mall, I had coffee with Dorji Wangchuk, a senior aide to the current king, Khesar Namgyel Wangchuck.

"It's not just about happiness as it is understood in the West," he explained, saying that a more accurate translation of the king's original concept might be "gross national contentment." "Bhutanese people are generally content. In the Buddhist tradition, wherever you are in this life is because of your previous life. Contentment leads to happiness."

Senior officials readily admit the experiment in trying to create a fairer, more humane society is far from complete. But a number of observers of Bhutan take heart from the fact that such a conversation is even taking place.

Francoise Pommaret is a French historian and anthropologist who has lived in Bhutan since 1981. When she arrived, Thimpu contained just 15,000 people, there were no telephones and mail took three weeks to arrive. "I think the concept is genius; it's the only alternative to the madcap development we have in the West," she said, over lunch in a smart Thimpu café. "But that does not mean everyone is happy, we are not Shangri-La. But we are trying to make a better country."

(1746 words)

---

[4] An NGO is a non-governmental organization, often a non-profit group, dedicated to promoting a particular cause.

Buncombe, A. (2012, Jan. 14). Is Bhutan the happiest place in the world? *The Independent.* Retrieved from http://www.independent.co.uk/life-style/health-and-families/healthy-living/is-bhutan-the-happiest-place-in-the-world-6288053.html.

Check Your Understanding

A. Are the following statements true (T) or false (F)?

                                                                          T   **F**

1. Bhutan is a small mountainous country in Africa.   ○ ○

2. The infrastructure in Bhutan is not yet fully developed.   ○ ○

3. Bhutan has full employment among its young people.   ○ ○

4. Bhutan may be losing some of its customs and traditions.   ○ ○

5. The king of Bhutan has absolute power.   ○ ○

B. Answer the following questions in your own words using information from the reading.

1. How does GNH (Gross National Happiness) differ from GNP (Gross National Product)?

   _____

   _____

2. How is GNH measured?

   _____

   _____

3. Who first coined the term Gross National Happiness?

   _____

   _____

4. What are the four central pillars of GNH?

   _____

   _____

5. What kind of attention has the concept of GNH received outside Bhutan?

   _____

   _____

C. Which of the following inferences does the author make? Check all that apply.

○ a) Bhutan is not a wealthy country.

○ b) The young people of Bhutan are generally happy with their lives.

○ c) The concept of GNH is responsible for Bhutan's rapid development.

○ d) There is a strong religious component to GNH.

○ e) The concept of GNH is more important to members of the government than to ordinary Bhutanese citizens.

Key Vocabulary

Find a word or expression in the text that means the same as each of the words and expressions below.

1 situation of being found everywhere
(para. 3, lines 9 to 18)   _____

2 obvious, easily seen (para. 6, lines 34 to 41)   _____

3 weakening as a result of something added
(para. 6, lines 34 to 41)   _____

4 movement of people to towns and cities
(para. 7, lines 42 to 50)   _____

5 politically neutral (para. 8, lines 46 to 53)   _____

6 things seem better somewhere else
(para. 11, lines 66 to 75)   _____

7 group of representatives (para. 15, lines 94 to 101)   _____

8 with terrible results (para. 15, lines 94 to 101)   _____

9 serious, detailed and time-consuming
(para. 17, lines 109 to 112)   _____

10 feeling of satisfaction with your life
(para. 21, lines 126 to 130)   _____

Analysis and Discussion

Discuss the following questions with your group.

1 How would you describe the author's reaction to his experiences in Bhutan?

a) He noticed that everyone seemed so happy and friendly. He was impressed by the results of Bhutan's emphasis on GNH.

b) He recognized that Bhutan had some of the same problems found anywhere. He was skeptical about whether GNH really made a difference.

2 What is your opinion about the four pillars of GNH? Are there any other factors that could be added to this list?

3 What do the research results being described by Tshokey Zangmo say about regional differences in GNH? How do these results compare to the findings of the happiness economists described in Reading 1? Which theory does Zangmo's results support?

4 It could be said that Bhutan has focused on happiness at the expense of investment in roads, electricity and other necessary improvements to the country's infrastructure. How do you think a member of the Bhutanese government would respond to this?

5 Dorji Wangchuk says, "Bhutanese people are generally content. In the Buddhist tradition, wherever you are in this life is because of your previous life. Contentment leads to happiness." What do you think is the role of religion in the pursuit of happiness? Do you think people in countries with a strong religious tradition are generally happier in countries where religion is less important? Why, or why not?

6 Have the Bhutanese formulated a new approach to measuring success? What, if anything, could world governments and economists learn from Bhutan's approach to national success?

Going Further
Focus on Language

A. The following chart contains ten words from the readings. Complete the chart with related words in the other categories and, where possible, in the same category. (There may not be a word for each category.)

	NOUN	VERB	ADJECTIVE	ADVERB
1				apparently
2		confront		
3			democratic	
4	equality			
5			global	
6	implication			
7			intense	
8			marginal	
9			original	
10			reliable	

B. In Reading 1 the phrase *per capita* is used several times, for example, in the sentence "Perhaps the most ambitious study on the relationship between average income and happiness ... comes from a 131-country examination of life satisfaction and GDP per capita ..." (lines 158 to 163). What do you think *per capita* means in this sentence?

The phrase *per capita* comes from Latin. Some other Latin phrases in use in English today are listed below. You may well come across these in your reading. Use your dictionary to find out what each of the following means.

PHRASE	MEANING
ad hoc	
ad nauseam	
bona fide	
curriculum vitae	
de facto	
per se	
status quo	
vice versa	

Consider the following questions.

> In what situations might you hear Latin phrases used in English?

> Why do you think these phrases are still in use today?

Note

The common abbreviations *e.g.* and *i.e.* also come from Latin:
> *e.g.* is short for *exempli gratia*, meaning "for example." It tells the reader that an *example* follows.
> *i.e.* is short for *id est*, meaning "that is." It tells the reader that an *explanation* is coming.

Independent Research

Choose a country that you know well; this could be the country where you grew up, or a country you have visited. Carry out some Internet research about that country. Find out the following information:

> The country's per capita GDP

> The country's wealth distribution

> The country's life expectancy

> The country's literacy rate

> The country's infant mortality rate

Now decide to what extent you think the people of this country are happy. If they are very happy, where does this happiness come from? If they are less happy, what could be changed to increase the GNH of the citizens of the country? You will present your findings to the class.

Synthesis and Written Response

Based on your reading of the three texts above as well as your own independent research into economics, development and happiness, write a short response to the following question:

> What is the relationship between the wealth of a country, its economic policies and the happiness of its citizens?

You may, if you wish, refer to one specific country in your response.

REVIEW
of the chapter ...

> Answer the following questions.

    1 Why is it important to consider the context in which a text was written?

    2 If you come across a text that seems to contradict everything else you have read on a topic, what are some questions you can ask yourself about the text?

Social Networks: A Magic Number?

FOCUS THE TEXT IN CONTEXT 2

How does the text compare with your own experiences and opinions?

In this chapter

YOU WILL LEARN ...

> why it is important to ask yourself whether the text supports your own experiences; and

> why it can be hard to do this.

Warm-up

Discuss the following questions with your group.

> Which of these are important in a friend? Choose all that apply and explain why each one is important.

○ common interests

○ a similar age

○ the same cultural background

○ shared beliefs and values

○ the same job

○ living near each other

○ a similar socioeconomic status

○ other: _____

> How is a friend different from an acquaintance, a colleague or a classmate? How do you know when someone has become a friend?

> In what way(s) has the Internet changed the nature of socializing? Do you think these changes are positive or negative?

Your Connection to the Text

> What is the value of social networks?

Imagine you have been given this essay topic in a course entitled *Introduction to Social Anthropology*. This topic, as with many in the social sciences, may well be something you have personal experience with. Don't discount your own experiences with the topic; these form part of the reading process.

The Writer, the Reader and the Text

Think of the reading process as a triangle: writer, reader and text. As the reader, you are the third component of the triangle, and it is important that you bring your own personal experiences and opinions to the text. Ask yourself questions like these:

> Does this text match my own experiences with this topic?

> If so, how does the text contribute to my understanding of the topic? What can I learn from it?

> If not, where are the differences?

> What might cause any differences? Here, you can come back to some of the questions asked in earlier chapters. Is the text current, or is it dated? Is the author qualified to write on this topic? Is the author biased and/or promoting a personal agenda? Is the information presented based on empirical research, or has the author used anecdotes found in some other—possibly unreliable—source?

Here are some examples:

> You read an article in a magazine about gender roles in a specific country. You happen to know this country very well, and you know the information presented is at least ten years out of date. Ask yourself where the author got this information from—empirical research or secondary sources? Don't be afraid to discount the information if you know it to be inaccurate.

> You are writing a paper about marriage customs in the part of the world where you grew up. You come across a journal article on this topic. While the author has done some empirical research, you feel that the information presented is not representative of all sectors of society and that the situation is more complex than it appears. Don't be afraid to point this out if you use the article in your paper.

Why is it hard to bring your own background to a text?

It may initially be hard to bring your own experiences to a text. You may well have grown up in a part of the world where students are not expected to critique a text written by someone older, better educated or more experienced. You may find yourself thinking, "I don't think this is true, but it would be impolite or disrespectful to say this."

Dutch researcher Geert Hofstede (see Chapter 6, Reading 3) calls this "power distance." In cultures with high power distance, students are not expected or encouraged to question what is taught or what they read. In low power-distance cultures (including Canada, the US, the UK, Australia and New Zealand), it is considered more acceptable to critique written texts. You will be rewarded for doing so, not frowned upon.

> **Be careful!**
>
> When you come across a text on a topic you are familiar with, you may well find statements in the text that you strongly disagree with or that you know to be factually inaccurate. When this happens, remember to look at the text objectively, not emotionally. Ask yourself to what extent the text is inaccurate and why this inaccuracy exists.

Put It into Practice

A. Read the following descriptions of types of friendships.

1 Rank the descriptions in order from 1 (strongest friendship) to 5 (weakest friendship).

2 Do these descriptions remind you of friendships in your own life?

_____ a) 66 I met L. four years ago when we were both studying overseas. We're from the same country, but from different cities. When we found ourselves in the same class, we connected. We started to hang out together on the weekends. We supported each other through homesickness and loneliness. Now that we're home, we keep in touch and see each other two or three times a year. 99

_____ b) 66 B. and I have been friends since we were five years old and lived in the same apartment building. As children, we were inseparable. As we grew older, our interests developed in different directions, and we both formed other friendships. Today, B. lives in another country, but we sometimes exchange e-mails. We're hoping to meet in our home town next year. 99

_____ c) 66 I met S. through sports; we're on the same team. We have known each other for about four years. We train together once a week, and we usually go out to celebrate after we win a game. S. is fifteen years older than I am and is married with children, but we get along really well. When I needed a place to stay, I slept on S.'s sofa for a month. I enjoy spending time with S. 99

_____ d) **“** I have never met K. in person. We met online through social media, and we soon found that we have lots in common. We had similar childhoods, we do similar jobs, and we like the same music and movies. We spend hours and hours chatting online about our careers and our relationships. I'd love to meet K. in person, but we live on opposite sides of the ocean! **”**

_____ e) **“** I have worked with D. for two years, and we've got to know each other really well. We often eat lunch together, and we usually go out for dinner on Friday nights after work. We don't usually talk about deep stuff; we just hang out, gossip about the office, complain about the boss … I am never lonely when D. is around; we always have a good time together. **”**

B. Read the following text and answer the questions below.

Social Networking Leads to Isolation, Not More Connections, Say Academics

By Ethan A. Huff

Modern society seems convinced that social networking sites like Facebook and Twitter keep them connected and thriving socially with their friends and peers. But a new book called _Alone Together_ by Massachusetts Institute of Technology (MIT) professor Sherry Turkle says otherwise, purporting that social networks are more like mutual isolation networks that detach people from meaningful interactions with one another and make them less human.

"A behaviour that has become typical may still express the problems that once caused us to see it as pathological," says Turkle in her book, referring to the near-total obsession with the digital world in today's society. She and others say that the online social world is destroying real communication, dumbing down society and leading to a society of people that have no idea how to actually function in the real world.

Turkle emphasizes her belief that more people need to put down their phones, turn off their computers and learn to communicate with one another face-to-face. She writes, "We have invented inspiring and enhancing technologies, yet we have allowed them to diminish us." And many others in research and academia share her views.

One major indicator of the chilling decline in communication values is the case of Simone Back, a Brighton, UK, woman who announced her suicide on her Facebook status. None of her more than 1,000 "friends" contacted her in response to the posting, and many simply argued with one another back and forth on her "Wall" about the legitimacy of her posting and whether or not Back had the freedom of choice to kill herself.

This sick display of meaningless Facebook "friendship" is only fuel for the fire to the many who say it represents the "writing on the wall" of worse things to come. If individuals cannot learn to interact and develop meaningful relationships outside the narcissistic, soap opera–environment of the Facebook "News Feed," then society is in for some major trouble down the road.

Sources for this story include: http://www.guardian.co.uk/media/2011/jan/22/…

Huff, E.A. (2011, Jan. 27). Social networking leads to isolation, not more connections, say academics. http://www.naturalnews.com/031128_social_networking_mental_health.html#ixzz3FBw4uZDU

1. Summarize the problem outlined by MIT professor Sherry Turkle.

2. What does Sherry Turkle think we should do to solve the problem?

3. How does the case of Simone Back exemplify the problem identified by Turkle?

4. Do your own experiences lead you to agree or disagree with Turkle's argument? Why?

C. The nature and meaning of interpersonal relationships often vary according to culture. Find a published article about relationships (friendships, marriage, interaction with colleagues, etc.) in a country you are familiar with. Answer the following questions.

1. What point is the author of the article making?

2. Does the author's argument match your own experiences?

3. If so, why? If not, why not?

The Magic Number

This reading presents the opinion of a well-known social anthropologist on the topic of friendship.

 As you read, think about whether the author's points are true in your own case.

Before You Read

Work in groups of three or four. Discuss the following questions.

1. Describe the place where you grew up. Did you experience a sense of community in this setting, or did you feel isolated? Explain your answer.

2. Do you have friends online that you have never met in person? Do you consider these people to be "real" friends? Why, or why not?

3. The author of this article describes a person's social network as "the number of people you wouldn't feel embarrassed about joining if you happened to find them at the bar in the transit lounge of Hong Kong airport at 3 a.m." Given this definition, how many people do you estimate that you have in your own social network?

Key Vocabulary

The words below are all in the reading. Fill in the space in each sentence with the correct word.

NOUNS	cohesion			
VERBS	decay			
ADJECTIVES	dispersed	dysfunctional	fragmented	homogenous
	integrated	nebulous	reciprocal	secular

1 When a group is _____, all members of the group are alike in some way.

2 A/An _____ society is one that does not function well; for example, there could be conflict, or there might be lack of communication. This word is also used to describe smaller groups, such as families.

3 If you describe a society as _____, you mean that it is broken into small, separate units, none of which has much contact with the others.

4 A/An _____ organization is one that is not connected to any kind of formal religion.

5 A/An _____ relationship is one in which there is give-and-take on both sides; both sides have something to contribute to the relationship and something to gain from it.

6 When people are _____, they are spread out over a large area. A family with members in different countries could be described in this way.

7 When members of a community feel connected and work well together, the community can be described as having _____.

8 A concept described as _____ is unclear, undefined and vague.

9 When something _____ s, it goes bad; this word is used to describe relationships, but it can also be used to describe food, teeth, and buildings that fall into a state of disrepair.

10 Societies that are _____ are those in which every group works effectively together and no group is marginalized or excluded.

The Magic Number

By Robin Dunbar

If social networks become too large, communities fail to function effectively—and we've got evolution to prove it, claims Robin Dunbar.

As a species, we have spent more than 95 percent of our evolutionary history in small-scale foraging societies in which no more than a few hundred people are **dispersed**
5 over a wide geographical area. But ever since the Industrial Revolution, with its voracious demand for large labour forces, human communities have become increasingly concentrated in urban centres. In 1800, just 2 percent of the world's population lived in cities, rising to 13 percent in 1900 and 60 percent in 2000. While we can obviously manage to live in very large communities, our psychology is not really designed to handle the
10 kind of densities and social pressures associated with urban centres. Our social world is still built on a very small scale, and the relative **cohesion** of traditional small-scale societies has become difficult to replicate in the urban environment, in part explaining our civic dysfunctionality.

Among primates in general, there is a simple relationship between a species' typical
15 social group size and the size of its neocortex (very roughly, the thinking part of the brain). Humans fit nicely on to the end of this line, with a predicted group size based on our neocortex size of about 150—the figure that is now known as "Dunbar's number." I remember being surprised at how small this figure was when I first predicted it. The apparent mismatch between this prediction and the fact that people now live in
20 "megacities" of ten million or more prompted me to set about finding out how big natural human groups actually were. Initially, I searched the literature on ethnographic societies—hunter-gatherers such as the !Kung San[1] of Namibia or many Amazonian Indian tribes—thinking that these would best reflect our natural ancestral state. Their typical community size turned out to be about 150. But in the industrialized world,
25 perhaps we had managed to break through this particular glass ceiling and found ways to live in much larger communities?

To see if this was at all likely, one obvious place to look was personal social networks—the number of people you know and have relationships with. Our first attempt to do this exploited the old Christmas card trick. Writing cards costs money and time and, at
30 the very least, implies that you think the recipients are worth the effort. We asked a number of people to tell us exactly whom they were sending cards to, and it turned out that, on average, there were about 148 recipients, taking into consideration all household members.

This looked sufficiently promising for us to begin sampling social networks in earnest.
35 We have now asked about 500 people about their social networks. And by this, we don't mean that they merely know the names of the people in their networks, but rather that they have a **reciprocal** relationship with a proper history. Informally, a good definition is the number of people you wouldn't feel embarrassed about joining if you happened to find them at the bar in the transit lounge of Hong Kong airport at 3 a.m. You know $\Rightarrow$

---

[1] The !Kung San people are a hunter-gatherer group living in the Kalahari desert in southwest Africa. The *!* at the beginning of their name is a phonetic symbol denoting a click sound that does not exist in English.

40 where they fit into your social world, and they know where you fit into theirs. This figure also turns out to be about 150.

In fact, the number 150 starts to emerge from all kinds of unexpected places once 45 you know what to look for. It is the average village size recorded in William the Conqueror's Domesday Book² of England in 1087, and it is the average size of the smallest stand-alone unit (the 50 company) in all modern armies. In business organizations, it turns out to be the point at which businesses start to need formal management structures if they are not to fall apart as they grow in 55 size. Intriguingly, it is also the typical size of communities among both the Hutterites and the Amish, both of which practise a communalistic form of fundamentalist Christianity in the USA. In sum, the number 150 seems to define the limit on the number of people with whom you can form personalized relationships that involve a sense of 60 mutual obligation, trust and reciprocity.

Circles of acquaintanceship

That said, the 150 people in your social world do not form a **homogenous** group. Our research has revealed that social networks actually consist of a series of layers, or circles, of acquaintanceship. The size of these layers tends to increase by a multiple 65 of three—an inner layer of five intimates, then fifteen good friends, fifty friends and 150 acquaintances, with each successive layer including those below it. As you go up through the layers, the average emotional intensity of the relationship declines, as does the frequency with which you see individuals. What seems to set the limit at 150—the outer layer—is that you run out of time and psychological capital to give to 70 more people.

Two things seem to be important in creating the relationships that give rise to this pattern.

When social psychologists have looked at intimate relationships, they consistently come out with two key dimensions, labelled "being close" and "feeling close." "Being 75 close" is clearly related to spatial proximity—that is, time spent together. "Feeling close" is an altogether more **nebulous** thing, but it has something to do with the emotional quality of our human interactions.

It's a small world

One characteristic of small-scale communities is that everyone knows everyone else 80 and, more importantly, there is almost complete overlap in people's social networks.

---

² The Domesday Book contains the results of an early population survey carried out by William I shortly after becoming King of England in 1066. The goal of the survey was to provide the new king with information about the country he had invaded.

The trends towards urbanization, economic migration and social transience that have come to dominate modern life have changed all that. We grow up in Huddersfield, go to university in Brighton, get our first job in London and move (or are moved by our employer) to Glasgow a few years later. At each step, we leave behind a small group of
85 friends until time and distance eventually dim our relationships with them beyond he point of rescue.

The effect of all this is that our networks of 150 people become increasingly **fragmented**, consisting of small clusters of friends who are forever associated with a particular time and place. These clusters rarely overlap; indeed, our social network only
90 partially overlaps with even that of our partner, despite the fact that we live in the same house and share a life together. The core clusters of best friends and family may overlap, but we tend to have separate friends for work, hobbies and so on.

In small-scale societies, the fact that the community is spatially and socially **integrated** means that its members can maintain social cohesion and social discipline. This doesn't
95 mean to say that they never fall out or quarrel, but it does mean that they will look out for one another. Peer pressure is usually sufficient to police everyone's behaviour and prevent individuals from stepping too far out of line. What bonds the community together is a common sense of obligation, reciprocity and trust. Religion often plays a seminal role in these societies, providing a common signal of community membership through
100 shared values and beliefs. Rituals such as trance dancing and sweat lodges are extremely effective at releasing the endorphins that seem to be so crucial for social bonding.

The fact that social networks in our urbanized world are fragmented and geographically distributed means that there is less to bind us into the fabric of our local community. We don't even know most of the people we pass in the street. This fragmentation may
105 be part—and perhaps a major part—of the reason why modern urban societies seem to be so **dysfunctional**. So we have a genuine problem—one to which we need to find a solution if we are not to be overwhelmed by the aspects of modern society that give rise to lack of social cohesion.

Might the Internet offer us a way of creating virtual communities that reinstate small-
110 scale society on a grand, global scale? There are several reasons for suspecting not. First, some exaggerated claims notwithstanding, most people have only their everyday, face-to-face friends on their Facebook page. The number of people with 500 or even 1,000 "Facebook friends" is in fact very small. Second, those who do have very large numbers of virtual "friends" do not know most of these people in any meaningful sense.
115 Third, social networking sites lack the everyday physical contact that seems to be so important in establishing real relationships of trust and obligation. They are very good for slowing down the rate at which relationships **decay**, but not for preventing that decay altogether. Sooner or later, you need to get to grips with people in real life. Nor do social networking sites really work well for establishing new relationships. In the
120 end, a touch in the real world is worth a thousand words in the virtual world. Finally, analysis of community sizes in virtual worlds such as Second Life and World of Warcraft suggests that they mirror exactly what we see in the world of real-life communities. Dunbar's number reigns supreme even here.

$\rightarrow$

Cohesive communities

125 So, if the Internet isn't any help, how do we create large, integrated communities? There are probably only two serious options: the stick or the carrot. It is always possible to enforce integration by resorting to draconian punishment. But the problem, as everyone who breaks the speed limit knows only too well, is that it is not the size of the punishment that makes you obey the rules, but how likely you are to get caught. The temptation to 130 cheat is always present. The punishment solution leads inevitably to a police state, which seems an unattractive option.

In fact, social cohesion is always more effective under "carrot" regimes: if people sign up to the rules voluntarily, their commitment to the community is greater and requires much less (if any) policing. In the end, small-scale communities work precisely because 135 everyone is signed up to the same grand project—survival and successful reproduction— and cannot afford to drop out or leave. We are all in it together, and we had better pull together or we all go down—even if we can't stand one another.

Modern life allows us more independence. If that is the root of our problem, then might the answer lie in inventing a new grand project that will pull us all together? 140 I have thought long and hard about this, but the only grand project that seems to work effectively in this kind of way seems, for better or worse, to be religion. Data on 19th-century American millenarian cults show rather dramatically that cults based on religious beliefs, however outlandish, survive for considerably longer than purely **secular** utopian cults.

145 Religion has undoubtedly played a central role in community bonding throughout the course of recent human evolution, but the prospect of its becoming the centrepiece of modern life again fills me with deep angst, not least because it can be (and has been) a very strong mechanism for social strife and for creating deeply divisive, "them-and-us" polarizations.

150 Another answer might lie in some kind of Swiss model: smaller, semi-independent, old-fashioned "city states" in which a sense of community can more easily be created at the local level. This would almost certainly require greater diversity than the current enthusiasm for central government control, from Westminster to Brussels, allows. As much as I like this idea, I suspect that, given the current level of job mobility, it may 155 still be difficult to create that sense of local commitment in smaller civic units. This is because belonging invariably arises out of history—being part of a community for a lengthy period.

Inevitably, most of the obvious solutions will either be difficult to achieve or have less than desirable consequences. But we cannot duck the problem, because it won't simply 160 go away. Our task in the century ahead must be to find a better alternative—before we get overwhelmed by the dysfunctionality of the urban state.   (1976 words)

Dunbar, R. (2010, spring). The magic number. *RSA Journal*. Retrieved from http://www.thersa.org/fellowship/journal/archive/spring-2010/features/the-magic-number

Check Your Understanding

A. Complete the sentence below.

"Dunbar's number" is _____

_____

_____

B. Use the words and phrases below to complete the following sentences. Use each word or phrase only once.

150	being close	businesses
cohesive	feeling close	fragmented
less-developed societies	meaningful	mobility
online	overlap	religion
small-scale societies	social networks	urban

1 Dunbar argues that human evolution took place in small societies. Now that we increasingly live in large _____ areas, our society has become less _____ and more dysfunctional.

2 Dunbar's number suggests that humans are best suited to living in _____. His research into _____, such as the !Kung San and the Amazonian tribal groups, bears this out. These groups typically function in units of around _____. This number also appears in armies, _____ and American religious communities.

3 Dunbar wonders whether we have been able to compensate for the loss of small-scale societies by creating these in an alternate form: _____.

4 Dunbar differentiates between "being close" and "feeling close." According to Dunbar, _____ is related to the amount of time you spend with your network, while _____ refers to the extent to which you feel emotionally connected.

5 Because people move around so much today, they tend to have clusters of friends that rarely _____. They may have friends in different locations, or friends for work or hobbies. For this reason, our groups of friends are more _____ than in the past.

6 In his research into _____ networks, Dunbar has found that people who have large numbers of Facebook friends do not have _____ relationships with these people. The Internet does not help us to create integrated communities.

7   One thing that encourages people to function in an integrated community seems to be _____; however, Dunbar recognizes that this can also create social strife. Another option might be the creation of semi-independent city-states, but the fact that people today have a lot of _____ might make this difficult.

Analysis and Discussion

Discuss the following questions with your group.

1   How do you respond personally to the following statements made by the author? Based on your own experiences, do you agree or disagree with these statements?

a) While we can obviously manage to live in very large communities, our psychology is not really designed to handle the kind of densities and social pressures associated with urban centres. (lines 8 to 10)

b) … the number 150 seems to define the limit on the number of people with whom you can form personalized relationships that involve a sense of mutual obligation, trust and reciprocity. (lines 58 to 60)

c) … social networks actually consist of a series of layers, or circles, of acquaintanceship. The size of these layers tends to increase by a multiple of three—an inner layer of five intimates, then fifteen good friends, fifty friends and 150 acquaintances … (lines 63 to 66)

d) … our networks of 150 people become increasingly fragmented, consisting of small clusters of friends who are forever associated with a particular time and place. These clusters rarely overlap …. The core clusters of best friends and family may overlap, but we tend to have separate friends for work, hobbies and so on. (lines 87 to 92)

e) What bonds the community together is a common sense of obligation, reciprocity and trust. Religion often plays a seminal role in these societies, providing a common signal of community membership through shared values and beliefs. (lines 97 to 100)

f) The fact that social networks in our urbanized world are fragmented and geographically distributed means that there is less to bind us into the fabric of our local community. We don't even know most of the people we pass in the street. (lines 102 to 104)

g) In the end, a touch in the real world is worth a thousand words in the virtual world. (lines 119 to 120)

h) … the prospect of [religion] becoming the centrepiece of modern life again fills me with deep angst, not least because it can (and has been) a very strong mechanism for social strife and for creating deeply divisive, "them-and-us" polarizations. (lines 146 to 149)

2   What questions would you like to ask the author if you met him?

3   Write a short letter to the author a) stating the extent to which your own experiences match his theory, and b) asking him any questions you may have.

Is Dunbar's Friend-Limiting Number Still Relevant in the Facebook Era?

This lighthearted text shows how one author tests Dunbar's theory.

 As you read, think about how the author's experiment shows how an individual can respond to a published academic theory.

Before You Read

Work in groups of three or four. Discuss the following questions.

1. The title of this reading asks: "Is Dunbar's friend-limiting number still relevant in the Facebook era?" What do you predict the answer to this question will be? Why?

2. What do you think would be a good way to answer this question? What kind of research could be carried out?

3. Describe your own involvement with social media such as Facebook. How many online friends do you have? How many of them have you communicated with recently?

Key Vocabulary

The words below are all in the reading. Match each word with the correct definition.

1. bully (n. line 24) _____ a) short and clear

2. calligraphy (n. line 21) _____ b) networks between people, that encourage the smooth functioning of society

3. concise (adj. line 14) _____ c) someone in the same professional or personal situation as you

4. condolences (n. line 56) _____ d) alone, with no help from anyone

5. executive decision (n. line 44) _____ e) artistic writing, sometimes done with a brush and ink

6. fellow (adj. line 17) _____ f) relating to ideas and concepts

7. mutual friend (n. line 41) _____ g) expression of sorrow, usually after someone's death

8. singlehandedly (adv. line 6) _____ h) someone who is a friend of both you and another person

9. social capital (n. line 75) _____ i) someone who is threatening to another, usually weaker, person

10. theoretical (adj. line 3) _____ j) decision made without consulting anyone else

Is Dunbar's Friend-Limiting Number Still Relevant in the Facebook Era?

By Rick Lax

Nineteen years ago, a British anthropologist took control of my social life. Robin Dunbar—he's the guy—said I could only have 150 friends.

Technically "Dunbar's number," a theoretical limit that pegs the number of social relationships one can maintain at somewhere between 100 and 230, applied to everyone,
5 but I couldn't help but take it personally.

Fast forward to late 2011. I had more than 2,000 Facebook friends. I'd singlehandedly disproved the Brit's sociological theorem. Did I interact with every one of those 2,000 people? No. But they showed up in my News Feed. And wasn't that enough?

Not for Dunbar, apparently. He was looking for individual interactions. Well, I thought,
10 if that's all it takes to disprove Dunbar's number, then that's what I'll do: I'll write personal letters to every one of my 2,000 Facebook friends.

Starting at A

I tackled the list alphabetically and kept the letters short. I don't write long letters to my best friends, so why pour my heart out to the casual ones? Concise, friendly, honest and
15 personal—that was the goal.

A.S., a girl I dated in Chicago, was engaged now. So I sent her a congratulatory note. A.J. Jacobs, a fellow "stunt journalist,"[1] got a note explaining that I was sending letters to each of my Facebook friends.

"I look forward to the letter!" came the response.

20 "That was the letter," I clarified.

"I was expecting something handwritten. Something with nice calligraphy and a wax seal on the envelope," Jacobs said.

Clearly the guy was shilling for Dunbar, so I moved on.

I went to high school with A.G. He was a bully and I only accepted his Facebook friend
25 request so I could monitor how miserable his life had become. The weight gain, the receding hairline, the recent breakup, the unemployment—just delightful. What friendly words did I have for him? None. So I de-friended him.

I'd forgotten so many As in the past decade: The girl who advised the MSU[2] Freshman Class Council, the guy from the ironic heavy metal band, the girl who requested my
30 friendship after seeing a photo of me wearing a fake muscle suit. Needless to say, they were all pretty surprised (and confused) to hear from me.

And then I made it to the Bs.

---

[1] A *stunt journalist* is someone who immerses himself in a situation and then writes about his experiences. For example, A.J. Jacobs is the author of *The Year of Living Biblically*, in which he describes his year spent trying to follow literally the teachings of the Bible.

[2] MSU is Michigan State University.

B.M., it turns out, is dead. It took me a while to realize this. Friends were still uploading photos of him and leaving comments on his page, like, "I miss you." At first, I figured he'd moved out of the country.

I wrote B.S. a long, apologetic note. I'd treated him rudely when we first met. A mutual "friend" of ours had said some pretty nasty things about him. B.S. accepted my apology.

Before I hit the Cs, I made an executive decision: I was going to start leaving wall posts in place of writing letters. For some people, not all. That's what I do with my best friends, I figured. And wall posts are still personalized.

If it was somebody's birthday, they got a "Happy Birthday." If somebody's birthday had recently passed, well, they got a "Happy Birthday," too. And if somebody's birthday had passed by a couple weeks, they got a "Sorry I missed your birthday!" So maybe they're not as personalized, I thought. But 2,000, in case you haven't heard, is a huge number.

Some random observations from the Cs through Is:

> C.L.'s six-month-old child had recently passed.[3] I gave her my condolences. Truth is, I had no clue who this woman was. But my sentiments were real.

> When I saw C.J., I thought, Who's the old guy? Is he a friend of my parents? And then I saw that C.J. was born in '83. Meaning he's younger than me.

> After I wrote Dvn Yan Kit, I assumed I'd completed the Ds. But apparently I have a Facebook friend named "Dyke Stabler," too.

> Two of my middle-school friends got married, to each other. Recently. And I wasn't invited to the wedding.

> Three years back, I asked this cute girl, K.C., if she could come to my party. She said that she couldn't because her parents had gotten in a big fight. "And it now is just a crazy mess," she wrote. I'd never written her back. So I asked whether the fight had ever been resolved. "My mom died, I got married, and I moved to Texas," came the response.

Enter Timeline

Before I hit the Js, I converted to Facebook's Timeline. As a result, I lost access to the alphabetical friend list, which brought my social experiment to a screeching halt.

---

[3] *Passed* is a polite way of saying *died*. It is also possible to say "passed away."

I only made it through 1,000 of my 2,000 Facebook friends. But that was enough.

In trying to disprove Dunbar's number, I actually proved it. I proved that even if you're aware of Dunbar's number, and even if you set aside a chunk of your life specifically to 75 broaden your social capital, you can only maintain so many friendships. And "so many" is fewer than 200.

Writing my Facebook "friends" had taken over my time. I was breaking plans with real friends to send meaningless messages to strangers. Some of the strangers didn't respond, and many of those who did respond only confirmed Dunbar's theory.

80 Quick examples: When I wrote A.F., a Malaysian magician, he responded: "hey rick i think you might've sent me this message by mistake lol." And when I wrote A.D., a friend of a friend, and asked how things were going, she replied, "Sorry but do i know you?:)"

I walk away from this experiment with a newfound respect for 1) British anthropology 85 and 2) my real friends. There aren't too many of them, I now see. So I'd better treat them well.

(958 words)

Lax, R. (2012). Is Dunbar's friend-limiting number still relevant in the Facebook era? Retrieved from http://gizmodo.com/5889894/is-dunbars-number-still-relevant-in-the-facebook-era

Check Your Understanding

A. Was your prediction from "Before You Read" correct? Did you predict anything that was not correct?

B. Write the following short summaries.

a) Summarize in three or four sentences the experiment the author decided to carry out and his reason for doing so.

b) Summarize in two or three sentences the results he found.

c) Summarize in one or two sentences the lesson he learned from his experiment.

C. Find examples of the following people.

a) Someone the author did not know _____

b) Someone who did not know the author _____

c) Someone who was deceased _____

d) Someone the author did not like _____

Analysis and Discussion

Discuss the following questions with your group.

1 The author states that he took Dunbar's theory personally and believed that he had more than 150 friends. How do you personally respond to the idea that you can only have 150 friends? Which statement best matches your own experience?

○ 150 is a lot! I don't think I know that many people.

○ 150 sounds about right.

○ I have more than 150 friends.

○ Other: _____

2 If you were to carry out this kind of experiment with your own social network, what results do you think you might find?

3 Why do you think people add "friends" on social media that they don't know personally? How do you respond to "friend" requests from strangers? Do you usually accept them, usually refuse them, or something else?

4 Do you think the author's experiment was a waste of time, or do you think it taught him a useful lesson? Explain your answer.

5 Write a response to the following message:

❝ I only have fifty-eight friends on Facebook. I feel like a social failure. **❞**

READING 3

Social Networks: A Learning Tool for Teams?

This reading shows how the use of online networks will help today's students to develop into effective leaders in their careers.

 As you read, think about how your own use of social media will help you to develop your career-related skills.

Before You Read

Work in groups of three or four. Discuss the following questions.

1 What do you understand by the term *digital native*? Do you think you are a digital native? Why, or why not?

2 How is the workplace different for today's graduates than it was for their parents?

3 What work-related skills might digital natives have that their parents' generation does not have?

Social Networks: A Learning Tool for Teams?

Patrick Tissington and Carl Senior

The modern-day student begins university life as part of a generation that is born into a world of ubiquitous computing. The sum of the world's knowledge can be accessed
5 through the Internet-enabled mobile phone in his/her pocket. However, with access to such knowledge comes the evolution of a mindset distinct from their parents. Although contentious, the term
10 "digital native" has been applied to describe people who have this information age mindset (Prensky, 2005). Such a mindset is defined not by over familiarity with various social networking sites but by a distinct
15 style of cognition with very specific characteristics (Frand, 2000). Amongst other things, the digital native has a zero tolerance for delays, multitasks at every opportunity and also needs to be part of a
20 social community throughout the day.

Perhaps one could argue that this information age mindset would flourish within higher education. Indeed, one of the most significant changes in students'
25 experience of university over the past twenty years has been the increased use of group work to deliver learning objectives. This change reflects the needs of the modern-day workplace, which often
30 requires its workforce to operate effectively in groups. However, as modern organizations increase in size, they require their workforce to operate in teams that span across national borders. This would also
35 mean that the modern-day undergraduate would need to be accustomed to working across cultural and religious boundaries. While universities have, in general, been active in developing teaching strategies
40 that encourage mobile learning, there is very little research if any into the possible factors that facilitate the ability to work in teams, virtually and across national or cultural boundaries (Alexander, 2004).
45 Thus, it is not known if the need for socializing that is inherent within the "digital natives" is counterintuitive to the lack of ecological social interaction that is seen in the geographically and culturally dispersed
50 virtual work team.

To address this question, our research looked at the relationship the current generation of undergraduates has with the use of social networking media. Students in one undergraduate module, introduction to organizational behaviour, were selected due to their cultural diversity. In this course, the current cohort came from fifty-seven countries which reflect the diversity of many international organizations. We asked a sample of 290 of these students how they interacted with social networking media. Our results were surprising, with nearly all of them indicating that they used Facebook everyday, swamping MySpace (1 percent regular use) and Twitter (4 percent). In fact, over a third log on to Facebook first thing every morning. We also discovered that they had easy access to the Internet, with over 90 percent owning a laptop and all but one student owning a mobile phone, with the majority of these phones having Internet connectivity. Nearly 60 percent indicated that they also use their mobile phones to access the Internet, and 84 percent indicated that they stayed in contact with friends/colleagues electronically throughout the day. Here, it is clear that even when most of their colleagues are physically not far away, social networking is used to add to the feeling of connectedness and support which one derives from an effective community of practice. Such social groups see its members becoming adept at its core competency merely by social interaction with its members (Wenger and Synder, 2000).

When considering the nature of the new workplace, these digital enhancements to socializing can provide alternatives to the traditional workplace social benefits such as the casual corridor chat or the combined work/social chat over coffee (Brown & Duguid, 1991). Whatever form it takes, we know that humans are driven to socialize as a very basic necessity—probably with its origins in our deep evolutionary past when it was discovered that hunting in packs was more efficient than alone (Nicholson, 1998). Natural selection has led to those humans who wanted to be part of a group being more likely to survive. Perhaps the strength of this drive is sufficient to overcome the very many shortcomings of electronic communication as compared to face to face.

These data show us that these undergraduates—who are in essence the workforce of the future—are immersed in a world of transglobal computing from birth, have not lost the evolutionary urge to socialize with each other. Indeed, they have readily adopted the technologies on hand and use social networking via the Internet or mobile telephony to remain in constant touch with each other. It further suggests that as these "Generation Y" individuals grow into the managers and chief executive officers of tomorrow, they will be uniquely placed to take on the challenges of virtual teams.

It has recently been noted that social networking sites and even participation in online social games facilitate the rapid dissemination of knowledge as well as serve to refine it via an iterative social peer process by which other digital natives act as modern-day Delphi experts (Kane, Fichman, Gallaugher & Glaser, 2009; van der Meij, Albers & Leemkuil, 2010). Indeed, the digital native also views knowledge as a utilitarian concept that is accessible everywhere at any time, and access to it is more way of life than a right. This, perhaps idiosyncratic, outlook has ensured that knowledge is fast becoming democratized and is no longer solely the preserve of a select few academics and policy makers. So we see that social networking sites such as Facebook not only serve a vital role in complementing the needs of the new generation of digital natives but also maintain our evolutionary imperative to socialize and share knowledge.

References

Alexander, B. (2004). Going nomadic: mobile learning in higher education. *Educause Review, 39,* 28–35.

Brown, J. S. & Duguid, P. (1991). Organizational learning and communities-of-practice: toward a unified view of working, learning, and innovation. *Organization Science, 2,* 40–57.

Frand, J. (2000). Information age mindset; changes in students and implications for higher education. *Educause Review, 35,* 15–24.

Kane, G. C., Fichman, R. G., Gallaugher, J. & Glaser, J. (2009). Community relations 2.0. *Harvard Business Review, 87,* 132–133.

van der Meij, H., Albers, E. & Leemkuil, H. (2010). Learning from games: does collaboration help? *British Journal of Educational Technology.* DOI: 10.1111/j.1467-8535.2010.01067.

Nicholson, N. (1998). How hardwired is human behaviour. *Harvard Business Review, 76,* 134–147.

Prensky, M. (2005). Listen to the natives. *Educational Leadership, 63,* 8–13.

Wenger, E.C. (2000). Communities of Practice and social learning systems. *Organization, 7,* 2, 225–246.

916 words (excluding references)

Tissington, P., & Senior, C. (2011). Social networks: a learning tool for teams? *British Journal of Educational Technology,* 42(5), E89–E90.

Check Your Understanding

A. Answer the following questions in your own words using information from the reading.

1 What three characteristics do digital natives display that distinguish them from their parents?

_____

_____

_____

2 In the authors' view of postsecondary education,

a) what change has been introduced to better prepare students for the workplace?

b) what form of training is still lacking?

_____

_____

3 The study described here was prompted by the following statement:

> Thus, it is not known if the need for socializing that is inherent within the "digital natives" is counterintuitive to the lack of ecological social interaction that is seen in the geographically and culturally dispersed virtual work team.

Paraphrase this statement in one or two sentences.

_____

_____

_____

_____

4 Look at the authors' description of their research.

    a) How many participants took part in the study? _____

    b) Where did they come from? _____

    c) What were they asked about? _____

    _____

    d) What results were found? _____

    _____

    _____

5 How do the authors connect their results to the needs of future workers?

_____

_____

6 How do the authors connect their results to what is known about human evolution?

_____

_____

Key Vocabulary

Find the following sentences in the text. Write a synonym for each of the words in **bold**.

1 The modern-day student begins university life as part of a generation that is born into a world of **ubiquitous** computing. (lines 1 to 3) _____

2 Perhaps one could argue that this information age mindset would **flourish** within higher education. (lines 21 to 23) _____

3 This would also mean that the modern-day undergraduate would need to be **accustomed to** working across cultural and religious boundaries. (lines 34 to 37)

_____

4 ... there is very little research if any into the possible factors that **facilitate** the ability to work in teams ... (lines 40 to 43) _____

5 Students in one undergraduate module, introduction to organizational behaviour, were selected due to their cultural **diversity**. (lines 54 to 57)

_____

6 Here, it is clear that even when most of their colleagues are physically not far away, social networking is used to add to the feeling of connectedness and support which one **derives** from an effective community of practice. (lines 78 to 83)

_____

7 Perhaps the strength of this drive is sufficient to overcome the very many **shortcomings** of electronic communication as compared to face to face. (lines 103 to 106)

_____

8 It has recently been noted that social networking sites and even participation in online social games facilitate the rapid **dissemination** of knowledge … (lines 122 to 125)

_____

9 Indeed, the digital native also views knowledge as a **utilitarian** concept … (lines 130 to 132)

_____

10 This, perhaps **idiosyncratic**, outlook has ensured that knowledge is fast becoming democratized and is no longer solely the preserve of a select few academics and policy makers. (lines 134 to 138) _____

Analysis and Discussion

Discuss the following questions with your group.

1 The authors say:

> These data show us that these undergraduates—who are in essence the workforce of the future—are immersed in a world of transglobal computing from birth, have not lost the evolutionary urge to socialize with each other. Indeed, they have readily adopted the technologies on hand and use social networking via the Internet or mobile telephony to remain in constant touch with each other.

How do you think the following people would respond to this statement?

> Sherry Turkle

> Robin Dunbar

> Rick Lax

2 The authors say:

… as these "Generation Y" individuals grow into the managers and chief executive officers of tomorrow, they will be uniquely placed to take on the challenges of virtual teams (lines 117 to 121).

a) If you consider yourself to be a digital native, do you agree that your use of social media has given you an advantage in the workplace? Why, or why not?

b) If you do not consider yourself to be a digital native, do you feel that you are disadvantaged in today's workplace? Why, or why not?

3 Can you think of any other situations in which digital natives behave differently from members of their parents' generation?

4 Do you think universities and colleges should modify their courses to prepare students better for a career in which they might have to work virtually with people in different parts of the world? If so, in what ways could this happen? If not, why not?

5 Think about the three readings in this chapter and discuss these questions.

a) Have you read anything you strongly agree with?

b) Have you read anything you strongly disagree with?

c) Have you read anything that has changed your mind about social networks?

d) Have you read anything you would like to learn more about?

Going Further

Focus on Language

A. The following chart contains ten words from the three readings. Complete the chart with related words in the other categories and, where possible, in the same category. (There may not be a word for each category.)

	NOUN	VERB	ADJECTIVE	ADVERB
1			apologetic	
2	behaviour			
3			divisive	
4				dramatically
5			dysfunctional	
6	necessity			
7	option			
8	polarization			
9		predict		
10		suspect		

B. In Reading 1, the German word *angst* is used, meaning "a feeling of anxiety and unhappiness." Many words from other languages are commonly used in English.

> Which language do you think each of these words comes from?

> Can you think of any other words that have come into English from other languages?

> Why do you think English has so many words from other languages?

algebra	canyon	elephant	flamingo
iceberg	piano	pyjamas	restaurant
sauna	shampoo	tattoo	tomato
tsunami	typhoon	yacht	yoghurt

Independent Research

Carry out an analysis of your own social network (or, if you prefer, interview a friend about his or her network). Ask yourself the following questions.

> How many people are in my social network?

> Is my network cohesive, or is it fragmented?

> How does my analysis of my network compare with what I have read in this chapter?

You will present your findings to the class.

Synthesis and Written Response

Based on your reading of the texts in this chapter as well as your own independent research into social networks, write a short response to the following question:

> What is the value of social networks?

REVIEW
of the chapter ...

> Answer the following questions.

1 Why is it important to bring your own experiences to the text?

2 Why can it sometimes be hard to do this?

CHAPTER 10

Looking at the Stars

 FOCUS **BRINGING IT ALL TOGETHER: WRITING A CRITICAL REVIEW**

Many undergraduate courses require students to submit a critical analysis of a text. What is the best way to do this?

In this chapter
YOU WILL LEARN ...

> the key components of a critical review;

> how a critical review is different from a research essay; and

> how to structure a critical review.

Warm-up

Discuss the following questions with your group.

> Should space exploration be prioritized by governments? If so, why? What form should space exploration take? If not, why not?

> Think back to the early days of space exploration in the time of the Cold War (see Chapter 1, page 4). What has changed since that time? What has stayed the same?

> Is there a role for private enterprises in space exploration? Why, or why not?

How to Write a Critical Review

> How can life on earth be improved by exploration and understanding of the universe beyond the earth?

Imagine you have been given an article on this topic in a course entitled *Introduction to Astronomy*. Your task is to write a critical review of the article, showing that you a) understand the article and b) are able to provide an analysis of it.

What is a critical review?

A critical review is a paper in which you provide two things:

> a brief summary, or overview, of the text; and

> an analysis of the text, commenting on the kinds of topics you have practised in earlier chapters.

A critical review is different from a research essay

> For a research essay, you go to library or online resources to find out as much as possible about your subject. You then synthesize all this information and present your own perspective on the topic of the paper. Your essay supports a thesis statement, which you formulate on the basis of extensive reading.

> For a critical review, you may want to check a few facts that the author has given, but you should not need to do extensive research. Your goal is to evaluate the argument presented by the author, not try to persuade the reader of your own point of view on the topic. Don't focus solely on the *topic*; focus on how *the author presents* his or her argument.

What does a good critical review include?

There is no single approach to writing the critical review, but a good outline is as follows. *Note that you do not normally need to label your sections.*

Introduction

In your introductory paragraph, do the following:

> Introduce the text, giving the title, the author's name, the place it was published (journal, magazine, newspaper, website or other source) and the date of publication.

> Give a sentence or two stating the main point of the text. Don't go into a lot of detail here; just give the main argument.

> Give a thesis statement showing what you think about the text. Again, this does not need to be detailed, but it should give your reader an idea of the direction your review will take.

Main section

A. Summary

Next, summarize the main points of the text. Remember the following:

> Do not make your summary too long; it should be no more than one third of the main section of your review.

> Do not copy large amounts of text from the original. Use your own words as much as possible.

> Do not provide a detailed analysis in this section; that comes later.

B. Analysis

This is the longest and most important section of your review. Remember the following:

> This section should be at least two thirds of your main section. If you write a long summary and include only a few comments at the end, you have not written a critical review.

> Think about the various aspects of critical reading you have learned about in Chapters 1 to 9. Think about where the text was published, how old it is, who wrote it, what we know about the author, whether the author's conclusions are justified and how the text fits in with other sources and your own experiences. Not all of these questions will be answered in detail (some will be more important than others), but you should keep these questions in mind as you plan your analysis.

> Your analysis section may be positive about the text, it may be negative, or it may contain a mix of positive and negative comments. Most critical reviews point out both positive features of the text and any shortcomings it may have.

> There are different ways to organize this section. You could, for example, move from positive points to negative comments. You could also pinpoint several sections of the text that you would like to focus on.

> It is often helpful to the "flow" of your review if you use linking words and phrases such as *however*, *moreover*, *similarly*, *consequently* and other devices of this nature.

> There are no "right" or "wrong" text analyses. You will have your own opinion about the text, and it may not be the same as your classmates' opinions.

> In western academic culture, it is not disrespectful to make negative comments about a text, as long as you can back them up. However, remember to use polite language— even if you strongly disagree with the author of the text.

Conclusion

Finally, end your review with a brief conclusion. Do the following:

> Restate your thesis statement; in other words, repeat your overall impression of the text.

> Provide some insight into how the text should be received; for example, does the text make a useful contribution to the body of knowledge on the topic? Does it provide a new perspective on the topic? Does it support existing literature on the topic? Is it inherently flawed in some way? Can it be safely disregarded?

Put It into Practice

Read the following short article.

NASA's SpaceX, Boeing Deal a Giant Leap for Space Flight

By Bob McDonald

It's about time governments turned to the private sector to build spacecraft, writes Bob McDonald.

The handover from expensive government space flight to commercial travel was completed this week, as NASA awarded two contracts to companies that will supply transportation to the International Space Station. Will this make space travel akin to cheap airline travel?

Spaceflight has traditionally been ridiculously expensive. Each mission to the moon cost billions, and even the space shuttles—which were touted as low-cost, reusable vehicles—were costing about $1.5 billion for every launch during their final years. That's because these were enormous, pioneering projects, involving thousands of people spread all over the continent and huge government bureaucracies.

Now, after fifty years of spaceflight experience, individual corporations can do it for ten times less money on their own.

And, the fact that NASA awarded the contract to two companies rather than one prime contractor means there will be competition, which should keep those costs down. Already, Space-X, the smaller start-up company, says it can offer flights at 40 percent lower cost than Boeing.

The heat is on for both companies to deliver on their promises.

The idea of selling space in space is not new. The Russians have been doing it for decades. In the 1990s, before the International Space Station was built, the US paid Russia $325 million to allow space shuttles to dock with their MIR Space Station and for American astronauts to live on board for long periods, as they had little experience of living in space.

Later, the Russians offered empty seats on their Soyuz capsules to tourists who paid $20- to $30-million each for a week on the Space Station.

And finally, since the space shuttles retired, NASA has been paying $70 million each for the same seats, as their only way to get their astronauts—including our own Chris Hadfield—up to the orbiting outpost. That commercial approach has kept the Russian space program alive since the collapse of the Soviet Union, when government funding all but vanished.

Commercial vehicles

The new arrangement, where NASA essentially becomes a paying customer for rides on commercial vehicles, is similar to the handover from government to the private sector that took place after World War II.

Governments had been paying huge sums to military contractors to develop fighters and large bombers, but when the war ended, the companies used the same technology to build airliners and sell them worldwide. This made flying cheaper and more available to anyone who could afford a ticket. And since then, the cost of a ticket, when compared to income, has dropped dramatically.

Likewise, we are entering a new era of space flight that is no longer in the realm of highly trained and specialized astronauts, who train for years for the opportunity of one or two flights.

Boeing, Space-X and the other companies that were bidding on the NASA contract also have their eyes on the tourism market. Bigelow Aerospace is designing an inflatable space hotel that can hold six people from ten to sixty days. It has already launched two successful prototypes as proof of concept and will soon send an inflatable module to the Space Station to show that people can actually live inside.

The Russians, not to miss a commercial opportunity, unveiled their own version a few years ago. And other countries have similar dreams. These are not flights of fancy; they are business operations with viable markets, overheads, operating costs and, hopefully, profits that will only succeed if they meet the bottom line.

It's about time governments get out of the business of building spacecraft that only go to low Earth orbit. Now that they've handed that off to the private sector, they can focus on researching the next big step beyond the Earth.

And you can be sure that once that leap has been made to deep space, the corporations will be soon to follow.

McDonald, B. (2014, Sept. 19). NASA's SpaceX, Boeing deal a giant leap for space flight. *CBC News, Technology and Science.* Retrieved from http://newsmaritimes.ca/2014/09/19/nasas-spacex-boeing-deal-a-giant-leap-for-space-flight/

Now read the following short critical review of this article and complete the exercise below it.

Critical Review of "NASA's SpaceX, Boeing deal a giant leap for space flight" by Bob McDonald

The article (1) __g__ "NASA's SpaceX, Boeing deal a giant leap for space flight" was posted on September 19, 2014 on Canadian science journalist Bob McDonald's blog (http://newsmaritimes.ca/2014/09/19/nasas-spacex-boeing-deal-a-giant-leap-for-space-flight/). McDonald's article presents a favourable response to the announcement that NASA has contracted two private companies to provide transportation to the International Space Station (ISS). (2) _____While this article does not provide an academic analysis of the situation, it serves a purpose in that it raises public awareness of this issue.

(3) _____ Space travel is, according to McDonald, "ridiculously expensive"; the solution appears to be privatization of some components of space travel, which can dramatically lower the costs for governmental organizations. The recent announcement of the privatization of travel to the ISS does not represent a new concept; the Russian space program has survived for many years by charging large fees for docking rights to their MIR Space Station as well as providing ISS transportation to astronauts and civilians alike. McDonald compares the privatization of space travel to the transfer of airplane technology from the public to private sector after World War II. The result in the post-war period was the increased availability of airline travel to civilians at affordable costs; McDonald suggests that a similar situation may arise with space travel—indeed, there are already plans to bring this about. McDonald concludes that the move towards privatization is the right decision at this time.

(4) _____ As an award-winning writer and broadcaster who has specialized in scientific issues since 1972, McDonald's goal is to present complex scientific matters in a manner accessible to lay readers. He accomplishes this by (5) _____ using language the average reader without a degree in astronomy can make sense of—short paragraphs, a casual, journalistic style and a notable absence of highly

technical jargon or complex statistical analysis. While the article is not intended for an expert audience, McDonald nevertheless shows evidence of a careful understanding and analysis of the topic. He uses numbers and examples to support his argument; for example, he tells the reader how much Russia has charged civilians for seats on their Soyoz capsules, and he describes how one company is planning an inflatable space hotel. He looks at the financial statistics and provides a reasonable response.

It is, however, important to remember that this is a journalistic text, not a peer-reviewed article. Since McDonald's audience is made up of "ordinary" people, he does not explore the topic in as much detail as a more academic text would have done. (6) _____ Specifically, no sources for his numbers are provided. The reader must trust him when he says that each space shuttle launch cost $1.5 billion or that private companies can provide flights into space for ten times less than governmental organizations. McDonald also shows no evidence of having spoken to anyone involved in space travel; there are no quotations from space industry experts, and his article appears to be based entirely on his own opinions.

(7) _____ Some key issues are not addressed in McDonald's text. Most notably, the text does not question whether low costs and increased competition will result in compromised personal safety in either the privately-owned spacecraft or the proposed hotel. Neither does it question what might happen if these spacecraft fall into the wrong hands; the era of space terrorism is perhaps not too far away. (8) _____ A second point of contention concerns the analogy McDonald draws between the privatization of space travel and the sale of aircraft after World War II. There are those—notably those involved in the design and manufacture of spacecraft, or those involved in legal aspects of space exploration—who might argue that the situation is far more complex than McDonald acknowledges.

McDonald summarizes his own opinions on the topic of the privatization of space travel in the sentence "It's about time governments get out of the business of building spacecraft that only go to low Earth orbit." Since he has no apparent commercial interest in spacecraft, it is reasonable to assume that this is an objective assessment rather than an attempt to sway readers to his point of view. Having said that, (9) _____ McDonald has written elsewhere about his support of exploration of Mars; he has even said, "I will volunteer to make the first boot prints in the red soil" (2014, June 6). McDonald's analysis may be influenced by his personal enthusiasm for space travel.

(10) _____ In sum, this is not a peer-reviewed publication, some of the information may be of questionable accuracy, and some key concerns are not addressed. However, McDonald's article provides a useful service in that it raises awareness of the issue among readers with a casual interest in space exploration, and for this he should be commended.

References

McDonald, B. (2014, June 6). Let's go to Mars, but make sure it's for the right reasons. http://www.cbc.ca/newsblogs/technology/quirks-quarks-blog/2014/06/lets-go-to-mars-but-make-sure-its-for-the-right-reasons.html.

McDonald, B. (2014, Sept. 19). NASA's SpaceX, Boeing deal a giant leap for space flight. http://newsmaritimes.ca/2014/09/19/nasas-spacex-boeing-deal-a-giant-leap-for-space-flight/.

Find the places in the review (numbered 1 to 10) where the writer of the review does the following. The first (1) is done for you.

a) comments on the author's use of language

b) brings up a key issue that the author has not addressed

c) addresses the credentials of the author and his ability to write on this topic

d) gives a final evaluation of the usefulness of the text

e) summarizes the article in one paragraph

f) points to an argument that others may not agree with

g) provides the title, author and publication details of the text

h) provides an introductory thesis statement

i) raises concerns about the author's lack of sources

j) relates this text to another article written by the author

Now, choose *either* Reading 1 *or* Reading 2 and follow the steps shown.

READING 1

Why It's Important to Look at the Stars—Literally

This reading presents one author's opinion on the value of astronomy.

 As you read the article, think about which points you will emphasize in a critical review of this text.

Before You Read

Work in groups of three or four. Discuss the following questions.

1. Have you ever looked up at the stars and wondered about life and the universe? What questions have you asked?

2. "Why spend so much money sending satellites into space when people around the world are starving?" How would you answer this question?

3. Can you think of any specific technological items we now have on Earth as a result of space exploration?

Key Vocabulary

The words below are all in the reading. Fill in the space in each sentence with the correct word.

NOUNS	enticement	navigation	predecessor	successor
VERBS	accelerate			
ADJECTIVES	fascinating	inquisitive	organic	
ADVERBS	inextricably	vehemently		

1. Something that develops in a/an _____ way develops naturally, without any form of planning.

2. Someone who argues _____ for or against a topic states his or her argument strongly with passion and conviction.

3. If we receive a/an _____ to do something, we receive something that encourages us and gives us a reason for doing it.

4. Our _____s are people who came before us in history; this word can also be used for earlier versions of a form of technology.

⑤ When two things are _____ linked, the connection between them cannot be broken.

⑥ _____ is the process of finding the way between two points, often using some kind of mechanical device.

⑦ When something _____s, it travels at a faster speed.

⑧ The _____s to a form of technology are the later versions of it; we can also use this word for a person who takes a job or position after someone has resigned or retired.

⑨ If you are _____, you always wonder about things and ask lots of questions.

⑩ Something that is _____ is extremely interesting.

Why It's Important to Look at the Stars—Literally

By Conor Farrell

*It's good to be curious about a world outside our own, because being **inquisitive** in the past has gotten us where we are today, writes Conor Farrell.*

Oscar Wilde[1] said, "We are all in the gutter—but some of us are looking at the stars."

In a time when the world has so many huge issues with society and economy, one
5 might ask why people spend time looking out into deep space when they might be able to contribute to our more earthly problems. However, can people be blamed for taking some time out from the madness to indulge in a **fascinating** pastime? And do astronomers and space scientists contribute more to society than we actually think?

Most—if not all—of us have done at some stage what our **predecessors** did in their
10 time: gaze up at the night sky and ask, "Where did all that come from, what is it and what does it mean?" Many of us had our passion for things, beyond our atmosphere, fuelled by the late Sir Patrick Moore,[2] who died last weekend after inspiring generations of people to look up.

As far back as I can remember, I was always interested in astronomy, and I'm still
15 finding out new things about it. I was lucky to live in a dark area, which meant that I could easily spend hours spotting passing satellites, noticing how the Moon changes from night to night and picking out star clusters with binoculars. My curiosity for science and astronomy was always encouraged, and it was the likes of Sir Patrick Moore who continued to give me and countless others that **enticement** to keep on watching the
20 night sky.

---

[1] Oscar Wilde (1854–1900) was an Irish writer known best for his novel *The Picture of Dorian Gray* and his play *The Importance of Being Earnest*. He died penniless after a period in prison for homosexual activity.

[2] Sir Patrick Moore (1923–2012) was a British astronomer famous for his popular television show *The Sky at Night*.

Finding Our Place in Space

It's a science that at first seems so separate and distinct from the "real world" yet is still **inextricably** linked to our everyday lives. It is thanks to those
25 who ventured into understanding the universe that we have so much technology that we take for granted today. Many people say that astronomy and the exploration of space are a waste of time. On the contrary, I believe that it is these things that
30 will drive our civilization forward on our own planet and beyond for a long time to come.

This deep interest and passion for astronomy has existed in people for thousands of years. With the inquisitive nature of people, the world began to
35 develop rapidly. With nations built and trade routes established, the citizens of Europe focused on survival and business on the ground. An improved version of a Dutch optical device, which helped spot enemy ships far out to sea from the towers in
40 Venice, was developed by Galileo. The device was, of course, the telescope. Galileo used his telescope to observe Jupiter, a bright object that's very easy to spot. Dotted around Jupiter he noticed four small specks of light. As he observed over hours and days, Galileo realized that these specks were moving around Jupiter, discovering what are now known as the Galilean moons: Europa, Io, Ganymede and Callisto. What he also
45 realized with this discovery was that he had found proof that the earth was not at the centre of the Universe, as Church-dominated Europe **vehemently** believed.

Over the next several centuries, curiosity drove humanity to look further and deeper into space to find out more about how the universe works and why Earth and the other planets exist. The 19th and 20th centuries saw huge leaps in our understanding of the
50 universe. Until recently it was thought that the expansion of the universe would eventually slow down and stop, before it started to contract and finally destroy itself in something of a "Big Crunch." However, in 1998, following a study of supernovae (exploding stars), it was found not only that the universe is still expanding but that the expansion is actually **accelerating**.

55 Continued observations of the cosmos will eventually provide us with the answers, and in the meantime doing so will push our technological limits even further. But is spending time and money on such endeavours worth it? Should we take our heads out of the clouds, so to speak, and take a look at issues here on our own planet first?

What's the Point?

60 There are people who feel that astronomy and space exploration is a waste of time and money. A regular opinion is the classic "why spend billions of euro sending that satellite into space when there are so many people starving in the world?" The problem of world hunger is a very serious one, but the argument that we should not explore space because people are hungry is a self-defeating one: by the same logic, we should also stop $\rightarrow$

65 spending millions on building motorways or undertaking computer technology research, because the same amount of money could feed a certain number of families for so long.

The fact is that space exploration and astronomy provide technologies that we use in our everyday lives, and spending money on such projects has a long-lasting benefit to society. Indeed, it is thanks to satellites in space that we can monitor weather conditions 70 and crops to help food production and decrease world hunger. Here are a few things that we probably take for granted, which were borne out of astronomy and space science.

> Sky TV and Internet data is transmitted using satellites in orbit.

> Lightweight carbon-fibre material was used for prosthetic limbs after being developed for use in the Alpha Magnetic Spectrometer on board the International 75 Space Station.

> The GPS and upcoming Galileo **navigation** systems are a network of space satellites that help stop us getting lost—and are vital for emergency and rescue services.

> The miniaturization of electronic components was advanced by the need to make 80 things small and light during the race to the moon.

> The camera chips in your phone or digital camera are the **successors** of imaging technology used to photograph distant stars and galaxies.

> Cronidur 30, the material developed for use in the Space Shuttle's fuel pumps, found another use in corrosive-resistant kitchen knives.

85 The list of spin-off technologies that have resulted from space science and astronomy is endless. While the everyday benefits may not always be apparent or immediate, the fact that as a species we are driven to push ourselves to understand more about the universe accelerates research and development, much of which ends up in the hands of you and me, even if we don't realize it.

90 Astronomers and astrophysicists try to understand the universe and how things within it work by making observations and applying the science that we know to those observations. To date, over 850 extra-solar planets have been discovered, and it's thought that there may be billions of planets in the galaxy. But we are now asking a new question: can—or do—any of them support life? This is a question we are in the midst of answering 95 and one I hope astronomers can answer soon.

You may be surprised to learn that we launched our first interstellar spaceship thirty-five years ago, and it's still making discoveries. Voyager 1 was launched in 1977 to firstly explore the outer solar system and its planets, but to also to eventually explore the interstellar medium. At this moment it is crossing what's known as the heliosheath, the 100 outermost region of the solar system. Once it passes this point within the next couple of years, Voyager 1 will be outside our solar system and in the space between the stars.

Very recently, Voyager discovered extremely high magnetic fields in this section of the edge of the solar system, something which can now be taken into consideration when designing and building new spacecraft—spacecraft that may carry humans in 105 the distant future. Of course, there is also the sense of wonder and amazement at the heavens that raises so many philosophical questions for each of us: why are we here? Are there other people on other planets? Even if there are, will we ever get to meet them? Where did all the stuff out there come from? Where will it go? What happens when the sun burns out? Will we have to find a new home?

110 **Keep Your Head in the Clouds**

Astronomy forces us to ask questions and to be curious. Many of these questions are very similar to those that were asked by our ancestors hundreds and thousands of years ago. By being so inquisitive in the past, we were driven to be as advanced as we are today. We must continue to be so curious, as it will be to our benefit in the 115 future. Eventually civilization will move away from Earth, whether by **organic** expansion or by necessity, and astronomy, astrophysics and space exploration will allow us to do that.

Gazing at the stars and wondering what's out there is certainly not something that has no real relation to or effect on life on Earth: watching the stars and asking questions 120 is what pushes our society to find out its capabilities and is most definitely something we should never stop doing. The stars will raise questions we may not be able to answer immediately, but in walking the path to the answer we will learn new things along the way.

Astronomy and science are not things to be left for others to explore; we can all take 125 part and enjoy it just as much as the greats themselves have done. As Sir Patrick Moore once said, "I'm only a four-dimensional creature. Haven't got a clue how to visualize infinity. Even Einstein hadn't. I know because I asked him."

Conor Farrell is an astronomer with Astronomy Ireland. He writes about science and astronomy on his blog conorfarrell.com.　　　　　　　　　　　(1574 words)

Farrell, C. (2012, Dec. 15). Why it's important to look at the stars—literally. *TheJournal.ie*. Retrieved from http://www.thejournal.ie/readme/patrick-moore-inspired-generations-to-explore-713644-Dec2012/

Check Your Understanding

Works in pairs or groups of three. Summarize the author's argument in 200–250 words.

Analysis and Discussion

Discuss the following questions with your group.

1. Where was this text published? Was it published in a peer-reviewed academic journal, or somewhere else? How can you tell? Why does it matter?

2. When was this text published? Is the publication date important? Is the material still relevant, or is it dated? Has anything changed since the date of publication?

3. Who wrote the text? What can you find out about this person? What credentials does this author have? What biases might he have?

4 What is the author's opinion of the topic being discussed? Why did the author write this text? Who is the intended audience for this text? What does the author want the reader to do as a result of reading this text?

5 Is this a purely factual piece, or does the author present a personal opinion here?

6 Does the text present a convincing argument about the topic in question? Has the author done empirical research?

7 If the author is not presenting the results of his or her own empirical research, how are the author's points supported? Are there statistics? If so, where from? How about quotations from others? If so, who is being quoted? Does the author rely on anecdotes? If so, are these convincing? How effective is the author's use of supporting detail?

8 If this text has no supporting evidence but is simply a presentation of the author's own opinion, how do you respond to it?

9 What is the larger context of this work? How does the text support or contradict other opinions on this topic? Who might agree with the text? Who might disagree?

10 How does the text compare with your own experiences and opinions? Does it support your own experiences, or does it contradict them? Does the text contain information that you know to be incorrect?

Your Critical Review

Use your summary from "Check Your Understanding" and the opinions you formed as a result of your group discussion to write a critical review of this text. You should aim for 800–1,000 words.

Make your notes on page 243.

© ERPI Reproduction prohibited

READING 2

Does Mars Have Rights?

Do humans have the right to explore and perhaps establish colonies on Mars? Read one science writer's opinion on this subject.

 As you read, think about which points you will emphasize in a critical review of this text.

Before You Read

Work in groups of three or four. Discuss the following questions.

1 Do you believe that, in your lifetime, people will travel to Mars and even establish a colony there? Why, or why not?

2 What could the human race gain by changing conditions on Mars to make the planet suitable for humans to live there? What might be the drawbacks of doing this?

3 Would you be interested in travelling to Mars? What kinds of people do you think would be best suited to this endeavour?

Key Vocabulary

The words below are all in the reading. Match each word or phrase with the correct definition.

1 aesthetic (adj. line 42) _____ a) someone who thinks about the future in an imaginative way

2 emulate (v. line 22) _____ b) related to beauty

3 hospitable (adj. line 29) _____ c) basic

4 intrinsically (adv. line 98) _____ d) having good conditions, e.g., a suitable environment

5 quarantine (v. line 11) _____ e) deliberate destruction of or damage to public property

6 rudimentary (adj. line 2) _____ f) disregard, e.g., a law or agreement

7 vandalism (n. line 44) _____ g) in itself, naturally

8 violate (v. line 38) _____ h) isolate someone until she/he is known to be free of disease

9 visionary (n. line 19) _____ i) do great damage

10 wreak havoc (phrase line 12) _____ j) copy someone or something that is known to be successful

Does Mars Have Rights?

By Ronald Bailey

Does Mars have rights? What about Europa, Ganymede and Titan—the moons of Jupiter and Saturn that may be home to rudimentary extraterrestrial life? The 1967 Outer Space Treaty requires space-faring nations to conduct exploration of the moon and other celestial bodies "so as to avoid their harmful contamination and also adverse changes
5 in the environment of the Earth resulting from the introduction of extraterrestrial matter." The goal of the treaty is to prevent both back contamination (the introduction of extraterrestrial life to Earth) and forward contamination (the introduction of Earth life to extraterrestrial environments).

The reason for avoiding back contamination is pretty clear. We want to prevent an
10 *Andromeda Strain*[1] scenario in which an unleashed alien life form harms life on Earth. →

___
[1] *The Andromeda Strain* is a novel (Michael Crichton, 1969) about a military satellite that brings a microorganism back to Earth from outer space, resulting in an outbreak of a fatal disease. It has been made into a movie and a TV series.

Returning Apollo astronauts and their hauls of moon rocks were quarantined for a couple of weeks, just to make sure that no lunar microbes escaped to wreak havoc. Years of testing found no indication of life hidden in the moon rocks.

The main reason to guard against forward contamination is to prevent equipment
15 designed to detect extraterrestrial life from getting confused. Consequently, NASA regularly sterilizes gear destined to land on other celestial bodies. So far no mission has detected life anywhere else in our solar system.

All this caution is reasonable, as long as we are just poking around and taking some readings. But what are our ethical obligations if, as some space exploration visionaries
20 urge, humanity begins the process of making other worlds fit for human habitation? British planetary scientist Martyn Fogg explains, "The ultimate in terraforming[2] would be to create an uncontained planetary biosphere emulating all the functions of the biosphere of the Earth—one that would be fully habitable for human beings."

Mars in its current condition is not a promising home for Earth life. The Red Planet's
25 average temperature is -60°C, well below Earth's average of 15°C. The pressure of its carbon-dioxide atmosphere is one-hundredth that of our planet's nitrogen-oxygen atmosphere, and it lacks an ozone layer, so its surface is blasted by DNA-destroying ultraviolet rays from the sun.

Can Mars be made more hospitable? The level of life-sustaining carbon dioxide could
30 be raised by pumping potent man-made greenhouse gases like perfluorocarbons into the Martian atmosphere or by directing extra sunlight from a space mirror 250 kilometres in diameter at the Martian South Pole. Either solution would take an estimated 100 years to build up an atmosphere thick enough so that the new warmth would prove hospitable to colonizing anaerobic microbes that thrive in extreme environments on Earth.

35 Later, we could genetically engineer Earth plants so that they could begin to pump oxygen into Mars' atmosphere. It might take another 10,000 to 100,000 years for the terraformed Martian atmosphere to contain enough oxygen for people to breathe unassisted. But assuming that terraforming Mars would work, would doing so violate a moral obligation to leave Mars and other worlds alone?

40 Yes, argued Australian philosopher Robert Sparrow in a 1999 article, "The Ethics of Terraforming," in the journal *Environmental Ethics*. An effort to terraform Mars, Sparrow asserted, "demonstrates two serious defects of moral character: an aesthetic insensitivity and the sin of hubris.[3] Trying to change whole planets to suit our ends is arrogant vandalism."

45 Developing what he called an agent-based virtue ethics, Sparrow argued that what makes actions right or wrong is the character of the moral agent. Terraforming Mars indicates an ethically significant aesthetic insensitivity reminiscent of a remote hiker wantonly whacking a transient but beautiful set of icicles on a wintry day. "What is significant is the blindness the hiker has displayed to beauty even though no one

_____

[2] *Terraforming* is the process of changing the surface of another planet (e.g., its temperature or its ecological system) to make it suitable for human habitation.

[3] *Hubris* originates in Greek mythology and means extreme arrogance and a sense of superiority over others.

50 else may suffer from its loss," he wrote. The blindness is a vice. Filling Mars' Valles Marineris, the largest canyon in the solar system, with genetically modified redwoods would indicate that 55 we do not properly appreciate its present desolate beauty.

The second moral defect demonstrated by terraforming, according to Sparrow, is hubris, which "occurs when humans 60 wilfully ignore their limits and seek to become like gods." Instead we should stay in our proper place. "A proper place is one in which one can flourish without too much of a struggle," Sparrow ex- 65 plained. So our proper place is Earth, and "we must show that we are capable of looking after our current home before we could claim to have any place on another."

Sparrow acknowledged that he did not offer an objective account of beauty, so the notion still resides in the eye of the beholder, as does desolate ugliness. And as awesome as the view down Valles Marineris might be right now, it would arguably be even more 70 so if it were teeming with life. With regard to the hubris of terraforming, one initial response should be a hearty "so what?" Terraforming offers the promise of helping humanity toward practical moral improvement by increasing our understanding of just how precious terrestrial life is, aiding us in managing it toward greater integrity, stability and beauty.

75 Mars may not be lifeless. Some researchers believe that Martian life may have retreated to warm underground refuges as the planet's oceans dried up and froze hundreds of millions of years ago. Do we have any moral obligations toward Martian microbes, should they exist?

"If life is present on another world, the introduction of terrestrial life forms could lead 80 to an ecological holocaust, a moral and aesthetic tragedy, as well as an immense loss to science," argued University of Oregon sociologist Richard York in a 2005 article, "Toward a Martian Land Ethic," in *Human Ecology Review*.

Martian life might indeed constitute a "second genesis," that is, life that has arisen independent of Earth life. Or it might be the result of transpermia, in which organisms 85 were spread via meteors between planets. Perhaps life originated on Mars and eventually reached Earth, where it thrived. If so, what we could learn from Martian life probably would be limited, and terraforming would not be ethically much different from colonizing terrestrial ecosystems uninhabited by humans.

NASA astrobiologist Christopher McKay, who first raised the question of whether 90 Mars has rights in a 1990 essay in the book *Moral Expertise: Studies in Practical and Professional Ethics*, argues that if Martian life is a second genesis, "its enormous potential for practical benefit to humans in terms of knowledge" might "exceed the opportunity ➔

cost of not establishing human settlements on Mars." But finding a second genesis so close to Earth also would suggest that the emergence of life is a relatively common
95 occurrence in the cosmos, reducing the moral force of arguments for preserving Martian microbes. Saving samples of Martian life for later study is a prudent precondition before embarking on terraformation.

Dead planets and moons are not intrinsically valuable. And as fascinating as they might be, Martian microbes are not moral agents, any more than are terrestrial microbes.
100 They simply do not have an ethical point of view that we must consider. On that account, there is no good moral reason why humans should limit the expansion of terrestrial life, including themselves, throughout the solar system.

Science Correspondent Ronald Bailey is the author of Liberation Biology *(Prometheus Books).*

(1179 words)

Bailey, R. (2012, Feb.). Does Mars have rights? An ethical case for terraforming the Red Planet. *Reason*, February 2012. Retrieved from http://reason.com/archives/2012/01/30/does-mars-have-rights.

Check Your Understanding

Work in pairs or groups of three. Summarize the author's argument in 200–250 words.

Analysis and Discussion

Discuss the following questions with your group.

1. Where was this text published? Was it published in a peer-reviewed academic journal, or somewhere else? How can you tell? Why does it matter?

2. When was this text published? Is the publication date important? Is the material still relevant, or is it dated? Has anything changed since the date of publication?

3. Who wrote the text? What can you find out about this person? What credentials does this author have? What biases might he have?

4. What is the author's opinion of the topic being discussed? Why did the author write this text? Who is the intended audience for this text? What does the author want the reader to do as a result of reading this text?

5. Is this a purely factual piece, or does the author present a personal opinion here?

6. Does the text present a convincing argument about the topic in question? Has the author done empirical research?

7. If the author is not presenting the results of her or his own empirical research, how are the author's points supported? Are there statistics? If so, where from? How about quotations from others? If so, who is being quoted? Does the author rely on anecdotes? If so, are these convincing? How effective is the author's use of supporting detail?

8. If this text has no supporting evidence but is a simply presentation of the author's own opinion, how do you respond to it?

9 What is the larger context of this work? How does the text support or contradict other opinions on this topic? Who might agree with the text? Who might disagree?

10 How does the text compare with your own experiences and opinions? Does it support your own experiences, or does it contradict them? Does the text contain information that you know to be incorrect?

Your Critical Review

Use your summary from "Check Your Understanding" and the opinions you formed as a result of your group discussion to write a critical review of this text. You should aim for 800–1,000 words.

Make your notes on page 243.

Going Further

Focus on Language

A. The following chart contains ten words from the three readings. Complete the chart with related words in the other categories and, where possible, in the same category. (There may not be a word for each category.)

	NOUN	VERB	ADJECTIVE	ADVERB
1	beauty			
2	civilization			
3	competition			
4			curious	
5		detect		
6			destined	
7	exploration			
8			inquisitive	
9	obligation			
10		observe		

B. a) This chapter contains some vocabulary that is specialized and is found only in texts related to astronomy and space exploration. This specialized vocabulary is called *jargon*; the presence or absence of jargon provides an indication of the intended reader of the text. The following are anagrams of words related to space exploration. Solve the puzzles.

1 TELIALETS   _ _ _ _ _ _ _ _ _

2 CHALNU   _ _ _ _ _ _

3 HUTLETS   _ _ _ _ _ _ _

4 TUNASROTA   _ _ _ _ _ _ _ _ _

5 TERAOHMSPE   _ _ _ _ _ _ _ _ _ _

6 TORIB   _ _ _ _ _

7 CERTKO   _ _ _ _ _ _

8 ALORS EMYSST   _ _ _ _   _ _ _ _ _ _

b) What jargon can you think of from your own area of study? Look back at earlier chapters of this book, look at online resources or use your dictionary. Make a list of some jargon that will be useful to you in your future studies.

> _____
> _____
> _____
> _____
> _____

> _____
> _____
> _____
> _____
> _____

REVIEW
of the chapter ...

> Answer the following questions.

1 What are the key components of a critical review?

2 How is a critical review different from a research essay?

Critical Review—Notes

Glossary

analyze: Carefully consider something in order to evaluate or respond to it.

anecdote: A short story about an individual case, often used to attract the attention of the reader.

assess: Judge, evaluate.

audience: The readers for whom a text is intended.

bias: Preference for one point of view or one side to an argument over another.

compare/contrast: Look for similarities and differences between two or more texts.

context: The body of work surrounding a text, i.e., the texts and other information to which the work in question will be compared or which will influence how it is judged.

credentials: An author's qualifications to write on a topic (education, experience, previous publications).

empirical evidence: Evidence obtained through empirical research.

empirical research: Research carried out through a process of experimentation or observation on the part of the author.

evaluate: Reach a decision on the quality, validity or usefulness of a text.

fact: A piece of information that can be confirmed by various independent sources, e.g., scientific, historical, biographical, geographical or statistical.

generalizable: Applicable to different situations, different parts of the world or different circumstances.

hedging: Use of language designed to "soften" an argument, e.g., to show caution when giving a conclusion.

hypothesis: An idea or theory that the researcher will try to prove; an "educated guess" about what the research will reveal.

imply: Suggest indirectly rather than state explicitly.

infer: Determine the intended meaning, which is not stated explicitly.

judgment: A decision made after a process of evaluation and analysis.

objective: Balanced, unbiased.

opinion: A personal belief of the author.

peer-reviewed: Evaluated by members of an academic community with expertise in the subject.

purpose: The author's reason for writing a text, e.g., to persuade, warn, advise, entertain or advertise.

qualitative: Based on data that cannot be measured, e.g., observations, interviews.

quantitative: Based on data that can be measured, e.g., surveys, questionnaires.

question: Not accept at face value; wonder about.

quotation: A piece of text copied directly from another source.

reliable: (Referring to a piece of research) producing the same results when carried out again.

school of thought: The theories put forward by researchers or writers who share the same approach to a subject.

scientific method: A systematic process used when carrying out an academic study.

stance: The opinion of an author; the position the author puts forward on a topic.

statistics: Numerical data used to make an argument sound more credible.

synthesis: The process of bringing together information from different sources in order to reach a conclusion or solve a problem.

visual items: Non-textual things such as photographs, illustrations, charts, graphs, maps, diagrams and tables.

Vocabulary

A	Reading
abolish (v.)	2-2
aboriginal (adj.)	1-1
abundant (adj.)	2-1
accelerate (v.)	10-1
accustomed to (adj.)	9-3
acknowledge (v.)	4-3
acoustic (adj.)	7-3
addiction (n.)	2-1
adequate (adj.)	4-3
adjustment (n.)	5-3
adverse (adj.)	4-3
advocate (n.)	8-2
aesthetic (adj.)	10-2
aggressive (adj.)	5-2
allegedly (adv.)	1-1
allegiance (n.)	3-3
ambient (adj.)	7-3
ambivalent (adj.)	7-2
anabolic steroids (adj.+n.)	3-2
ancestor (n.)	2-1
apparent (adj.)	8-3
arrogant (adj.)	5-2
assertive (adj.)	5-2
assess (v.)	7-1
asset (n.)	7-3
associated (adj.)	2-3
assumption (n.)	5-3
attitude (n.)	7-3
audible (adj.)	7-3
auspicious (adj.)	7-1
austerity (n.)	3-3
authority (n.)	2-2

B	
bacteria (n.)	4-1
benefits (n.)	7-3
betray (v.)	2-2
bold (adj.)	5-2
boon (n.)	4-1
bottom line (n.)	7-1
brand (n.)	5-1
bully (n.)	9-2

C	
calculate (v.)	6-3
calligraphy (n.)	9-2
calorie (n.)	2-1
canine (adj.)	1-1
catastrophic (adj.)	8-3
charismatic (adj.)	5-2
cognition (n.)	7-2
cohesion (n.)	9-1
collect (v.)	6-3
commodity (n.)	3-3

	Reading
commute (v.)	8-2
compelling (adj.)	6-1
complex (adj.)	5-3
complicate (v.)	2-3
concise (adj.)	9-2
condolences (n.)	9-2
conduct (v.)	6-2
confidentiality (n.)	7-3
conjunction (n.)	2-3
conservation (n.)	4-1
consist of (v.)	6-3
contemplate (v.)	7-1
contentious (adj.)	8-1
contentment (n.)	8-3
controversial (adj.)	1-1
conveniences (n.)	4-2
conventional (adj.)	1-2
conventional wisdom (adj.+n.)	2-3
correlate (v.)	8-1
corruption (n.)	8-2
counterpart (n.)	5-3
credible (adj.)	1-2
crowdfunding (n.)	5-1

D	
DNA (n.)	1-2
decay (v.)	9-1
decisive (adj.)	5-2
deficiency (n.)	2-1
delegate (v.)	5-1
delegate/delegation (n.)	8-3
derive (v.)	9-3
device (n.)	6-2
digestion (n.)	2-1
dilution (n.)	8-3
discount (v.)	4-3
dismiss (v.)	4-3
dispersed (adj.)	9-1
disruptive (adj.)	7-3
dissemination (n.)	9-3
distracted (adj.)	7-2
diversity (n.)	9-3
dominant (adj.)	5-2
doping (n.)	3-2
dose (n.)	3-2
downsize (v.)	4-2
dynamics (n.)	7-1
dysfunctional (adj.)	9-1

E	
eccentric (n.)	1-2
egocentric (adj.)	5-2
elite (n., adj.)	3-3
embellish (v.)	6-1
embrace (v.)	3-1

	Reading
empathetic (adj.)	4-3
emulate (v.)	10-2
endangered (adj.)	4-1
enticement (n.)	10-1
entrepreneur (n.)	5-1
enzyme (n.)	4-1
epiphany (n.)	4-2
epitomize (v.)	3-3
erosion (n.)	10-2
eschew (v.)	6-1
euphemism (n.)	2-3
euthanize (v.)	2-2
evolution (n.)	3-1
evolve (v.)	4-3
executive decision (n.)	9-2
exploitation (n.)	3-3
express (v.)	6-3

F

fabrication (n.)	3-3
facilitate (v.)	9-3
fascinating (adj.)	10-1
feasibility (n.)	2-2
fellow (adj.)	9-2
ferment (v.)	4-1
fidget (v.)	7-2
fiscal (adj.)	2-3
flourish (v.)	9-3
forecast (v.)	5-1
fragmented (adj.)	9-1

G

gauge (v.)	6-3
generalize (v.)	6-3
generosity (n.)	8-2
grasp (n.)	7-1
grass grows more greenly (idiom)	8-3
grieve (v.)	2-2

H

have a thing for (idiom)	4-2
hierarchy (n.)	3-3
homogenous (adj.)	9-1
hone (v.)	5-1
hospitable (adj.)	10-2
humanely (adv.)	2-2
hypothesis (n.)	2-3

I

ideology (n.)	3-3
idiosyncratic (adj.)	9-3
ignorant (adj.)	6-1
implication (n.)	8-1
improvise (v.)	6-1
incapacitated (adj.)	3-1
incentive (n.)	7-3

indicate (v.)	6-3
inextricably (adv.)	10-1
influx (n.)	6-2
injustice (n.)	4-3
inquisitive (adj.)	10-1
inspiring (adj.)	7-1
instinct (n.)	5-3
integral (adj.)	3-2
integrated (adj.)	9-1
intense (adj.)	8-3
intrepid (adj.)	1-2
intrinsically (adv.)	10-2
intuition (n.)	5-1
intuitive (adj.)	8-1
isolation (n.)	1-2

K

kinship (n.)	6-1

L

legitimate (adj.)	7-2
lethargic (adj.)	2-1
let off the hook (phrase)	5-3
liberation (n.)	4-2
life expectancy (n.)	2-3

M

mainstream (adj.)	3-1
malinger (v.)	7-2
mammal (n.)	1-2
mandatory (adj.)	3-3
marsupial (n.)	1-2
maturation (n.)	3-1
median (adj.)	6-2
mentor (n.)	5-3
merit consideration (v.+n.)	2-3
microbe (n.)	4-1
mitigate (v.)	8-2
mobile (adj.)	6-2
modulate (v.)	5-3
monitor (v.)	3-2
morale (n.)	5-1
mutual friend (n.)	9-2

N

naivety (n.)	3-2
navigation (n.)	10-1
nebulous (adj.)	9-1
negotiate (v.)	5-3
non-aligned (adj.)	8-3
notorious (adj.)	1-1

O

optimal (adj.)	2-1
organic (adj.)	10-1
overlook (v.)	4-3

P

pacify (v.)	2-2
paradox (n.)	8-1
paranoid (adj.)	7-1
parity (n.)	8-2
performance-enhancing drugs (adj.+n.)	3-2
perseverance (n.)	3-1
pervasiveness (n.)	8-3
plummet (v.)	4-2
podium (n.)	3-2
pragmatic (adj.)	7-2
precedent (n.)	3-1
predator (n.)	1-2
predecessor (n.)	10-1
premise (n.)	7-1
prioritize (v.)	8-2
proactive (adj.)	5-2
prolific (adj.)	7-2
proponent (n.)	2-1

Q

quarantine (v.)	10-2

R

racial (adj.)	6-2
rational (adj.)	3-2
rebuke (n.)	8-1
recipient (n.)	8-2
reciprocal (adj.)	9-1
redistribute (v.)	8-1
relevance (n.)	6-1
relic (n.)	6-1
rely on (v.)	6-2
reputedly (adv.)	7-1
reserved (adj.)	5-2
retro (adj.)	6-1
reveal (v.)	6-3
rivalry (n.)	1-1
rudimentary (adj.)	10-2

S

sabotage (v.)	2-3
second-guess (v.)	6-1
secular (adj.)	9-1
sedentary (adj.)	7-2
self-esteem (n.)	3-1
seminal (adj.)	8-1
set an example (phrase)	4-2
setback (n.)	5-1
settle (v.)	1-1
shortage (n.)	4-1
shortcomings (n.)	9-3
singlehandedly (adv.)	9-2
skeptic (n.)	1-1
social capital (n.)	9-2
social studies (n.)	6-2

solar panel (n.)	4-2
something's got to give (idiom)	4-2
spectator (n.)	1-1
speculate (v.)	1-1
spontaneous (adj.)	4-3
staple (adj.)	2-2
startup (n.)	5-1
stationary (adj.)	7-2
stimulating (adj.)	7-3
subjective (adj.)	8-1
successor (n.)	10-1
sustainable (adj.)	4-1

T

tally (v.)	6-2
tantamount to (adj.)	2-2
theoretical (adj.)	9-2
transition (v.)	2-1

U

ubiquitous (adj.)	9-3
unanimously (adv.)	6-2
undertake (v.)	6-3
undocumented (adj.)	1-2
uninsured (adj.)	8-2
unique (adj.)	5-3
urbanization (n.)	8-3
utilitarian (adj.)	9-3

V

validation (n.)	3-1
vandalism (n.)	10-2
vehemently (adv.)	10-1
violate (v.)	10-2
visionary (n.)	10-2
voluntary (adj.)	8-2
vulnerable (adj.)	3-1

W

welfare state (n.)	8-1
widespread (adj.)	4-1
wind turbine (n.)	4-2
wreak havoc (phrase)	10-2

Z

zero-tolerance (n.)	3-2

Photo Credits

ISTOCKPHOTO
p. 146 & 171

Janice Hudson
p. 85

SHUTTERSTOCK
p. 1 & 20 A. Pix
p. 16 AlessandroZocc
p. 21 & 47 stockcreations
p. 48 & 73 Iurii Osadchi
p. 62 sainthorant daniel
p. 74 & 97 A. Crimi
p. 123 & 145 Monkey Business Images
p. 192 frizt16
p. 199 & 222 (foreground) Rido
p. 199 & 222 (background) Andrekart
Photography
p. 233 Triff
p. 239 Tristan3D

THINKSTOCK
p. 10
p. 29
p. 34
p. 67
p. 80
p. 98 & 122
p. 105
p. 115
p. 130
p. 135
p. 154
p. 172 & 198
p. 186
p. 206
p. 213
p. 223 & 242